ANALYSING LANGUAGE IN CONTEXT:
A STUDENT WORKBOOK

Analysing language in context: a student workbook

This book is part of a course: *Language and Literacy in a Changing World* (E844), that is itself part of the Open University Masters programme, and a core component in the MA in Applied Linguistics degree offered by The Open University.

The Open University Masters in Education

The Open University Masters in Education is now firmly established as the most popular postgraduate degree for education professionals in Europe, with over 3,000 students registering each year. The Masters in Education is designed particularly for those with experience of teaching, the advisory service, educational administration or allied fields.

Structure of the Masters in Education

The Masters in Education is a modular degree, and students are therefore free to select from a range of options the programme which best fits in with their interests and professional goals. Specialist lines in management, applied linguistics and special/inclusive education are also available. Study in the Open University's Advanced Diploma can also be counted towards the Masters in Education, and successful study in the Masters Programme entitles students to apply for entry into the Open University Doctorate in Education programme.

OU Supported Open Learning

The Masters in Education programme provides great flexibility. Students study at their own pace, in their own time, anywhere in the European Union. They receive specially prepared study materials, supported by tutorials, thus offering the chance to work with other students.

The Doctorate in Education

The Doctorate in Education is a part-time doctoral degree, combining taught courses, research methods and a dissertation designed to meet the needs of professionals in education and related areas who are seeking to extend and deepen their knowledge and understanding of contemporary educational issues. The Doctorate in Education builds upon successful study within the Open University Masters in Education programme.

How to apply

If you would like to register for this programme, or simply find out more information about available courses, please write for the *Professional Development in Education* prospectus to the Course Reservations Centre, PO Box 724, The Open University, Walton Hall, Milton Keynes, MK7 6ZW, UK (Telephone +44 (0) 1908 653231). Details can also be viewed on our web page http://www.open.ac.uk.

ANALYSING LANGUAGE IN CONTEXT: A STUDENT WORKBOOK

Theresa Lillis and Carolyn McKinney

Trentham Books
Stoke on Trent, UK and Sterling, USA

in association with

Trentham Books Limited

Westview House, 734 London Road
Oakhill, Stoke on Trent
Staffordshire, England ST4 5NP

22883 Quicksilver Drive, Sterling
VA 20166-2012, USA

First published 2003

British Library Cataloguing-in-Publication Data
A catalogue record for this book is available from the British Library

ISBN: 1 85856 287 2

Designed and typeset by Trentham Print Design Ltd., Chester and printed in Great Britain by Cromwell Press Ltd., Wiltshire.

Acknowledgements

Grateful acknowledgement is made to the following sources for permission to reproduce material within this volume.

Text

Extract from Giles, H., Robinson, P. and Smith, P. (eds) *Language: Social Psychological Perspectives*, Pergamon Press, 1980

Extracts from Hutchby, I. and Wooffit, R. (1998) *Conversation Analysis: Principles, Practices and Applications*, Polity Press, by permission of Blackwell Publishing Ltd

Extracts from Mercer, N. (1995) Chapter 5 – A Theory of Practice and Chapter 6 – Talking and Working Together, *The Guided Construction of Knowledge*, Multilingual Matters Ltd

Extracts from Alexander, R. (2000) *Culture and Pedagogy – International Comparisons in Primary Education*, Blackwell Publishing Ltd

Extract reproduced by kind permission of The Guide Association UK

Extract from Stubbs, M. (1996) *Text and Corpus Analysis – Computer-assisted Studies of Language and Culture*, Blackwell Publishing Ltd

Extract from Swann, J. (1988) Chapter 9 – Talk Control: an illustration from the classroom', in Coates, J. and Cameron, D., *Women in Their Speech Communities*. Copyright © Longman Group UK Limited 1988. Reprinted by permission of Pearson Education Limited

Extracts reprinted from *Linguistics and Education*, Vol. 9, No. 3, 'Voice, Appropriation and Discourse Representation in a Student Writing Task, Scollon, R., Tsang, W. K., Li, D., Yung, V. and Jones, R., pp.231 and 233, 1977, with permission from Elsevier Science

Extract from Connor, U., Davis, K. W. and De Rycker, T. (1995) 'Correctness and clarity in applying for overseas jobs: a cross-cultural analysis of US and Flemist application', in *TEXT: an interdisciplinary journal for the study of discourse*, 15 (4), pp.457-475, Walter de Gruyter and Co., Berlin

Extract from Hall, N. (1999) Young Children's use of Graphic Punctuation, *Language and Education*, Vol. 13 (3), pp. 184-5, Multilingual Matters Ltd

Extract from Haas Dyson, A. *Written Communication*, Vol 14, No. 3, pp.293-8, Copyright © 1997 by Sage Publications, Inc. Reprinted by Permission of Sage Publications, Inc

Extract from Rampton, B. (1995) Chapter 3 – Stylised Asian English, *Crossing: Language and Ethnicity Among Adolescents*, Longman Group Limited. Reprinted by permission of Ben Rampton

Extract from Zubair, S. (1999) Women's Literacy in a Rural Pakistani Community, *Language and Literacies*, Multilingual Matters Ltd

Extract from Lee, A. (1996) *Gender, Literacy, Curriculum: Re-writing school geography*, Taylor and Francis Books Ltd

Tables

Table from Coates, J. and Cameron, D. (eds) (1988) *Women in Their Speech Communities*. Copyright © Longman Group UK Limited 1988. Reprinted by permission of Pearson Education Limited

Tables from Iedema, R. (2001) Analysing Film and Television, in Van Leeuwen, T. and Jewitt, C., *Handbook of Visual Analysis*, Sage Publications Ltd

Table from Hawisher, G.E. and Selfe, C. L. (eds) (2000) *Global Literacies and the World-wide Web*, Routledge

Table from Connor, U., Davis, K. W. and De Rycker, T. (1995) Correctness and clarity in applying for overseas jobs: a cross-cultural analysis of US and Flemist application, in *TEXT: an interdisciplinary journal for the study of discourse*, 15 (4), pp.457-475, Walter de Gruyter and Co.,

Table from Lippi-Green, R. (1997) *English with an Accent*, Routledge

Figures reprinted by permission of Sage Publications Ltd from Ormerod, F. and Ivanic, R. Materiality in children's meaning-making practices, in *Visual Communication*, 1,1, 2002, Copyright © 2002 Sage Publications

Figures

Five figures from Lippi-Green, R. (1997) *English with an Accent*, Taylor and Francis Books Ltd

Figure from Alexander, R (2000) *Culture and Pedagogy – International Comparisons in Primary Education*, Blackwell Publishers Ltd

Figure from Iedema, R. (2001) Analysing Film and Television, in Van Leeuwen, T. and Jewitt, C., *Handbook of Visual Analysis*, Sage Publications Ltd

Figure from Hawisher, G.E. and Selfe, C. L. (eds) (2000) Global Literacies and the World-Wide Web, Routledge

Figure © *The Big Issue*

Figures from Barton, D., Hamilton, M. and Ivanic, R. (eds) (2000) *Situated Literacies – Reading and Writing in Context*, Routledge

Figures from Hall, N. (1999) Young Children's use of Graphic Punctuation, *Language and Education*, Vol. 13 (3), pp.182-3, Multilingual Matters Ltd

Figure from Kress, G. Ogborn, J. and Martins, I. (1998) A Satellite View of Language, *Language Awareness*, Vol. 7 (2) and (3), pp.75-6, Multilingual Matters Ltd

Figures reprinted by permission of Sage Publications Ltd from Ormerod, F. and Ivanic, R. Materiality in children's meaning-making practices, in *Visual Communication*, 1,1, 2002, Copyright © 2002 Sage Publications

Every effort has been made to contact copyright holders. If any have been inadvertently overlooked the publishers will be pleased to make the necessary arrangements at the first opportunity.

Contents

Introduction • ix

PART 1: APPROACHES TO SPOKEN INTERACTION
Introduction • 1

1: Sociolinguistics: accent and dialect in film • 3
Example: LIPPI-GREEN, R. (1996) *English with an Accent*, London, Routledge.

2: Interactional sociolinguistics: gender and informal talk • 11
Example: FISHMAN, P. (1998) 'Conversational insecurity', reprinted in D. Cameron (ed.) *The Feminist Critique of Language* (2nd edn), London, Routledge, pp.253-8.

3: Sociolinguistics: codeswitching at school • 17
Example: NCOKO, S.O.S., OSMAN, R. and COCKCROFT, K. (2000) 'Codeswitching among multilingual learners in primary schools in South Africa: an exploratory study', *International Journal of Bilingual Education and Bilingualism*, vol.3, no.4, pp.225-41.

4: Conversation analysis: radio talk • 23
Example: HUTCHBY, I. and WOOFFITT, R. (1998) *Conversation Analysis. Principles, Practices and Applications*, Cambridge, Polity Press.

5: Sociocultural approach: talk and learning • 31
Example: MERCER, N. (1995) *The Guided Construction of Knowledge*, Clevedon, Multilingual Matters.

6: Sociocultural approach: teacher-student interaction in different cultural contexts • 39
Example: ALEXANDER, R. (2000) *Culture and Pedagogy*. International Comparisons in Primary Education, Oxford, Blackwell.

PART 2: APPROACHES TO WRITTEN TEXTS

Introduction • 51

7: Corpus linguistics: official letters • 53
Example: STUBBS, M. (1996) *Texts and Corpus Analysis*, Oxford, Basil Blackwell.

8: Systemic functional linguistics: information texts in a museum • 61
Example: PURSER, E. (2000) 'Telling stories: text analysis in a museum', in E. Ventola (ed.)
Discourse and Community. Doing Functional Linguistics, Tubingen,
Gunter Narr Verlag, pp.169-98.

9: Bakhtinian discourse analysis: students' written texts • 67
Example: SCOLLON, R., TSANG, W.K., LI, D., YUNG, V. and JONES, R. (1998)
'Voice, appropriation and discourse representation in a student writing task',
Linguistics and Education, vol.9, no.3, pp.227-50.

10: Talk around texts: punctuation in young children's writing • 00
Example: HALL, N. (1999) 'Young children's use of graphic punctuation',
Language and Education, vol.13, no.3, pp.178-93.

11: Contrastive rhetoric: job applications • 73
Example: CONNOR, U., DAVIS, K.W. and DE RYCKER, T. (1995) 'Correctness and
clarity in applying for overseas jobs: a cross-cultural analysis of US and
Flemish applications', *Text*, vol.15, no.4, pp.457-75.

12: Bernsteinian discourse analysis: educational policy • 85
Example: LEUNG, C. (2001) 'English as an additional language: distinct language focus
or diffused curriculum concerns?', *Language and Education*, vol.15, no.1, pp.33-55.

13: Critical discourse analysis: a magazine text • 91
Example: CHOULIARAKI, L. and FAIRCLOUGH, N. (1999) *Discourse in Late Modernity.*
Rethinking Critical Discourse Analysis, Edinburgh, Edinburgh University Press.

PART 3: MULTIMODAL APPROACHES

Introduction • 97

14: Non-verbal behaviour and interaction: teacher gaze and student participation • 99

Example: SWANN, J. (1998) 'Talk control: an illustration from the classroom of problems in analysing male dominance of conversation', in J. Coates and D. Cameron (eds) *Women in Their Speech Communities. New Perspectives on Language and Sex*, London, Longman, pp.122-40.

15: Verbal and visual analysis: textbooks in the science classroom • 107

Example: KRESS, G., OGBORN, J. and MARTINS, I. (1998) 'A satellite view of language: some lessons from science classrooms', *Language Awareness*, vol.7, no.2/3, pp.69-89.

16: Texts as material objects: children's project writing • 113

Example: ORMEROD, F. and IVANIČ, R. (2002) 'Materiality in children's meaning-making practices', *Visual Communication*, vol.1, no.1, pp.65-91.

17: A social semiotic approach: television film • 125

Example: IEDEMA, R. (2001) 'Analysing film and television: a social semiotic account of Hospital: An Unhealthy Business', in T. van Leeuwen and C. Jewitt (eds) *Handbook of Visual Analysis*, London, Sage, pp.183-204.

18: New literacy practices: email communication • 133

Example: SUGIMOTO, T. and LEVIN, J.A. (2000) 'Multiple literacies and multimedia: a comparison of Japanese and American uses of the Internet', in G.E. Hawisher and C.L. Selfe (eds) *Global Literacies and the World-Wide Web*, London, Routledge, pp.133-53.

PART 4: ETHNOGRAPHIC APPROACHES

Introduction • 139

19: Ethnography and new literacy studies: women's literacy practices • 141
Example: ZUBAIR, S. (1999) 'Women's literacy in a rural Pakistani community', in
T. O'Brien, (ed.) *Language and Literacies, Selected Papers from the Annual General Meeting
of the British Association for Applied Linguistics*, University of Manchester,
September 1998, BAAL/Multilingual Matters, pp.114-25.

20: Ethnography and visual data: community literacy • 147
Example: HAMILTON, M. (2000) 'Expanding the new literacy studies. Using photographs
to explore literacy as social practice', in D. Barton, M. Hamilton and R. Ivanič (eds)
Situated Literacies. Reading and Writing in Context, London, Routledge, pp.16-34.

21: Ethnography and talk around texts: student academic writing • 153
Example: LILLIS, T.M. (2001) *Student Writing: Access, Regulation and Desire*,
London, Routledge.

**22: Ethnography and a Bakhtinian approach:
writing in the primary classroom • 159**
Example: DYSON, A.H. (1997) 'Rewriting for, and by, the children: the social and
ideological fate of a Media Miss in an urban classroom', *Written Communication*,
vol.14, no.3, pp.275-312.

**23: Ethnography and critical discourse analysis:
gender and school geography • 167**
Example: LEE, A. (1996) *Gender, Literacy, Curriculum. Re-writing School
Geography*, London, Taylor and Francis.

**24: Ethnography and interactional sociolinguistics:
language and identity • 175**
Example: RAMPTON, B. (1995) *Crossing: Language and Ethnicity Among Adolescents*,
London, Longman.

References • 187

Index • 193

Introduction

Aims of this workbook

The aim of this workbook is to provide an accessible, hands-on introduction to the analysis of language in context. The book can be used in a number of ways; for example, as a student reference text to briefly review a particular kind of language analysis or as a course textbook to introduce students to a variety of approaches to language data analysis.

In writing this book we set out to be:

- *Accessible*: we assume no previous knowledge on the part of the reader so we define key terms, provide theoretical background on the approaches discussed and guide readers through detailed data analysis.

- *Practical*: we use a step-by-step approach, with directions, questions and activities, to take readers through a range of analytical methods.

- *Authentic*: the data examples analysed and discussed are drawn from published work by experts in specific fields of language study.

- *Academically rigorous*: the examples discussed in the workbook are drawn from authentic research projects in the field of language study. Readers are not only introduced to particular analytic approaches but are also given the opportunity to 'hear' the expert voices in an accessible way.

- *Wide ranging*: in line with the current state of the field of language study, the examples are wide ranging in terms of both the methods represented and the contexts exemplified. Analytical methods are drawn from sociolinguistics, sociocultural approaches, ethnography, multimodal approaches and discourse analysis. Contexts include education, the media, informal communication and new technologies, with child, youth and adult participants. Data examples are from a range of national contexts including the UK, the USA, Australia, South Africa, Hong Kong, Japan and Pakistan.

This book will most obviously be of interest to those who are studying applied linguistics, communication studies, language and education, literacy studies, and the teaching and learning of English as a foreign/second language. It assumes no prior knowledge of data analysis, so will be suitable for beginners in this area, yet the range covered ensures that it has something to offer the more experienced reader. It is thus equally relevant to undergraduate and postgraduate students. The book will also be of interest to schoolteachers and trainers in English at primary and secondary levels, particularly given the increasing emphasis on the importance of teachers' linguistic subject knowledge.

How to use this workbook

We assume that this book will be used in different ways, according to readers' specific interests at a particular time. Lecturers can use this book as a resource, selecting examples of analytic approaches to discuss with students or even as a course textbook to introduce students to the range of analytical approaches that are available. Students can use this book as a resource or reference text, selecting the examples to read depending on the course being studied or specific research interests.

There are four main parts to the workbook, organised around the four main types of language data that researchers collect and analyse: Part 1 'Approaches to spoken interaction', Part 2 'Approaches to written texts', Part 3 'Multimodal approaches' and Part 4 'Ethnographic approaches'. Within each part, different approaches to data analysis are exemplified by focusing on authentic data extracts drawn from published research. Each specific approach is structured in the same way, as outlined in Table 1.

Table 1 The structure of each of the approaches examined in this workbook

1 **Key features of this approach.** The key features of each approach are briefly summarised

2 **Example.** Full details are given of the specific example of the approach to be considered

3 **The aims of the researchers.** The main aims of the researchers are listed

4 **Data extracts.** Data extracts are provided from researchers' published work

5 **Questions for you about the data.** We direct you to examine the data, asking you to consider some specific questions

6 **Some points from the researchers' analysis.** We summarise some of the main points made by the researchers in their analysis

7 **More questions for you about the data.** We ask you to look again at the data or to consider an additional data extract with specific questions in mind

8 **Further discussion and conclusions.** We summarise the main conclusions reached by the researchers

9 **Your view.** We ask you to consider the value of the approach exemplified

10 **Examples of studies using a similar approach.** We list some studies following a similar approach for further reading

---

Approaches to language analysis in the workbook

Throughout this book we use the word 'approach' to indicate in broad terms the particular methodological tradition that the researcher is drawing on. While they differ in important ways, all the approaches focus on *language in context*; that is, language is not treated as an abstract system of signs or symbols but rather as embedded in social contexts which profoundly influence the kind of language that is used, and how it is used and understood. Some of the approaches in the workbook are widely recognised in the various academic fields of language study, for example: sociolinguistic approaches to the study of dialect and codeswitching; critical discourse analysis; conversation analysis. Others are less easily definable because they draw on a number of approaches or combine approaches in new ways. For example, ethnography as an approach to researching and analysing language is increasingly being explicitly combined with a range of theoretical or analytic frameworks, such as critical discourse analysis, or the work of a particular social theorist. In labelling the approaches and the specific research examples we have tried to make them as transparent as possible to readers. Where a researcher has referred to her or his analysis as representing a particular approach, we have generally used their terms. For example, the approach used by Hutchby and Wooffitt (1998) to analyse radio talk between a presenter and a caller is explicitly called 'conversation analysis' by the authors and we have used this term (see Example 4 in this workbook). However, in some instances we have coined our own labels in an attempt to make explicit to the reader the specific features of the analytic framework being used by the researchers. For example, we have labelled the work by Scollon, Tsang, Li, Yung and Jones (1998) on professional writing by students as 'Bakhtinian discourse analysis', because of the prominent way in which they use the work of Bakhtin in their analysis (see Example 9 in this workbook).

About the examples

We use the word 'example' to refer to the specific study from which the data extracts are taken and the particular researcher's analysis we are discussing. There are 24 specific examples in the workbook illustrating different approaches to analysing language data. The 24 examples are drawn from authentic, publicly available academic research studies. Full references are provided for all the studies. We have used authentic examples in order to introduce readers to real academic research on language in context. In doing so we have aimed to represent as fairly as possible the main points of analysis of the original researchers. We have consciously tried not to critique the approaches but we encourage readers throughout to ask questions about different approaches and to consider their own perspectives on the approaches and examples discussed (in Step 9 outlined in Table 1) in the workbook. Our main aim is to introduce readers to the range of available ways of analysing language data and to emphasise what each approach has to offer.

Of course there are dangers in presenting others' analyses and it is important that readers bear in mind that we have had to be selective in the following ways:

- *The data extracts.* We have selected data extracts which illustrate the kinds of data that the researchers are working with. In many examples the data extracts are from larger research projects – for example, we may use one 15-line conversation to exemplify a study where more than 1000 lines were analysed.

- *The analysis.* We have aimed to summarise what we see as the main points of analysis, rather than attempting to provide a detailed overview of all the points made by the original researchers.

- *Conclusions.* We give an overview of the principal conclusions reached by the researchers. However, it is important to bear in mind that the conclusions reached by researchers are usually based on far more than the actual data extracts that are discussed in the examples in this workbook.

What kinds of data are included?

The data extracts discussed in the workbook represent a wide variety of contexts: *education* (for example, primary- and secondary-level schooling, English as a foreign language classrooms, higher education); *informal settings* (for example, home, communities, playtime at school); *media* (for example, magazine texts, television, film).

Many of the data extracts included and discussed in this workbook are from spoken and written verbal language. Spoken data includes naturally occurring language in informal contexts, the scripted language of film and the spoken language of teacher-pupil interaction. Written data includes primary school children's writing, students' academic writing, magazine texts and official letters. However, acknowledging the growing interest in the multimodal nature of communication, particularly with the advent of new technologies, several examples include data in a number of modes, such as visual as well as verbal. This raises difficult questions about representation: in this predominantly monomodal book, it is impossible to represent certain aspects of language data, such as sound or the three-dimensional nature and moving images. Thus, where necessary, we have followed the strategy of the original authors by representing the different modes in ways afforded by a verbal written text. So, in Example 17, in order to offer a representation of a television documentary film, we include a copy of the author's line drawing alongside his description of the action.

Ethnographic data, such as descriptions of particular people, contexts and places, are also included in some of the examples in this workbook, but it is always analysed alongside the analysis of other texts. For instance, Dyson (1997) draws on her ethnography of a primary classroom to explore the production of written texts (Example 22), and Hamilton (2000) draws on a longitudinal ethnographic study in focusing specifically on photographs of community literacy practices (Example 20).

Terminology used in the workbook

We have tried to keep specialist terminology to a minimum. However, becoming familiar with some specialist terminology is a key aspect of engaging in language research and analysis, so we have used relevant terms where necessary. In such cases we have aimed to provide appropriate definitions and explanations.

Two terms which are used throughout the workbook and which may seem confusing to readers new to this field are 'text' and 'discourse'. Following the practice in most applied linguistics research, we use the term text to refer to all the different kinds of spoken, written and multimodal data discussed (rather than the more common-sense use of the term to refer only to written language). The term discourse is more complex. Briefly, discourse in the area of language studies has three principal and, at times, quite distinct meanings: a stretch of language longer than a single sentence or utterance; a particular way of using language in a particular context; a particular way of constructing knowledge and representing the world. If we adopt and combine the first and second definitions, then all the data discussed in this workbook could be called discourse because the focus is always on actual stretches of language in context. In some examples, the third, more abstract, level of discourse is the focus of analysis, as in Example 13. Where the term discourse is explicitly used in an example as an analytic approach to data analysis, the specific way in which it is used is labelled and discussed; as in 'critical discourse analysis' (Example 13) and 'Bakhtinian discourse analysis' (Example 9).

About the four parts

The four parts of the book are organised broadly around the different kinds of data that are discussed. In many instances the reasons for a particular example being in a particular part of the workbook is obvious. For example, the analysis of talk between men and women by Fishman (Example 2) obviously fits well in Part 1 'Approaches to spoken interaction'. But some examples could have been placed in any one of several parts because they combine approaches and/or focus on several kinds of data. For instance, there are two examples we have labelled 'talk around text', which involve the use of spoken and written data – those by Hall (Example 10) and Lillis (Example 21). We decided to place the example by Hall in Part 2 'Approaches to written texts' because of Hall's principal emphasis on one aspect of the text – punctuation – and the example by Lillis in Part 4 'Ethnographic approaches' because of her emphasis on student perspectives alongside their written texts. In many studies more than one mode of data is collected and analysed and this is illustrated in several examples. However, we think the four main headings and parts are a useful starting point for considering different ways of analysing language data.

Part 1 'Spoken interaction' consists of six approaches to the analysis of spoken language – three from distinct approaches within the field of sociolinguistics, one from conversation analysis and two from a sociocultural approach. The contexts from which the data are analysed include informal conversation, student-teacher interaction and the media.

Part 2 'Approaches to written texts' consists of seven approaches to the analysis of written language including corpus linguistics, systemic functional linguistics and several discourse analytic approaches. Contexts illustrated are student writing at school and university level, and English as a foreign language classrooms; educational policy documents; the media.

Part 3 'Multimodal approaches' consists of five examples of multimodal approaches to language analysis, each of which combines analysis of one mode, verbal language, with other modes, such as visuality, materiality, movement and sound. Contexts include school classrooms, documentary film and Internet use.

Part 4 'Ethnographic approaches' consists of six examples of ethnographic approaches to the study of language and literacy. Ethnography is combined with a range of analytic approaches, including discourse analysis, interactional sociolinguistics and the use of visual data. Contexts include school classrooms, higher education and informal adolescent communication.

Acknowledgements

The authors would like to thank all those who have been involved in the production of this book. In particular we are grateful to all the researchers whose data we include and discuss in this book, the members of the team who produced the course of which this book is a part – **E844 Language and Literacy in a Changing World** – Sharon Goodman, Janet Maybin, Neil Mercer; Virginia Alitta, Elaine Ware, Andrew Coleman and Gill Gowans, and also Roz Ivanič who acted as external assessor for the course. We would also like to express our warm appreciation to Xiao Junhong for his detailed comments on earlier drafts.

Y como siempre a John, Guillermo, Carmen y Liam les damos las gracias por su apoyo y su alegría.

PART 1
APPROACHES TO SPOKEN INTERACTION

Introduction

The study of spoken language is a key interest for researchers from a number of disciplines. In Part 1 of the workbook we illustrate approaches from sociolinguistics, conversation analysis and sociocultural studies. The study of spoken language is at the heart of sociolinguistics and a wealth of research has been carried out in this area, ranging from a focus on the way specific aspects of language use (for example, sounds) vary in relation to speakers' social profiles and geographic context, to looking at the different ways in which people engage in conversation. The first three examples in this section are from the sociolinguistics tradition. The data analysed within such sociolinguistics studies is usually drawn from naturally occurring talk (or real conversation), which is illustrated in Examples 2 and 3. In Example 2 we discuss Fishman's analysis of the informal, private conversation of mixed-sex couples, which focuses on features of conversational strategies by men and women. The analysis in Example 3 is from Ncoko *et al.*'s exploration of how and why multilingual primary school children in South Africa switch in their conversation between the different languages they know. The data in Example 1 is not from real conversations but from Disney films. Lippi-Green explores the link between avvent and dialect and characerisation in these films (for an overview of sociolinguistics, see Mesthrie *et al.*, 2000, Chapter 1; Holmes, 2001, Chapter 1).

The fourth example in this part uses a conversation analysis approach. Conversation analysis developed from an interest by US sociologists in explaining how people make sense of everyday behaviour. Rather than focusing on large-scale social patterns, they were interested in exploring the detail of interactions in context (see Sacks, 1984). The focus in the example in the workbook is Hutchby and Wooffitt's analysis of the spoken interaction between a presenter and a caller on a radio phone-in talk show. The final two examples in Part 1 are from the area of psychology, and illustrate a sociocultural approach to the study of classroom talk. This approach relies heavily on the work of Vygotsky, who emphasised the important relationship between language, social interaction and learning (see Vygotsky, 1986). Example 5 outlines Mercer's analysis of teacher-pupil talk to explain how talk is used in classroom learning; in Example 6 we take you through Alexander's approach to analysing teacher-student interaction in the different cultural contexts of India, Russia and the UK.

There are a number of tricky questions facing researchers of spoken language. One of these is: how should spoken language be transcribed? Deciding how much detail to include or how much of the non-verbal aspects to observe and record will depend largely on the purpose of the analysis. Some approaches require far more detailed transcription than others. For example, in conversation analysis the exact length of each pause and the duration of each overlap in talk is viewed as crucial. Two transcription keys are provided in Part 1 (p.26, p.47) to illustrate the different features researchers choose to describe. For the most part, non-verbal aspects of spoken interaction are not recorded or commented on in the examples in Part 1; the transcription of some non-verbal aspects is discussed in Part 4 (Example 14). Another key question is: how much transcription detail should be presented to the reader? Most researchers want as many readers as possible to read transcriptions of their spoken language, without burdening them with too much detail. There are no easy answers to questions about transcription, but it is important to be aware of some of the decisions researchers face.

1: Sociolinguistics: accent and dialect in film

1.1 Key features of this approach

The study of accent and dialect is a key area in sociolinguistics. 'Accent' refers to pronunciation or the sound features of language; 'dialect' refers to particular uses of vocabulary and grammar. In many studies of accent, quantitative methods are used – that is, the amount of data (the database) is usually large and the data is quantified in some way. The assumption is that it should be possible for other researchers to carry out the same kind of analysis using the same data, and to reach the same conclusions (that is, it should be replicable).

Recording naturally occurring talk makes it possible to identify patterns of pronunciation and to map these against social variables such as age, gender, occupation and geographical location. For example, one of the sounds that Labov explored in his famous study carried out on Martha's Vineyard, an island off the New England coast, was the *ai* sound in words such as *white, right, kind* (Labov, 1963). By documenting the range of pronunciations of these words, Labov was able to identify distinct patterns of usage across different sectors of the island's population. He was also able to offer an explanation for why one group, younger people, seemed to be using a more distinctly island pronunciation of these words (*right* pronounced more like *rute*); to assert their identity as islanders in contrast to the increasing number of tourists visiting the island. This study exemplifies what is known as a 'linguistic variationist' approach, which involves, briefly stated, treating variation in the sounds of spoken language as being explicable in terms of patterns of social differentiation (for an overview of Labov's study as an example of a variationist approach, see Mesthrie *et al.*, 2000, Chapter 3).

1.2 Example

LIPPI-GREEN, R. (1996) *English with an Accent*, London, Routledge [Chapter 5 'Teaching children how to discriminate what we learn from the Big Bad Wolf'].

In this example, Lippi-Green uses a combination of approaches to analyse the representation of characters in Disney films. First, she draws on a 'variationist approach', focusing on particular features of the language spoken by Disney characters. This includes: accent – that is, the different kinds of English accents used (which she classifies in specific ways, as we discuss below); and dialect – sentence or syntactic structure; the use of marked lexical items – that is, words which would not be considered to be standard American English. Second, she uses 'content analysis', which involves looking at who the characters are and what they represent. While the linguistic analysis is concerned with *how* certain characters speak, the content analysis is concerned with *what* they say and with what kind of person they represent, based on their role in the film and their actions – for example, are they 'goodies' or 'baddies'?.

Because the analysis is of media representations, the data is pre-existing rather than specifically designed or collected for the research. In this example the actual data is not made available, only the researcher's analysis.

1.3 The aims of the researcher
Lippi-Green aims to:

- explore how characters are represented in Disney's animated films, with a specific focus on how stereotypes function sociolinguistically

- find out how the language varieties spoken by different characters are used to stereotype different social groups, and thus offer particular messages to children about different social groups.

1.4 Data extracts *(see data extracts 1.1-1.6)*
In this example, the data consisted of all available full-length Disney animated films produced between 1938 and 1994. All the characters with speaking roles of more than one word were analysed (a total of 371 characters). Here Lippi-Green does not provide examples of this data but rather provides her analysis of the data in a quantified form.

1.5 Questions for you about the data
(i) Look at Data Extract 1.1. Can you think of specific Disney characters who would exemplify the categories used by Lippi-Green here?

(ii) Are you surprised by the breakdown of accents that Lippi-Green offers here?

(iii) Look at Data Extracts 1.2 and 1.3. In which setting is the highest number of Disney characters located? In Data Extract 1.3, which setting has the highest percentage of 'foreign-accented' English characters?

(iv) Based on the breakdown of characters with negative motivations in Data Extract 1.4, do you think that there is any relationship between 'foreign-accented' and characters represented as evil?

(v) Based on the comparison of major characters in Data Extract 1.5, can you see any relationship between 'foreign-accented' and characters represented as evil?

(vi) What can you conclude based on your reading of Data Extracts 1.1-1.5?

1.6 Some points from the researcher's analysis
Lippi-Green uses a range of terms to describe the accents of the Disney characters. In Data Extract 1.1, a key distinction she makes is between mainstream United States English (MUSE) and regional or socially marked varieties. She explains MUSE as a variety 'which is not stigmatised in social or regional terms' (Lippi-Green, 1997, p.87),

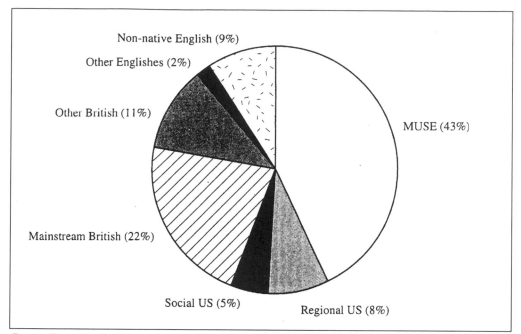

Data Extract 1.1 *Three hundred and seventy-one Disney animated characters by language variety used (Source: Lippi-Green, 1996, Figure 5.3, p.88) [MUSE: Mainstream United States English]*

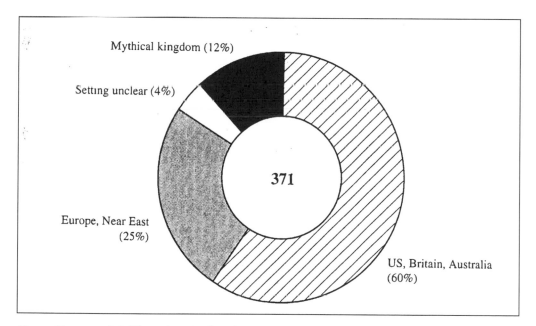

Data Extract 1.2 *Three hundred and seventy-one Disney animated characters by story setting (percentage figures rounded up) (Source: Lippi-Green, 1996, Figure 5.4, p.88) [MUSE: Mainstream United States English]*

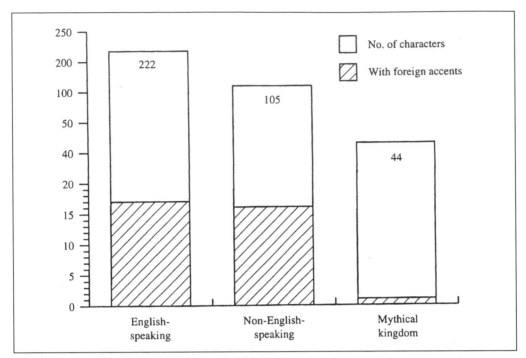

Data Extract 1.3 *Three hundred and seventy-one Disney animated characters by language spoken in the country in which the story is set, and the number of characters with foreign-accented English (Source: Lippi-Green, 1996, Figure 5.5, p.89)*

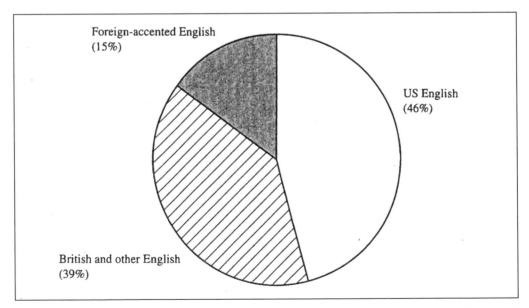

Data Extract 1.4 *Seventy-two Disney animated characters with negative motivations and actions by major language group (Source: Lippi-Green, 1996, Figure 5.7, p.91)*

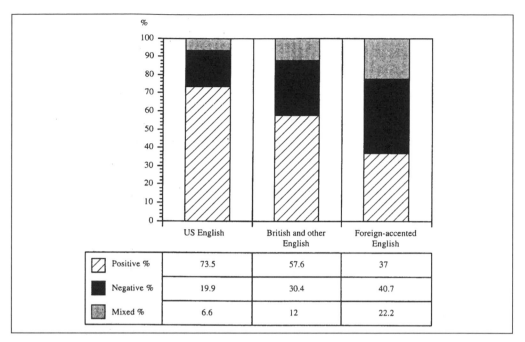

	US English	British and other English	Foreign-accented English
Positive %	73.5	57.6	37
Negative %	19.9	30.4	40.7
Mixed %	6.6	12	22.2

Data Extract 1.5 *Two hundred and eighty-five Disney animated characters of positive, negative or mixed motivations and actions, by major language group (Source: Lippi-Green, 1996, Figure 5.8, p.92)*

Language variety	Film	Male	Female
Mainstream US	Beauty and the Beast	Gaston	(no mate)
		The Beast	Belle
	Rescuers	Bernard	–
	Rescuers Down Under	Bernard	–
	Cinderella	Prince Charming	Cinderella
	Sleeping Beauty	Prince Philip	Aurora
	Little Mermaid	Prince Erik	Ariel
	Snow White	Prince	Snow White
	Lion King	Simba	Nala
	Lady and the Tramp	–	Lady
Socially marked US	Lady and the Tramp	Jock	–
	Aristocats	O'Malley	–
Non-US English	Robin Hood	Robin Hood	Maid Marion
	Rescuers Down Under	Jake	(no mate)
	101 Dalmations	Pongo	Perdita
		Roger Radcliff	Anita Radcliff
Foreign-accented English	Rescuers	–	Miss Bianca
	Rescuers Down Under	–	Miss Bianca
	Aristocats	–	Duchess

Data Extract 1.6 *Lovers and potential lovers in Disney animated films (Source: Lippi-Green, 1996, Table 5.4, p.95)*

preferring to use the less evaluative term 'mainstream' in place of 'standard'. 'Social US' or 'Socially marked US' refers to a non-mainstream use of English that is socially marked in some way – for example, as having features associated with working class speech. 'Regional US' refers to a non-mainstream variety that is associated with a particular geographical region.

In Data Extract 1.3, Lippi-Green divides the films according to their language setting as 'English-speaking' (for example, USA, Britain), 'non-English speaking' (for example, France) and 'Mythical Kingdom' (for example, the unspecified, possibly Mediterranean, setting of *The Little Mermaid*), and shows the number of characters with what she refers to as 'foreign-accented English'. She points out that the highest proportion (16/105) of foreign-accented characters occurs in films located in non-English settings, probably because foreign accents are often used to indicate that the language spoken in that setting would not usually be English. But, Lippi-Green emphasises, even more characters (17) with foreign accents appear in the English-setting stories.

In Data Extract 1.4, Lippi-Green takes all the characters that are negatively motivated, that is, those that are representative of evil in stories which draw a clear line between good and evil, and classifies them according to major language group. She includes all characters in this figure, even those in minor roles, and points out that the figure seems to indicate that there is no relationship between the portrayal of good and evil and non-native accents.

However, Lippi-Green argues that this conclusion is complicated by Data Extract 1.5, in which she removes the marginal characters and compares the proportions of positive, negative and mixed motivations in each major language group. This comparison shows that the general representation of characters with foreign accents is far more negative than that of US or British English accented characters. While about 20% of US English speakers are bad characters, 40% of non-native speakers of English are evil. Lippi-Green concludes that characters with clearly positive actions and motivations overwhelmingly speak US and British mainstream varieties of English, while characters with strongly negative motivations and actions often speak varieties of English linked to marginalised social groups and to specific geographical regions.

1.7 More questions for you about the data

(vii) Look at Data Extract 1.6, which categorises characters who are 'lovers' or 'potential lovers' in Disney films according to gender and the variety of English used. What variety of English do the majority of male lovers speak?

(viii) How many male lovers speak with 'foreign' accents?

1.8 Further discussion and conclusions

Lippi-Green concludes that, regardless of the setting of the story or the individual character's ethnicity, the majority of lovers speak mainstream US or British English, and that there are no male romantic leads with 'foreign' accents. Thus ideal lovers and potential mates are consistently portrayed in a way that lacks 'otherness' of any kind. The two female characters with 'foreign' accents are both voiced by Eva Gabor, an actress well known in the USA, and thus Lippi-Green argues that the association of the audience with the famous actress overrides considerations of accent. Lippi-Green concludes that 'to be truly sexually attractive and available in a Disney film, a character must not only look the idealised part, but he or she must also sound white and middle class American or British' (p.97).

Lippi-Green carries out similar analyses with the use of African-American Vernacular English (AAVE) in Disney animated films. She finds that almost all of these characters are animal rather than humanoid and are either unemployed or show no purpose in life other than making music and pleasing themselves. Her analysis shows that the distribution of language varieties in Disney films is such that those varieties that are marked in terms of national origins, ethnicities and races are linked with social norms and characteristics that are at best non-factual, and, often, overtly discriminatory. Characters with the widest variety of life choices and possibilities available to them are overwhelmingly male and speakers of MUSE or a non-stigmatised variety of British English.

Lippi-Green argues that 'what children learn from the entertainment industry is to be comfortable with *same* and to be wary about *other*, and that language is a prime and ready diagnostic for this division between what is approachable and what is best left alone' (p.103). She feels that this is extremely worrying when one considers that, for some children, this is the only contact they have with 'others'.

1.9 Your view

(ix) To what extent are you convinced by the categories Lippi-Green uses to organise her analysis of the data – 'English-speaking', 'non-English-speaking', 'mainstream United States English', 'mainstream varieties', 'foreign-accented'?

(x) What do you think of Lippi-Green's argument that ideologies regarding language variation and stereotypes are perpetuated through children's animated films?

(xi) What do you think the strengths of this approach are? What are the weaknesses or tensions?

(xii) Can you think of an example of research that could be carried out using this approach in your own context?

1.10 Examples of studies using a similar approach

A considerable amount of work on accent and dialect has been carried out. For classic studies, see:

LABOV, W. (1972) *Language in the Inner City: Studies in the Black English Vernacular,* Philadelphia, University of Philadelphia Press.

TRUDGILL, P. (1975) *Accent, Dialect and the School*, London, Edward Arnold.

For a further study on ethnicity and representation in Disney films, see:

BURTON, J. (1992) 'Don (Juanito) Duck and the imperial-patriarchal unconscious: Disney studios, the good neighbour policy, and the packaging of Latin America', in A. Parker, M. Russo, D. Sommer *et al.* (eds) *Nationalisms and Sexualities*, New York, Routledge, pp.21-41.

2: Interactional sociolinguistics: gender and informal talk

2.1 Key features of this approach

Interactional sociolinguistics (IS), as the name suggests, focuses on the ways in which participants interact in conversation. Researchers working within this approach believe that communication is not simply about decoding what participants mean, but is an on-going process of negotiation. In negotiating specific interactions, participants draw on their background knowledge about other participants and the sociocultural context of the interaction. A key aim of interactional sociolinguistics is to show how participants in interaction achieve their communicative goals through talk 'by concentrating on the meaning-making processes and the taken-for-granted background assumptions that underlie the negotiation of shared interpretations' (Gumperz, 1999, p.454).

Much work in interactional sociolinguistics centres on diversity. For example, IS is often used to examine how participants from diverse social and cultural backgrounds engage in spoken interaction. The approach is often used to analyse cross-cultural interaction and to explain failures in such interaction, or to explain how problems are often produced in interactions when communicative assumptions are not always shared by participants. Because interactional sociolinguistics aims to understand real-life conversation, data consists of naturally occurring spoken interaction which is usually tape-recorded and carefully transcribed to mark many aspects of spoken interaction, including, for example, overlaps in conversation and pauses.

2.2 Example

FISHMAN, P. (1998) 'Conversational insecurity', reprinted in D. Cameron (ed.) *The Feminist Critique of Language* (2nd edn), London, Routledge, pp.253-8. [Article first published in 1980.]

This example illustrates a relatively recent but rich area of language study: the relationship between language and gender. Fishman's example focuses on some specific features of language used by women in mixed-sex conversation. She aims both to describe where these features occur and to offer an explanation for their occurrence.

2.3 The aims of the researcher

Fishman aims to:

- challenge the idea that women's extensive use of 'you know' in spoken interaction reflects insecurity, which derives from the notion of a 'female personality'

• propose a different explanation for this feature of women's language by analysing the specific function that 'you know' serves in actual instances of spoken interaction.

2.4 Data extracts *(see data extracts 2.1-2.2)*

Data Extracts 2.1 and 2.2 are two samples of male/female conversation recorded by Fishman focusing on the use of 'you know'.

These extracts are taken from a much fuller analysis that Fishman conducts of 52 hours of tape recorded naturally occurring conversation between three male/female couples who agreed to have tape recorders placed in their apartments for 4-14 days.

The numbers in brackets indicate the length of pauses in seconds.

1	F	he's talking about the differences, that the women [1.3] uhm [0.8]
2		that the black women represent to the black men, [0.5] white
3		society [0.8] and that uhm [1.5] they stand for all the white values
4		like they're dressed much neater than the men. They're obviously
5		trying much harder, y'know, and they're more courteous and polite
6		etcetera, etcetera, you know. [1.5] It seems to me that the women
7		because of our [0.7] chauvinism in this society are constantly being
8		put down for things that the same set of the same traits in a man
9		would be put up. [1.5] Like this – he uses different words, you
10		know? [1.5] uhmm [1]. For instance you know they try more
11		they're more conscientious. This sort of thing the goddam blighter
12		used to say about a man, 'n'-, and so on. [1] It's just obvious that
13		– [3] uhh [1], he doesn't know what to do with the fact that the
14		women, the black women [1] uh you know, for a multitude of
15		reasons probably, have come out to be much stronger in many
16		ways than black men. [1] Y'know they hold families together,
17		they're also the bread earners, [1] they just have to go through a
18		lot more shit then the men it seems, and they're stronger for it.
19		[1] and uhm [1.5] he doesn't know what to make of the fact that
20		[0.9] they do all these things, [2] y'know, and so he just puts them
21		down. In a blind and chauvinistic way. [2.5] In other words black
22		women are white. [2] Y'know it's really a simplistic article [0.5]
23		you know he starts off saying – this – [1] y'know, [0.8] sort of
24		this gross, indiscriminate, black versus white [1] vison and .. ..

Data Extract 2.1 Male-female talk (Source: Fishman, 1998, pp.256-7)

2.5 Questions for you about the data

(i) Underline or circle the use of the phrase 'you know' in Data Extracts 2.1 and 2.2.

(ii) What purposes do you think the phrase 'you know' serves in the two extracts?

(iii) Do you think 'you know' is serving different purposes in Data Extracts 2.1 and 2.2, and if so, what might these be?

1	F	Many of the men I've met have been incredibly uhh provincial [2]
2		in a sense [1] Umm and it also you know you've got a-, mind you,
3		I know that Richard has had a very good education [2] but he's a
4		very taciturn man and very bitter about the way he's been treated.
5		He's ve-, you know old family in regards
6	M	umphhh
7	F	Well you know some people got caught up in it I mean
8	M	oh of course [1.1]
9	F	You know I mean [0.6] yes I'm sure I mean he's very conserva-
10		tive, right? I mean I'm [1] he hates everything [0.7] and I am I am
11		sure he didn't before but [1] whenever you talk to his father about
12		it [0.6] he [1.5] he is very confused. I mean apparently he, he was
13		[0.7] very active [0.6] hated Germany [2] and yet turned around
14		afterwards [1] you know which is sort of
15	M	Oh the trouble is that he turned against everything, even the war.

Data Extract 2.2 *Male-female talk (Source: Fishman, 1998, pp.257-8)*

(iv) How would you describe the nature of men's participation in these conversations?

2.6 Some points from the researcher's analysis

In her analysis, Fishman finds that women's use of 'you know' is concentrated in longer speaking turns in which the speaker is unsuccessfully attempting to carry out a conversation. The conversation is unsuccessful because there is very little, or no, response from the men in the conversation

In Data Extract 2.1, Fishman shows that eight out of the ten 'you know's cluster around pauses in the woman's speech, either before or after pauses – see lines 5, 6, 14, 16, 20, 22 and 23. She explains that these are often pauses where the man might have responded to the conversation or taken a conversational turn. The phrase 'you know' is therefore functioning as an explicit invitation to the (male) conversational partner to respond and plays the role of displaying the man as co-participant, even though he isn't responding. Fishman argues that in the absence of the man's responses, the woman uses 'you know' both to invite a response and to take the place of his responses.

In Data Extract 2.2, Fishman shows that two out of the five uses (lines 2 and 14) occur after internal pauses in the woman's speech, similar to Data Extract 2.1 and with a similar function. But she says the other three uses are a little different, as 'you know' clusters around the man's minimal responses (lines 5, 7 and 9). Fishman points out that minimal responses indicate minimal rather than full participation from the conversational partner in the extract as they fill the necessity of a turn but don't add anything to the context and progress of the conversation. Thus the use of 'you know' around minimal responses fulfils a similar function to its use around pauses: in both cases there is a 'speaker change' problem. Fishman explains that, in both extracts, the women are unsuccessfully attempting to elicit a response to their turn.

Fishman argues that the use of 'you know' is evidence not of women's insecurity but rather of the work that women are doing in order to 'turn insecure conversations into successful ones' (p.258). This results from men often not doing the conversational work necessary to keep the conversation going.

2.7 More questions for you about the data

(v) Look again at the data extracts. Can you identify differences in the ways in which the men and women participate in the conversations?

(vi) If yes, how would you explain these differences?

2.8 Further discussion and conclusions

The data extracts we discussed are a small part of the data Fishman analyses in her attempt to challenge the work of Robin Lakoff on women's language use (Lakoff, 1979). Briefly stated, Lakoff argued that women's linguistic behaviour is influenced by a female personality that is more insecure, emotional and dependent than men, acquired through socialisation.

Fishman did find, in support of Lakoff's work, that women used more questions than men – two and a half times as many – as well as more hedges, for example, five times more 'you know's. But Fishman hypothesised that if Lakoff's socialisation argument were correct, the women's use of 'you know', and questions, should be randomly scattered evenly across their conversation. Her analysis shows that rather than being used randomly, 'you know's cluster around points in the conversation where there is little response and thus they perform a particular role in helping women to solve conversational difficulties. Fishman also found – though this cannot be shown by the short data extracts here – that women had more difficulty in getting their topics taken up and responded to by men in conversation. Thus Fishman explains women's linguistic behaviour in terms of the interactional situation in which it is produced, rather than as a feature of female personality.

Fishman concludes that

> Socially-structured power relations are reproduced and actively maintained in our everyday interactions. Women's conversational troubles reflect not their inferior social training [as Lakoff argues] but their inferior social position. (p.258)

2.9 Your view on this approach

(vii) What do you think the value of this kind of analysis is?

(viii) Do you accept Fishman's argument that the conversational trouble women experience follows from their inferior social position?

(ix) What do you think the limitations of this approach are?

(x)   What other kinds of research do you think you could use this approach for?

(xi) Can you think of ways in which this approach might be used to explore an aspect of interaction in your own context?

2.10 Examples of studies using a similar approach

For discussion and exemplification of interactional sociolinguistics, see:

GUMPERZ, J. (1999) 'On interactional sociolinguistic method', in S. Sarangi and C. Roberts (eds) *Talk, Work and Institutional Order*, Berlin, Mouton de Gruyter, pp.453-71.

For an example of a study focusing explicitly on gender and interaction, see:

CAMERON, D., MCALINDEN, F. and O'LEARY, K. (1988) 'Lakoff in context: the social and linguistic functions of tag questions', in J. Coates and D. Cameron (eds) *Women in Their Speech Communities*, London, Longman.

For an example of a study focusing explicitly on male conversation, see:

JOHNSON, S. and FINLAY, F. (1997) 'Do men gossip? An analysis of football talk on television', in S. Johnson and U.H. Meinhof (eds) *Language and Masculinity*, Oxford, Blackwell.

3: Sociolinguistics: codeswitching at school

3.1 Key features of this approach

The study of codeswitching is an area of sociolinguistics that analyses naturally occurring interaction in which people change from using one language (code) to another. Codeswitching can take place at different points in any spoken exchange; for example, switches can be made by the same speaker both within the same sentence – intra-sentential – and between different sentences – intersentential – as well as switches occurring according to the speaker being addressed.

Codeswitching is viewed as a dynamic phenomenon that can only be explained in relation to the social context in which it is used. The social negotiation of rights and obligations of the speaker, based on the norms of particular speech communities and power relationships, are important in understanding why and how codeswitching occurs. The choice of language can depend on the social goals to be achieved in a particular speech situation (for an overview, see Myers-Scotton, 1993). Despite the reasons for codeswitching often being framed in terms of linguistic 'choices', it is not necessarily a conscious action. There are a number of social dimensions that are perhaps being negotiated in codeswitching, including 'identity, interpersonal relationships, social positions, group solidarity, ethnic identity, exploring new relationships, status, level of education, authority, neutrality, distancing or intimacy' (Ncoko *et al.*, 2000, p.229).

3.2 Example

NCOKO, S.O.S., OSMAN, R. and COCKCROFT, K. (2000) 'Codeswitching among multilingual learners in primary schools in South Africa: an exploratory study', *International Journal of Bilingual Education and Bilingualism*, vol.3, no.4, pp.225-41.

In this example, Ncoko, Osman and Cockcroft focus on codeswitching by schoolchildren in a multilingual South African context, both inside and outside the school classroom. They document where codeswitching occurs and offer explanations as to why.

3.3 The aims of the researchers

Ncoko *et al.*'s aims are to:

- analyse 'the effects of an English-language setting on the occurrence of codeswitching between multilingual learners in a primary school' (p.229)

- establish the extent of codeswitching taking place and to analyse the different reasons for codeswitching in both formal settings (the classroom) and informal settings (the playground).

3.4 Data extracts *(see data extracts 3.1-3.3)*

Data Extracts 3.1, 3.2 and 3.3 record the conversation of primary school children between the ages of 6 and 10 from two different English medium of instruction schools in South Africa. Half of the children at the schools used English as a second language and were multilingual in indigenous South African languages.

It is important to note that the controversies surrounding the use of the term 'ethnic'/'ethnicity' in any context are particularly complex in the South African context. 'Ethnic group' is often used in present day South Africa to refer to different language groups among African people (e.g. isiZulu, isiXhosa) although this term is not used unproblematicially due to the artificial construction of 'racial' groups during apartheid.

1	A:	Can I use your koki pens?
2	B:	No, they dry quickly.
3	A:	Oh! Please *ngizowavala mangiqeda ukuwa-user* (isiZulu). [I will close them
4		after using them.]
5	B:	No, I don't want you to use them.
6	A:	*Ngiyakucela, toe* (isiZulu). [Oh, please, I beg you.]
7	B:	No.
8	A:	*Kulungile* (isiZulu) [It's fine], I am not going to let you use my wax crayons.
9	B:	Who cares.

Data Extract 3.1 *Codeswitching in a formal setting (in the classroom) (Source: Ncoko et al., 2000, p.232)*

1	A:	If you do not go out I will lock you in.
2	B:	*Uthi uzokhiya* (isiZulu). [She says she is going to lock.]
3	C:	*Wantina* (seSotho). [She irritates me.]
4	A:	What are you saying?
5	B:	*O nahanang? O nahana hore o-boss wa rona. Nna ke tla o hijacka ke ye le*
6		*wena locationing* (seSotho). [What do you think? You think that you are our
7		boss. I am going to hijack you and take you to the township.]

Data Extract 3.2 *Codeswitching in an informal setting (Source: Ncoko et al., 2000, p.234)*

1	A:	*Uyazi ama-prefects ayakhetha* (isiZulu). [You know prefects discriminate.]
2	B:	I know, *thina abanandaba nathi* (isiZulu). [I know, they do not care about us.]
3		They like *ama*-Grade 1 prep *nama*-Grade 1 (isiZulu). [They like Grade 1 prep
4		and Grade 1.]
5	A:	*Thina bayasi-*shout-*a* all the time (isiZulu). [They shout at us all the time.]
6	C:	What did you say?
7	A:	We are talking about the prefects. They are always in favour of Grade 1 prep
8		and Grade 1s.
9	B:	It's not fair because they do allow Grade 1s to play on our playground.
10		*Asambe manje* (isiZulu). [Let's go now.]
11	A:	*Kulungile* (isiZulu). [It's fine.]

Data Extract 3.3 *Codeswitching in an informal setting (Source: Ncoko et al., 2000, p.233)*

3.5 Questions for you about the data

(i) Look at Data Extract 3.1. This interaction takes place in the English language classroom between two multilingual children. What kind of interaction is this?

(ii) Why do you think A codeswitches from English to isiZulu in line 3?

(iii) Why do you think B refuses to respond in isiZulu, despite her ability to do so?

(iv) Look at Data Extract 3.2. This interaction takes place outside class time and involves three children: A, who is a prefect and monolingual in English, and B and C, who are multilingual in isiZulu-seSotho-English. What kind of interaction is this?

(v) Why do you think B uses isiZulu in line 2?

(vi) Why do you think C responds to B in seSotho in line 3 and that B answers A in seSotho in lines 5-7?

(vii) Look at Data Extract 3.3. This interaction takes place in the playground. A and B are multilingual and C is monolingual in English. What kind of interaction is this?

(viii) Why do you think A and B codeswitch in the first three turns of the conversation?

(ix) Why does A switch to English in line 7?

(x) Why do B and A codeswitch to isiZulu again in lines 10 and 11?

3.6 Some points from the researchers' analysis

Ncoko *et al.* explain that in the interaction in Data Extract 3.1, A uses codeswitching to change the tone of the conversation. Thus codeswitching here serves a 'phatic', or emotional, function. The phatic function can be positive – narrowing social distance – or negative – increasing social distance. In this instance, the conversation starts off in the language that is permitted in the classroom: English. When B is unsuccessful in her request, she switches to isiZulu, thus reminding A that they belong to the same ethnic group, that is, language group, and so hoping that A might reconsider. B, however, rejects A's attempt at solidarity, that is, her attempt to arouse sympathetic feelings based on shared language background, and shows this by refusing to loan the *koki* (felt-tipped) pens as well as refusing to switch into isiZulu. In Data Extract 3.2, Ncoko *et al.* show that the use of codeswitching is exclusive, that is, it serves to exclude the monolingual English-speaking prefect and to narrow the social distance between the multilingual children. In this example, the codeswitching is conscious and serves to hide negative comments made about A. In line 2, spoken by B in isiZulu, the codeswitching is not negative, as it merely repeats A's words, but in lines 3 and 5-7 B and C use seSotho to speak unfavourably about the prefect. A and B explained to the researchers that they switched to seSotho to make sure that the prefect could not understand, as isiZulu is taught at the school and the prefect might have understood it.

In Data Extract 3.3, Ncoko *et al.* describe the codeswitching as having a directive function to specify who is being addressed – that is, the recipient – in the conversation. The researchers explain that here A switches from isiZulu to English to accommodate a monolingual speaker C in the conversation and to invite her to comment on the issue. The codeswitch to English in line 7 thus serves an *inclusive* function. However, B then switches back to isiZulu in line 10 to show that C is not invited to go with them and A responds in isiZulu. The switch in lines 10 and 11 thus seems to serve an *exclusive* function.

3.7 More questions for you about the data
   (xi) Can you think of any further reasons for codeswitching apart from those illustrated and discussed above?

3.8 Further discussion and conclusions
Ncoko *et al.* identify a number of further reasons for codeswitching apart from phatic, solidarity and directive – either inclusive or exclusive. They also found that the children used codeswitching to show defiance in the classroom, that is, using codeswitching to defy the English-only setting, though this kind of deliberate defiance was rare. They found that outside the classroom codeswitching was sometimes used to find out what the addressee's language was (exploratory choice), to quote and report what another person had said in a different language (for example, reporting what the teacher said in English in an otherwise isiZulu conversation) and to emphasise, reinforce or clarify an idea, that is for reiterative reasons. As already stated, codeswitching is often related to individual and group identity. Ncoko *et al.* show that codeswitching was used to hide one's identity in a case where a child did not want people to know his or her home language. It was also used as a strategy of neutrality when interaction between children with different home languages took place in order to avoid allowing one language to dominate – this would typically involve codeswitching among about four languages in the conversation. Finally, the researchers argue that codeswitching occurred as an indictor of ethnic identity and solidarity, particularly intragroup when children switched

between certain languages, even if they were not very competent in them, because they wanted to be associated with members of this language group.

Ncoko *et al.* thus conclude that whether it is used consciously or not, codeswitching is used frequently by multilingual learners in English medium of instruction schools and has specific aims. Their research provides support for Makoni's (1999) argument about the interconnectedness of languages. Makoni argues that in South Africa codeswitching is the norm and pure Zulu or Tswana, for example, are rare. South Africa has eleven official languages: isiZulu, isiXhosa, isiNdebele, siSwati, seSotho, sePedi, seTswana, tshiVenda, xiTsonga, and the languages of the whites, English and Afrikaans. The first four languages make up the Nguni language group, which is most common in urban areas. The next three make up the Sotho group, also common in urban areas. TshiVenda and xiTsonga are spoken mostly in rural areas. Ncoko *et al.* point out here that it is relatively easy for speakers of Nguni languages to communicate with each other, as it is for speakers of any of the Sotho languages.

Ncoko *et al.*'s codeswitching research serves the purpose of making sense of a particular linguistic phenomenon, that is, codeswitching by multilingual children in an English medium of instruction primary school. It also feeds into a political debate about multilingualism in South Africa and debates concerning language policy. It shows codeswitching as a valuable resource for multilingual learners that needs to be tapped as a strategy for teaching and learning.

3.9 Your views

(xii) What problems might you anticipate in the collection of naturally occurring language data necessary for research like this?

(xiii) How convincing do you find Ncoko *et al.*'s analysis of codeswitching?

(xiv) How do you think codeswitching can be used as a resource in a classroom of multilingual learners?

(xv) Can you think of a way you could research codeswitching in your own context?

3.10 Examples of studies using a similar approach

A classic study is:

POPLACK, S. (1980) 'Sometimes I'll start a sentence in Spanish y termino en Español: towards a typology of codeswitching', *Linguistics*, vol.18, no.7/8, pp.581-618.

For a further example of classroom-based research, see:

MARTIN, P.W. (1996) 'Codeswitching in the primary classroom: one response to the planned and unplanned language environment in Brunei', *Journal of Multilingual and Multicultural Development*, vol.17, pp.128-44.

A further example of a specifically South African study is:

KAMWANGAMALU, N.M. (1998) "We-codes', 'they-codes', and 'codes-in-between": identities of English and codeswitching in post-apartheid South Africa', *Multilingua*, vol.17, no.2/3, pp.277-96.

4: Conversation analysis: radio talk

4.1 Key features of this approach

Conversation analysts view talk-in-interaction as an ordered social activity that is not reducible to individual character, mood, and so on. Researchers working within a conversation analysis (CA) approach aim to uncover and describe the nature of this order by focusing on the ways in which participants engage in interaction.

Because of the emphasis on describing the order of spoken interaction, the aim in CA is for analysis to be 'data-driven'. This means that the questions to be asked should arise from the interaction itself and never be developed prior to analysis. This contrasts with other kinds of analysis, where one might examine the role of a particular pre-existing factor, such as gender, in the interaction (as in Example 2 in this workbook). Conversation analysis focuses on how utterances are designed to do particular things, for example, to elicit a positive response to a suggestion or to decline an invitation. Importantly, CA examines how utterances link together to form an identifiable sequence of conversation. Thus, crucial to CA is an examination of how one conversational turn follows on from another, as conversation analysts believe that this patterning reveals participants' own interpretations within the conversation, even if these are unconscious. The data collected is usually naturally occurring conversation, which is transcribed in a very particular and detailed way (see the transcription glossary on page 24).

4.2 Example

HUTCHBY, I. and WOOFFITT, R. (1998) *Conversation Analysis. Principles, Practices and Applications*, Cambridge, Polity Press [Chapter 4 'Analysing phenomena'].

In this example, Hutchby and Wooffitt focus on talk between a radio presenter and callers. They use a conversation analytic method for identifying key interactional features of disagreements between callers and the host presenter.

4.3 The aims of the researchers

Hutchby and Wooffitt aim to:

- find out what 'interactional business' is being accomplished through the use of a particular sequential pattern in conversation

- examine how participants show their active orientation to this interactional business.

Figure 1: Transcription glossary *(Source: Hutchby and Wooffitt, 1998, pp.vi-vii)*

(0.5)	The number in brackets indicates a time gap in tenths of a second.
(.)	A dot enclosed in a bracket indicates a pause in the talk of less than two-tenths of a second.
=	The 'equals' sign indicates 'latching' between utterances. For example:

Si: yeah September ⌈seventy six=
S2:   ⌊September
Si: =it would be
S2:   yeah that's right

[ ]	Square brackets between adjacent lines of concurrent speech indicate the onset and end of a spate of overlapping talk.
.hh	A dot before an 'h' indicates speaker in-breath. The more h's, the longer the in-breath.
hh	An 'h' indicates an out-breath. The more h's the longer the breath.
(( ))	A description enclosed in a double bracket indicates a non-verbal activity. For example ((banging sound)).
	Alternatively double brackets may enclose the transcriber's comments on contextual or other features.
-	A dash indicates the sharp cut-off of the prior word or sound.
:	Colons indicate that the speaker has stretched the preceding sound or letter. The more colons the greater the extent of the stretching.
!	Exclamation marks are used to indicate an animated or emphatic tone.
()	Empty parentheses indicate the presence of an unclear fragment on the tape.
(guess)	The words within a single bracket indicate the transcriber's best guess at an unclear utterance.
.	A full stop indicates a stopping fall in tone. It does not necessarily indicate the end of a sentence.
,	A comma indicates a 'continuing' intonation.
?	A question mark indicates a rising inflection. It does not necessarily indicate a question.
*	An asterisk indicates a 'croaky' pronunciation of the immediately following section.
↓↑	Pointed arrows indicate a marked falling or rising intonational shift. They are placed immediately before the onset of the shift.
a:	Less marked falls in pitch can be indicated by using underlining irriniediately preceding a colon:

S: we (.) really didn't have a lot'v cha:nge

a:	Less marked rises in pitch can be indicated using a colon which is itself underlined:

J: I have a red shi:rt,

Under	Underlined fragments indicate speaker emphasis.
CAPITALS	Words in capitals mark a section of speech noticeably louder than that surrounding it.
° °	Degree signs are used to indicate that the talk they encompass is spoken noticeably quieter than the surrounding talk.
Thaght	A 'gh' indicates that the word in which it is placed had a guttural pronunciation.
> <	'More than' and 'less than' signs indicate that the talk they encompass was produced noticeably quicker than the surrounding talk.
→	Arrows in the left margin point to specific parts of an extract discussed in the text.

4.4 Data extracts *(see data extracts 4.1-4.4)*

```
 1    Caller:   I think we should (.) er reform the la:w on
 2              Sundays here, (0.3) w- I think people should have
 3              the choice if they want to do shopping on a
 4              Sunday, (0.4) also, that (.) i-if shops want to
 5              open on a Sunday th- th- they should be given the
 6              choice to do so.
 7    Host:     Well as I understand it thee: (.) the la:w a:s
 8              they're discussing it at the moment would allow
 9              shops to open .h for six hou:rs, .hh ⌈e:r ⌉on a=
10    Caller:                                       ⌊Yes.⌋
11    Host:     =Sunday,
12    Caller:   That's righ⌈t.
13    Host:                ⌊From:, midda:y.
14    Caller:   Y⌈es,
15    Host:      ⌊They wouldn't be allowed to open befo:re that.
16              .hh Erm and you talk about erm, (.) the rights of
17              people to: make a choice as to whether they
18              shop or not, ⌈o:n ⌉a Sunday,=what about .hh the=
19    Caller:               ⌊Yes,⌋
20    Host:     =people who may not have a choice a:s to whether
21              they would work on a Sunday.
```

Data Extract 4.1 Radio talk (Source: Hutchby and Wooffitt, 1998, p.105)

```
 1    Host:     You sa:y that you would not force people to do
 2              it. You do however accept that there is prejudice
 3              against .hh er certain kinds of, homes and
 4              er, ⌈hh ⌉hospitals in communities ⌈.hh ⌉ so .h=
 5    Caller:      ⌊Yeh⌋                          ⌊Yeh⌋
 6    Host:     =if: that prejudice exists people aren't going
 7              to gi:ve ti:me. Or money for that matter.
```

Data Extract 4.2 Radio talk (Source: Hutchby and Wooffitt, 1998, p.107)

```
 1    Caller:    U:sually when a dog fouls:, .hh e::r it, it
 2               lea:ves-=the scent that is left behind even if
 3               you, clean up with boiling water an'
 4               disinfectant,.hhh is a marker. .h An' when 'e
 5               comes on 'is e::r, w:-wa:lk the next da:y, when
 6               'e gets to that ma:rk, he does the same thing
 7               again.((...))
 8    Host:      er you s-seem to be suggesting that they go to
 9               the same place every ti:me. Because they've been
10               there before.
11    Caller:    Ooh yes,=quite often ye:s.=
12    Host:      =Yeah but er(h)n(h) then:, .h e:r=
13    Caller:    =An⌈d other dogs will °also°.⌉
14    Host:          ⌊this- this mea:ns that ⌋they never go in
15               a different pla:ce,=doesn't it.
```

Data Extract 4.3 *Radio talk (Source: Hutchby and Wooffitt, 1998, p.107)*

```
 1    Caller:    Uh, what was supposed to happen yesterda:y, it
 2               was an org- it was an o:rganised lobby of
 3               Parliament by: the National Union of Students.
 4    Host:      °M:mm,°
 5    Caller:    And the idea was to make, .hh the public of
 6               England, an' Great Britain, .h awa:re, .h of
 7               thee loans proposals.((...))
 8    Host:      You say it was an organised demonstration by the
 9               National Union of Students.= ⌈do y-
10    Caller:                                 ⌊No it was an or- it
11               was an organised lobby, .hh a:nd a ma:rch, which
12               was supposed to go ⌈to ( )
13    Host:                          ⌊Well you- you can organise a
14               lobby or a march it still amounts to a
15               demonstration=d'you think it got out of hand?
```

Data Extract 4.4 *Radio talk (Source: Hutchby and Wooffitt, 1998, pp.108-9)*

4.5 Questions for you about the data

(i) Read through Data Extracts 4.1 and 4.2 and make a note of anything you find interesting or significant in trying to understand the interaction. You will find it useful to look at Figure 1, the Transcription glossary, as you do so.

(ii) How would you describe these interactions – for example, as requests, invitations, arguments, counselling?

(iii) What kinds of participants are involved in the interactions?

(iv) How many speaking turns are there? Try to work out the relationship between speaking turns; look at what precedes a turn and how the next turn follows on from this.

(v) How are the data extracts similar? How are they different?

(vi) Can you identify any similar patterns in the interactions?

4.6 Some points from the researcher's analysis

Both extracts are taken from Hutchby's work on radio phone-in shows in which callers present arguments or points of view (Hutchby 1992). Hutchby and Wooffitt work through the interaction turn by turn, analysing the function of each turn and deciding what 'business' is being done, that is, what is being achieved through each turn in the conversation. Through this process of analysis, they identify a particular device used by the radio talk-show hosts to indicate scepticism about a caller's argument. This device consists of the host reformulating a caller's statement and then undermining it. The device or pattern Hutchby and Wooffitt identified can be simplified as the host saying to the caller: 'You say x, but what about y?'

Re-read the extracts and try to identify this 'You say x, but what about y?' pattern in each one before continuing to read.

In their analysis of Data Extract 4.1, Hutchby and Wooffitt describe what is being achieved throughout the conversation. The caller begins by stating his opinion on British laws regarding Sunday trading (lines 1-6) and the host responds by clarifying a point of detail (lines 7-15). The host begins reformulating what the caller has said in line 16 'you talk about erm, (.) the rights' and follows this with a challenge which demonstrates his scepticism regarding the caller's point of view (line 18 'what about .hh the= =people who may not have a choice'). Thus the device 'you say x, but what about y' is used by the host in lines 16-21 to undermine the caller's argument.

Hutchby and Wooffitt argue that the 'you say x but what about y' device is an argumentative device of which the caller is aware. Their evidence for this is that the callers show awareness that the device is compound, or two-part, and takes two conversational turns to complete. In line 19, the caller inserts a 'Yes' at the point where the first turn could end, showing that he knows that the host has not yet completed his speaking turn. The 'Yes' here is used as a continuer – other responses might be 'right' or 'uh huh' – which shows that the caller knows the turn is not complete even though a possible transition point, that is, a point where he could come in with a turn, has been reached and the host then continues with his attempt to undermine the caller's position.

In Data Extract 4.2 the host begins with a reformulation of the caller's position 'You sa:y that you would') and in lines 6-7 offers his contrasting position ('=if: that prejudice exists'). In line 5, the caller uses two continuers ('Yeh' and 'Yeh' again). The first comes after the host has indicated that he will continue his turn with 'and er' and thus performs both the function of acceptance of the reformulation on the part of the caller, as well as his understanding that the host's turn will continue. The second comes at the point where the host could finish his turn but is going on to add new information. This shows the caller's recognition that the host is going to continue and is going to do more than merely reformulate his position. Hutchby and Wooffitt argue that the continuers clearly show the caller's awareness of the compound nature of the argumentative device.

4.7 More questions for you about the data

(vii) Read through Data Extracts 4.3 and 4.4. Can you identify the same argumentative device 'You say x, but what about y?'?

(viii) Can you identify any differences between the way this interactional pattern is used in Data Extracts 4.3 and 4.4 and how it is used in Extracts 4.1 and 4.2? If yes, what are the differences?

4.8 Further discussion and conclusion

Hutchby and Wooffitt show that in both Data Extracts 4.3 and 4.4, the same argumentative device as described in Data Extracts 4.1 and 4.2 is present. However, in Data Extracts 4.3 and 4.4, the callers respond to the host's introduction of scepticism with an attempt to resist it, rather than with a continuer.

In Data Extract 4.3, the caller states his position in lines 1-7 and the host attempts to reformulate the caller's claim in a much stronger way: 'you s-seem to be suggesting that they go to the same place every ti:me' provides the 'you say x' formulation. The caller then attempts to modify this stronger reformulation, replacing the host's 'every time' with 'quite often ye:s.=' in line 11. The host, however, ignores the caller's attempt at resistance and ends by stating that the caller implies that dogs 'never go in a different pla:ce' (line 15) even though 'never' is not equivalent to 'quite often'.

In Data Extract 4.4, the host attempts to undermine the caller by reformulating his words 'o:rganised lobby' (line 2) to his own stronger 'organised demonstration' (line 8). The caller resists in line 10 with 'No', which overlaps with the host's attempt to begin a question ('do y-') and attempts to reassert his description of a 'lobby' rather than a demonstration. The host rejects the caller's attempt at resistance, returns to his preferred term 'demonstration' (lines 14-15) and continues with the question he wants to ask, which focuses on a lack of organisation in the lobby/ demonstration: 'd'you think it got out of hand?'

To sum up, in all four of the data extracts, Hutchby and Wooffitt identify a particular pattern of interaction, which is the argumentative device of 'you say x, but what about y'. Hutchby and Wooffitt state that they were not looking for this particular device in the data, and did not even have it in mind before their analysis. Rather, their identification of the device emerged from their open-ended analysis of the data. They found, through analysing a large corpus of radio phone-in show data, that this argumentative device can be responded to by the callers in different ways: Data Extracts 4.1 and 4.2 show the callers merely indicating awareness of the compound nature of the device and in Data Extracts 4.3 and 4.4 callers offer some resistance to the host's use of the device.

4.9 Your view

(ix)   Do you agree with Hutchby and Wooffitt's identification of the 'you say x, but what about y' pattern?

(x)   Do you agree with Hutchby and Wooffitt's analysis that the callers are aware of the 'you say x, but what about y' pattern as an argumentative device?

(xi)   What do you think are the advantages of this approach?

(xii) Can you think of any limitations to this approach?

(xiii) How might this approach be useful in your specific context?

4.10 Examples of studies using this approach

Conversation analysis has been used to analyse talk in a wide range of settings. For an example of CA analysis of doctor-patient consultations:

HEATH, C. (1992) 'The delivery and reception of diagnosis in the general practice consultation', in P. Drew and J. Heritage (eds) *Talk at Work: Interaction in Institutional Settings*, Cambridge, Cambridge University Press.

It has also been used to analyse political rhetoric and audience response to this. An example of this is:

ATKINSON, J.M (1984) *Our Masters' Voices: The Language and Body Language of Politics*, London, Methuen.

For an example of the use of CA in an educational context, see:

STOKOE, E. (1994) 'Constructing topicality in university students' small-group discussion; a conversation analytic approach', *Language and Education,* vol.14, no.3, pp.194-203.

5: Sociocultural approach: talk and learning

5.1 Key features of this approach

The term 'sociocultural' is often used to refer to approaches to talk and learning that draw on the work of Lev Vygotsky, a Russian psychologist (1896-1934). His work has become increasingly influential over the past twenty years in many parts of the world, particularly in research on language and learning in formal schooling. Vygotsky starts from the premise that language is a cultural tool for meaning-making and argues that this has profound implications for how we conceptualise the relationship between thought and language, which can be summarised as follows: (a) thought is refracted through language, rather than language simply reflecting thought; (b) language is a socially and culturally shaped resource, bound up with the cultural practices of a society; (c) learning to talk is very much about learning to think.

An important Vygotskian concept of particular relevance to teaching and learning is that of the zone of proximal development (ZPD). The ZPD is a notion Vygotsky uses to question the widespread assessment practice of focusing on children's individual performance and to emphasise the importance of looking at what a child can do with the help of an adult – a parent or teacher. Vygotsky defined the zone of proximal development as follows:

> It is the distance between the actual developmental level as determined by independent problem solving and the level of potential development as determined through problem solving under adult guidance or in collaboration with more capable peers. (Vygotsky, 1978, p.86)

Bruner famously refers to the guidance or support that adults and more capable peers can offer as 'scaffolding' (Bruner, 1978).

Research drawing on this approach typically focuses on naturally occurring data in teaching and learning contexts: the talk between teacher and student, the talk between peers as they engage in a particular activity, and the talk between a teacher and a whole class.

5.2 Example

MERCER, N. (1995) *The Guided Construction of Knowledge*, Clevedon, Multilingual Matters [Chapter 6 'Talking and working together'].

Mercer draws on Vygotsky in his extensive research into talk in primary classrooms – both talk between pupil and teacher and between peers. Mercer emphasises the importance of the notion of scaffolding in his focus on what he calls 'the guided construction of knowledge', that is, the ways in which pupils come to learn school-based knowledge through talk. Mercer is keen to identify where and how this happens in classroom talk and to suggest ways in which particular kinds of talk can be encouraged.

5.3 The aims of the researcher

Mercer's principal aim is to demonstrate which kinds of talk in the classroom enable successful teaching and learning to take place. In particular, he aims to:

- identify ways in which teachers' talk can successfully scaffold pupils' learning
- identify ways in which pupils can use, and could be encouraged to use further, a particular kind of talk – exploratory talk for learning

5.4 Data extracts (see data extracts 5.1-5.4)

1	Teacher:	OK right Paul, I'm going to give you a sum, right, and I want
2		you to just tell me how you are doing it. OK this is the sum.
3		You (to Gary) can do it as well and then I'll give you a different
4		one – um – try and think of a nice...
5	Paul:	(interrupting) hard one
6	Teacher:	Hard one, OK.
7	Paul:	Oh no, oh no.
8	Teacher:	OK that's it (writing) and it's a subtraction.
9	Paul:	Oh no.
10	Teacher:	Now tell me what you actually do to start
11		with. What do you say to yourself?
12	Paul:	Well, 3 minus 9 you can't do.
13	Teacher:	Yes.
14	Paul:	Cross that out and make that 2?
15	Teacher:	Yes.
16	Paul:	So now you've got 13.
17	Teacher:	Correct.
18	Paul:	So that's 4.
19	Teacher:	Yes, correct.
20	Paul:	So that's 2 minus 6 you can't do so
21		that's 1 take that's – down to zero.
22	Teacher:	Yes.
23	Paul:	And you get 120. Is that – is it 4 and 4?
24	Teacher:	Say that again, 120, what do you mean 120?
25	Paul:	Well (loud noise occurs in background).
26	Teacher:	That Mrs Hemington, she's so helpful, isn't she, with her
27		stapler. Go on, say it again, just...
28	Paul:	Well, you've crossed that out (indicating
29		the '1' in the 'hundreds' column).

$$133 - 69$$

$$1\overset{2}{\cancel{3}}\overset{1}{\cancel{3}} - 69 \over 4$$

$$\overset{0}{1}\overset{2}{\cancel{3}}\overset{1}{\cancel{3}} - 69 \over 4$$

30	Teacher:	Yes. What are you going to do with it, now you've crossed it
31		out?
32	Paul:	Move it on to here (*indicating 'tens' column*).
33	Teacher:	Go on then. You haven't done that yet. I can't see it in there.
34		It's vanished.
35	Paul:	So that's three.
36	Teacher:	Well, is it though?
37	Gary:	Hang on, put a one there, Paul.
38	Paul:	Right, OK.
39	Teacher:	What did you say Gary?
40	Gary:	Put a one.
41	Teacher:	What is that one? Where have you got that from?
42	Paul:	From the hundreds.
43	Teacher:	Right. So what number is that there now?
44		(*indicating the 'tens' column*)
45	Gary:	That is now 13.
46	Paul:	Um, what's that, oh, 12, oh (*makes choking noises*) sixty-four.
47	Teacher:	Is he right?
48	Gary:	Yes.

$$
\begin{array}{r}
^{012}133\,^{1} \\
69 \\
\hline
4 \\
\end{array}
$$

$$
\begin{array}{r}
^{012}133\,^{1} \\
69 \\
\hline
64 \\
\end{array}
$$

Data Extract 5.1 *Subtraction using decomposition (Source: Mercer, 1995, Sequence 5.2, pp.76-6)*

5.5 Questions for you about the data

(i) Read through Data Extract 5.1.

(ii) What do you notice about the teacher's interventions? What kinds of things is the teacher doing in talk?

(iii) What do you notice about Paul's contributions? What kinds of things is he doing in talk?

(iv) What do you notice about Gary's contributions?

5.6 Some points from the researcher's analysis

Mercer states that this sequence represents for him successful teacher-pupil guided support or 'scaffolding'. The teacher encourages Paul to talk his way through the sequence of operations, thus making visible to her what he thinks he is doing and why. The teacher encourages Paul's talk through the use of what Mercer calls 'prompts' or 'elicitations', such as 'What do you say to yourself?' (line 11) and 'what do you mean 120?' (line 24), and confirmations 'Yes, correct' (line 19) and queries 'Is it though?'

1	**Lester:**	1, 2, 3, 4, 5 (*counting grid squares on the screen with his finger,*
2		*before he takes his turn*).
3	**Sean:**	1. It's there.
4	**Lester:**	So it has got to be…
5	**Sean:**	5, 4 (*suggesting co-ordinates*).
6	**Lester:**	(*ignoring Sean*).
7		4,3. No, we have had 4,3.
8	**Sean:**	4,5. No, 4, 4.
9	**Lester:**	4, 3 (*presses keys for his turn*) What! (*he fails to find the elephant*)
10		That's easy, I know where it is, opposite.
11		(*both sit silently for a while, looking at the screen*)
12	**Lester:**	I can do it.
13	**Sean:**	(*still staring at the screen*) No, not up, down.
14	**Lester:**	It can't be.
15	**Sean:**	It can.
16	**Lester:**	I know where it is.
17		(*Sean eventually takes his turn, but fails to find the elephant*)
18	**Lester:**	I told you it weren't over there. (*He then takes his turn, without*
19		*success*)
20	**Sean:**	Eh, heh heh heh (*laughing gleefully*).
21	**Lester:**	Which one just went on? I don't know (*says something*
22		*unintelligible*).
23	**Sean:**	1, 2, 3, 4,5, 6 (*counting squares*).
24	**Lester:**	I know where it is.
25	**Sean:**	I got the nearest.
26	**Lester:**	(*counting squares*) 1, 2, 3, 4, 5, 6, 7, 8.
27	**Sean:**	I got the nearest, 5.
28	**Lester:**	So it has got to be 1, 8.
29	**Lester:**	2, 8.
30	**Sean:**	Oh, suit yourself.

Data Extract 5.2 *Finding the elephant (Source: Mercer, 1995, Sequence 6.1, p.100)*

(line 36). Throughout the interaction, Paul is able to seek support from the teacher 'Cross that out and make that 2?' (line 14)

While Gary, a peer, also talks in this sequence, Mercer argues that his is a different kind of help, more akin to direct instruction than scaffolding.

5.7 More questions for you about the data

As well as attempting to find and describe ways in which teachers can successfully support pupils' learning, Mercer is interested in how pupils can support each other's learning. In particular, he is keen to explore ways in which children can be encouraged to engage in what he calls 'explicit reasoning' in talk, where participants not only make a claim or state an opinion but justify it too.

1	**Katie**:	Okay, so right then. What shall we write?
2	**Anne**:	We can have something like those autograph columns and
3		things like that and items, messages.
4	**Katie**:	Inside these covers. (*pause*) Our fun-filled...
5	**Anne**:	That's it!
6	**Katie**:	Something...
7	**Anne**:	Something like that!
8	**Katie**:	Yeah.
9	**Anne**:	Inside this fabulous fun-filled covers are - how can we have
10		a fun-filled cover? Let me try.
11	**Katie**:	Inside these (*long pause*)...
12	**Anne**:	Hah huh (*laughs*).
13	**Anne**:	You sound happy on this. Fantabuloso (*laughs*).
14	**Katie**:	Inside these, inside these fant, inside these fun-filled, no
15		inside these covers these fantastic these brilliant...
16	**Anne**:	Brilliant...
17	**Katie**:	Is it brilliant?
18	**Anne**:	No.
19	**Katie**:	No. Fantast fantabuloso, shall we put that?
20	**Anne**:	Yeah (*says something inaudible*) fantabuloso.
21	**Katie**:	Fan-tab-u-lo-so.
22	**Anne**:	Loso. Fantabuloso.
23	**Katie**:	Fantabuloso oso.
24	**Anne**:	Fantabuloso ho!

Data Extract 5.3 Fantabuloso (Source: Mercer, 1995, Sequence 6.2, p.101)

(v) Now look at Data Extracts 5.2, 5.3 and 5.4. In what ways do you think the kind of talk in each extract is similar and/or different?

(vi) To what extent do you think the talk in each extract represents successful learning?

5.8 Further discussion and conclusions

Mercer argues that the three sequences illustrate three very different kinds of talk. In Data Extract 5.2, while the participants are enthusiastic and on task – that is, doing what the teacher expects them to be doing – they engage in what Mercer refers to as 'disputational talk', which is characterised by short assertions, rebuttals and ignoring each other's remarks. In this kind of talk there are, in Mercer's words, 'few attempts to pool resources' (p.104) for the purposes of learning. The supposedly collaborative task amounted in practice to a competitive one and it is difficult to see what either boy is learning.

In Data Extract 5.3, the participants engage in what Mercer refers to as 'cumulative talk'. In contrast to what occurs in Data Extract 5.2, the participants do seem to listen to each other. They make suggestions, offer some reasons for their decisions and they

1	**Diana:**	Let's discuss it. Which one shall we go for?
2	**All:**	(*inaudible – reading from instructions*)
3	**Peter:**	1, 2, 3 or 4 (*reading out the number of options available*). Well
4		we've got no other chance of getting more money because...
5	**Adrian:**	And there's a monastery.
6	**Diana:**	And if we take number 2 there's that (*inaudible*)...
7	**Peter:**	Yeh but because the huts will be guarded.
8	**All:**	Yeh.
9	**Adrian:**	And that will probably be guarded.
10	**Diana:**	It's surrounded by trees.
11	**Peter:**	Yeh.
12	**Adrian:**	And there's a rock guarding us there.
13	**Peter:**	Yes there's some rocks there. So I think, I think it should be 1.
14	**Adrian:**	Because the monastery might be unguarded.
15	**Diana:**	Yes 1.
16	**Adrian:**	I yeh.
17	**Peter:**	Yeh but what about 2? That, it might be not guarded. Just
18		because there's huts there it doesn't mean it's not guarded,
19		does it? What do you think?
20	**Diana:**	Yes, it doesn't mean it's not. It doesn't mean to say its **not**
21		guarded does it. It may well be guarded. I think we should
22		go for number 1 because I'm pretty sure it's not guarded.
23	**Adrian:**	Yeh.
24	**Peter:**	Ok, yes, number 1 (*he keys in 1 on keyboard*). No (*computer
25		responds inappropriately*).
26	**Adrian:**	You have to use them numbers (he points to the number keys on
27		right of board, and Peter uses them to obtain the right result. Adrian
28		begins to read from screen display). 'You have chosen to raid
29		area 1.'

Data Extract 5.4 *Planning a raid (Source: Mercer, 1995, Sequence 6.3, p.102)*

confirm each other's statements. They therefore construct a 'common knowledge by accumulation' (p.104). While this is an improvement on what we saw in Data Extract 5.2, a criticism Mercer has of this kind of talk is that the justifications for decisions are often left implicit and are not articulated in the children's talk.

In Data Extract 5.4, the participants engage in what Mercer refers to as 'exploratory talk'. This kind of talk is characterised by the children asking each other questions, commenting and making suggestions. Mercer states that there is a great deal of explicit reasoning in this talk: suggestions are made for joint consideration and challenges are justified rather than just stated. Mercer states that it is in this exploratory talk that 'knowledge is made more publicly accountable and reasoning is more visible in the talk' (p.104). It is this kind of talk, Mercer argues, that is valued in formal education and that we should be encouraging in classrooms.

It is important to note Mercer's comment on the three categories of disputational, cumulative and exploratory talk. He says that these

> are not meant to be descriptive categories into which all observed speech can be neatly and separately coded. They are analytic categories, typifications of the ways in which children in the SLANT [Spoken language and new technology] project talked together (Mercer, 1995, p.104). (p.104)

5.9 Your view on this approach

(vii) Looking back at Data Extract 5.1, do you agree with Mercer that this sequence represents successful scaffolding?

(viii) Mercer uses three terms to categorise the talk in Data Extracts 5.2, 5.3 and 5.4. These are 'disputational', 'cumulative' and 'exploratory'. To what extent do you think these terms usefully categorise each episode?

(ix) Can you think of other ways in which these three episodes could be categorised? And, if so, how would you justify your categories?

(x) How might you use this approach to carrying out research in your own context?

5.10 Examples of studies using a similar approach

For an overview of a sociocultural approach to language and thinking, see:

WERTSCH, J.V., DEL RIO, P. and ALVAREZ, A. (eds) (1995) *Sociocultural Studies of Mind*, New York, Cambridge University Press, pp.1-34.

An example of further work by Mercer in classroom talk is:

WEGERIF, R., ROJAS-DRUMMOND, S. and MERCER, N. (1999) 'Language for the social con-struction of knowledge: comparing classroom talk in Mexican pre-schools', in *Language and Education*, 1999, vol.13, no.2, pp.133-50.

For an example of a sociocultural approach to reading, see:

PALINCSAR, A.S. and BROWN, A.L. (1988) 'Teaching and practising thinking skills to promote comprehension in the context of group problem solving', *Remedial and Special Education*, vol.9, no.1, pp.53-9.

6: Sociocultural approach: teacher-student interaction in different cultural contexts

6.1 Key features of this approach

A sociocultural approach to the study of talk and learning emphasises the fundamental relationship between language as a collective cultural tool and individual thought. As discussed in Example 5, the work of Vygotsky has been drawn on by many writers wishing to establish a theoretical basis for this relationship. One key writer is Bruner, who argues that it is through interaction with others, especially through speech, that we construct and make sense of our world:

> That world is a symbolic world in the sense that it consists of conceptually organised, rule-bound belief systems about what exists, how to set goals, about what it is to be valued. There is no way, none, in which a human being could possibly master that world without the aid and assistance of others, for, in fact, that world is others. The culture stores an extraordinarily rich file of concepts, techniques and other prosthetic devices. (Bruner, 1995, p.32)

The emphasis on 'assistance' or, to use Bruner's widely quoted term, 'scaffolding' has led to an interest in analysing the specific ways in which scaffolding occurs in school classrooms (see Example 5) as well as to discussions about exactly what students are being scaffolded into, in different contexts.

6.2 Example

ALEXANDER, R. (2000) *Culture and Pedagogy. International Comparisons in Primary Education*, Oxford, Blackwell [Chapter 16 'Learning discourse'].

Much work in sociocultural studies focuses on talk and learning in one specific cultural context. In contrast, Alexander compares classroom discourse practices (that is, ways in which teachers and students talk in the classroom) from a number of different cultural contexts: Russia, the UK, the USA, France and India. He is interested in exploring the precise nature of these classroom discourse practices in order to understand which kinds of talk constitute teaching and learning in different contexts. One of the specific frameworks that Alexander uses to identify what is going on in teacher-student talk is the well-known exchange pattern identified by Sinclair and Coulthard (1975); that is, I (initiation – by teacher), R (response – by student), F (feedback – by teacher). Alexander is interested in exploring not only how teachers and students from distinct cultural backgrounds interact in classrooms but also what these discourse practices tell us about cultural and national identity:

If we listen to what teachers and children in these five countries [UK, USA, Russia, India, France] say we may understand a little more about what it is to be English, American, Russian, Indian or French. Values will out; identity too perhaps. (p.432)

The main study involves audio and video recordings of naturally occurring classroom talk in some 30 primary classrooms in the five countries. The data extracts here are from three countries: India, Russia and the UK.

6.3 The aim of the researcher

In this example we focus on one of the many aims that Alexander has in carrying out research into classroom interaction in the five distinct cultural and geographical contexts. This is to:

- 'identify which sorts of discourse are associated with the culturally specific patterns of classroom organisation and interaction' (p.433).

6.4 Data extracts *(see data extracts 6.1-6.3)*

1	T	*[Raises her left hand above her head]* One hand up. *[Pupils raise their left*
2		*hands above their heads]*
3	T	*[Raises her right hand]* Second hand up. *[Pupils raise their right hands]*
4	T	Start clapping. *[Pupils clap, their hands still above their heads]*
5	T	Stop! *[Pupils stop clapping and lower their arms]* How many of you like
6		school?
7	PPP	*[Raising hands and shouting]* I do!
8	T	Hands down. *[Pupils lower their hands]* How many of you had a shower
9		before you came here?
10	PP	*[Some raise hands]* I did!
11	T	Hands down. *[Hands are lowered]* // What did mummy give you to eat?
12	PP	Chappati.
13	T	What else?
14	PP	Vegetable curry.
15	T	Did you have some milk?
16	PP	*[Some raise hands]* Yes!
17	T	Children, do you eat fruit?
18	PP	Yes!
19	T	What kind of fruit do you eat?
20	PP	*[Calling out, excitedly]* Aam *[mango]*
21		Kele *[banana]*
22		Sev *[apple]*
23		Tadbuch *[melon]*
24		Narangi *[orange]*
25	T	Do you like *aam*?
26	PP	Yes.
27	T	*[Looks towards A]* What does A like?
28	A	*Aam.*

28	A	*Aam.*
29	T	You also like *aam.*
30	PP	Yes I like *aam* too.
31	T	What does B like?
32	B	[*Raising her hand*] I like banana.
33	T	And what does C like?
34	C	I like *aam.*
35	T	And D?
36	D	I like banana.
37	T	You like bananas better. And E? [*E does not reply. Teacher walks between*
38		*rows to where she is sitting*] What do you like best? Which fruit do you
39		like? I Don't you like any fruit at all? Don't you even like banana? [*E*
40		*shakes her head, smiling*]
41	T	What does F like?
42	F	[...]
43	T	[*Walks further down the row and turns to face G*] G?
44	G	*Aam.*
45	T	You like *aam.*
46	T	[*Walking back towards the front of the class*] What does H like?
47	H	*Aam.*
48	T	*Aam.* Can anyone draw a picture of *aam?*
49	I	[*Raises hand and calls out*] I can draw *aam.*
50	T	Right. [*Gestures towards the blackboard*] Come forward and draw an
51		*aam.* [*I goes to the board and starts writing the word 'aam'. Teacher*
52		*points out she should draw a picture of a mango, which she does. She then*
53		*puts the chalk on the teacher's desk and returns to her place. The sequence*
54		*is repeated with other pupils and other fruit*].
		[...]
55	T	[*Bends down and gestures to B, who stands up. Teacher takes her arm and*
56		*turns her to face the class*] What is her **name**?
57	PPP	Aarti!
58	T	Is it Aarti?
59	PPP	Yes!
60	T	[*Steers Aarti back to her place. Then inclining her head towards the class*
61		*and saying the word slowly and with rising inflexion*] **Aam.**
62	PP	*Aam.*
63	T	[*Spoken Aar-ti*] Aarti.
64	PP	*Aar-ti.*
65	T	What can you hear?
66	PP	*Aam,* Aarti. [*In strict rhythm: common time, semibreve-crotchet-crotchet,*
67		*all accented*]
68	T	What can you hear?
69	PP	*Aam,* Aarti.
70	T	What are the same sounds you can hear in these two words? [*Holds*
71		*out hands as if to weigh the two words*]
72	PP	[*Calling out*] We can hear 'aa'.

72	PP	[*Calling out*] We can hear 'aa'.
73	T	[*To pupil sitting at front of one row*] What can you hear?
74	J	I can hear 'aa'.
75	T	'Aa'?
76	J	Yes.
77	T	[*Raises voice*] Which sound can you hear?
78	PPP	I can hear 'aa'.
79	T	Which sound can you hear
80	ppp	I can hear 'aa'.
[...]		
81	T	You stay clean don't you?
82	PPP	Yes!
83	T	Do you have a bath everyday?
84	PPP	Yes!
85	T	Is that a good [*acchi*] or a bad habit?
86	PPP	*Acchi.*
87	T	*Aam.*
88	PPP	*Aam.*
89	T	*Aarti.*
90	pp	*Aarti.*
91	T	*Aadat.*
92	PP	*Aadat.*
93	T	Which sound can you hear the most in these words?
94	PP	'Aa'.
95		[*Other answers, not individually decipherable, but certainly not 'aa'*].
96	T	Again, what can you hear?
97	PP	'Aa.'
98	T	Again, what can you hear?
99	PPP	'Aa.'
100	T	And how do we write the sound 'aa'? [*Pupils raise their hands and point,*
101		*ready to trace the letter. Teacher raises her hand. Together they trace the*
102		*letter A in the air*].
103	T	// How do we write 'aa'? [*Teacher and pupils trace the letter again. Teacher*
104		*then points to a child to come to board and write it*]
105	T	Does anybody else know? Anamika, will you come and show me?
106		[*Anamika comes to the board and does so*] Well done! Everyone, clap for Anamika.
107		[*Teacher and pupils applaud*]

Data Extract 6.1 *India – Chanderi Primary School (Source: Alexander, 2000, Sequence 6.2, pp.443-6)*

1	T	[*Pointing to magnetic letters on blackboard*] Now these letters, YO [Ю]
2		and YA[Я], are sometimes called soft consonants, and there is a connection
3		here. What is the connection? [*A few pupils raise their hands*] Shush. /
4		Please. Anyone? A? [*Gestures towards A, who stands up*] Listen carefully
5		please, the rest of you. [*Raises finger to reinforce this injunction*]
6	A	When we pronounce the sound '**ya**'....... /[*the sound is spoken very emphatic-*
7		*ally*]
8	T	The sound '**ya**'?
9	A	... the sound the sound is soft.
10	T	Well done so far, you're doing well. Carry on.
11	A	//And when we pronounce the sound '**a**'...
12	T	[*Nods encouragingly*] Mm....
13	A	... that's called a hard sound because it's not connected to any consonant.
14		The sound '**ya**', when it's pronounced, is similar, but it's joined up to a
15		consonant sound...
16	T	Right, yes.
17	A	... and it works in a totally different way.
18	T	Mm....
19	A	...Therefore you can't put A and YO together [*In the Russian, A actually*
20		*juxtaposes the letter names*].
21	T	Correct, yes. If you read all four of them . . . I'll put them all together.
22		[*Rearranges the letters А, Я, О, Ю - A, YA, 0 and YO — on the board*] It
23		will help us if we put them all together. Now A, which is the better pair? I
24		think they should be arranged in this way [*pointing to letters on board*]
25		because the way they are pronounced is similar. That's my opinion. Now
26		these are the pairs that really work together, I believe. Right, next question.
27		Why are they together? B? [*Gestures to B, who stands up*]
28	B	Because the pronunciation of '**ya**', the way you pronounce it, is very similar
29		to the pronunciation of the sound, the sound '**a**'.
30	T	Yes, correct. [*Points to Я on board*]
		[...]
31	T	Let's do some work with words now and everything will become clear. Let's
32		start with one word – roza [rose]. No [*raises finger as if to check herself*],
33		rozy [roses]. Let's do that one first. One of you out to the board, please.
34		[*Points to C*] C? [*Teacher walks to the back of the room while C goes to*
35		*board*]
36	T	Rozy [*emphatically rolls the R*] rrrr-ozy.
37	C	Rozy.
38	T	Rrrr-ozy.
39	C.	Rrr.
40	T	[*She watches while C writes the phonetic symbol for a consonant –* □ *– then*
41		*adds a diagonal line from bottom left to top right to indicate that it is hard.*
42		*The other pupils write it in their exercise books*] What kind of sound is
43		that? Anybody, tell me what kind of sound that is?
44	C	A consonant.
45	T	A consonant, good.// [*Briefly monitors a pupil's writing of cyrillic P(R)*]
46		Now, what kind of consonant? Is it a hard sound? Is it voiced? [*Walks back*
47		*to C at board*]
48	C	Hard.

Data Extract 6.2 Russia – Kirsk School (Source: Alexander, 2000, Sequence 6.4, pp.405-2)

49	T	Hard, yes, and is it voiced or unvoiced? Touch your throat, your throat.
50		[*Puts her hand to her own throat*] Feel your throat with your hand, 'rrrr'.
51	C	[*Imitates T, with fingers on her throat to feel her vocal cords vibrating*]
52		'Rrrr'.
53	T	What kind of sound is that?
54	C	Voiced.
55	T	Voiced, yes, good. [*C places a dot within the left segment of the consonant*
56		*symbol*] So what do you put into the picture? [*M makes the dot larger*] A
57		little bell, yes. Now let's go a bit further. What is the second sound in the
58		word?
59	C	[*Puts her hand to her throat*] 'o' - 'o' - 'o'.
60	T	[*Hurriedly*] Say the word, the **word**. The word.
61	C	Ro-o-o-zy.
62	T	What is the sound?
63	C	'o' [*Draws symbol -* **O** *- for a vowel. Puts hand to her throat*]. 'z'.
64	T	The word, say the word.
65	C	Ro-zzz-y.
66	T	Ro-zy // Is that a consonant sound? [*Quickly*] Consonant, consonant.
67	C	Consonant.
68	T	Consonant, yes. [*C draws the symbol for a second hard consonant*] And it's
69		voiced. [*C adds the 'bell' for voicing*]
70	T	'z' - that's the third sound of R-O-Z-Y [*P-O-З-Ы*], so it's a consonant, and
71		a voiced one. And the last sound?
72	C	Ro-z-**y** [*Stresses last syllable*]
73	T	Sound?
74	C	Vowel.
75	T	Pronounce it.
76	C	'y'.
77	T	'y'. Correct, a vowel, good. [*C draws symbol for a second vowel, adds a line*
78		*to separate the syllables, then places a diacritical mark over the first vowel*
79		*symbol to signify where the stress falls*]
80	T	Right. [*To C*] Wait a minute. [*To class*] Now the sounds are as follows.
81		What's the first sound? [*Points to first phonetic symbol on board and holds*
82		*up her other hand, outstretched*]
83	PP	'r'.
84	T	The sound is 'r'. [*Makes a grasping gesture with her outstretched hand*] Yes,
85		and 'r' indicates which letter?
86	PP	R [*C writes cyrillic letter P under the first of the four phonetic symbols*]
87	T	And the second sound is?
88		[*Teacher, C and the class follow the same procedure with the remaining*
89		*three letters*]
90	T	Good, well done. Read it please.
91	C	R-o-z-y [*C adds brackets below each pair of symbols and letters to indicate*
92		*the two syllables of PO3Ы*]
93	T	Good, that is written correctly. Well done C, thank you very much. Sit
94		down please. [*C returns to her seat*]

Data Extract 6.2 Russia – Kirsk School continued (Source: Alexander, 2000, Sequence 6.4, pp.405-2)

6.5 Questions for you about the data

The data extracts that Alexander discusses are longer than many extracts included in academic publications of research. He argues that if we wish to read and understand specific instances of teacher-student interaction as 'coherent acts of teaching' (p.439), extracts need to be long enough to enable the reader to see and make sense of what is going on. The three main extracts included here are examples of literacy teaching with younger students.

    (i)   Read through the transcription conventions in Figure 2 before reading the data extracts of classroom talk.

   (ii)   Now read Data Extract 6.1. What do you notice about the teacher's interventions? How would you describe them?

  (iii)   What do you notice about the students' interventions? How would you describe them?

  (iv)   Now read Data Extract 6.2. What do you notice about the teacher's interventions? How would you describe them.

   (v)   What do you notice about the students' interventions? How would you describe them?

  (vi)   What are they key differences and similarities between the teacher-student interactions in the two extracts?

6.6 Some points from the researcher's analysis

Alexander notes that the whole-class instruction in Data Extract 6.1 involves an exchange structure of two moves: initiation (I) and response (R). The teacher requires students to repeat *aam* (lines 25ff) and *Aarti* (lines 58ff), a child's name, and at lines 86ff and 92ff she introduces further sounds *acchi* and *aadat*. This particular pattern of rote learning, in which the teacher seeks a correct response from one or more students that is then gradually echoed by all the other students, is, according to Alexander, a common feature of classroom interaction in India. The extract also illustrates how this kind of rote learning takes place alongside a more open interaction pattern. At the beginning of the extract the teacher tries to engage students' attention by using open questions, for eample, 'How many of you like school?', 'What did mummy give you to eat?', rather than the closed questioning that is a feature of most of her talk. This is successful, with many students responding enthusiastically to talk about their breakfasts. Overall, however, Alexander classifies this as a 'transmission' lesson:

> The mode of instruction is ritualised, the two-move discourse exchange structure precludes feedback on answers – questioning remains largely closed, key words are chanted. (p.450)

Data Extract 6.2, while also a whole-class direct instruction, differs from Data Extract 6.1 in that it has a three-part exchange structure: initiation (I), response (R) and feedback (F). An example of this is at lines 1-10 where the teacher elicits a response from

1	(1)	*[Tables 1 and 2 have prominent signs announcing 'We are working with*
2		*the teacher']*
3	T	*[To tables 3, 4 and 5]* Right, I'm closing the magic curtain *[Mimes clos-*
4		*ing a curtain. Some pupils laugh]* / which doesn't work. *[Smiles, puts*
5		*finger to lips]* Now, if it's a curtain I can still hear you. And I'm working,
6		going to try and work with these two tables and you're trying, / *[frowns*
7		*at pupil who is talking loudly]* trying to work on your own. *[Goes to*
8		*table 1]*.
	[...]	
9	(2)	*[Teacher is walking towards table 4 to help B]*.
10	C	*[Sitting at table 3, calls out as teacher passes]* Miss, um Miss Newton, can
11		A be in our group?
12	T	A. / We'll work out where A is sitting. *[To B]* Oh, you've done it! *[Mov-*
13		*ing to table 5]* Well done! *[Places her hands on D's shoulders]*
14	D	Miss, can of, off be ...?
15	T	Of, off, it needs 'f' not 'v': of. *[Moves to table 3]*
16	E	*[Calls out from table 4]* Miss Newton, Miss Newton, *[Teacher stops,*
17		*looks and smiles in E's direction]* shall I do a short one?
18	T	*[Nods and moves on to table 1]*
19	(3) C	Miss, Miss, Miss Newton, Miss Newton...
20	F	*[Table 1, pointing to a word in her word book]* Is it that one?
21	T	*[Leaning over to look at F's work]* It is, well done! Good girl. 'I want...
22		*[Moves to table 2]*
23	(4) G	Miss Newton, Miss Newton, can you spell 'what'?
24	T	*[Leaning towards G with her hands resting on the table]* 'What'? There's
25		a hat in 'what'. *[Picking up G's wordbook, moves round to stand behind*
26		*him]* Shall we see if it's in here?
27	G	*[Nods]*
28	T	*[Notices F is not working, but staring at the teacher's radio microphone]*.
29		Hello F, shall we get on with the third word?
30	F	*[Pointing to the microphone]* I've seen that on the television, on Count
31		Me In.
32	T	*[Smiling]* It's listening to you, F. *[Continues to scan G's wordbook. To*
33		G] We're looking for 'w'. Help me find 'w'. *[To F]* No you are. 'w', 'w',
34		'w', 'w', what! It's the 'w'-'h' page. Sh-sh. *[To F, while walking towards*
35		*her]* Come on now, the best thing you can do <u>would be</u>...
36	H	<u>Mrs Newton, Mrs Newton</u>, *[Reads from his own writing]* 'I will help
37		you.'
38	T	'I will help you. Very good. *[Moves to table 2, touches I's shoulder. I*
39		*leans back from J]* Let's sit separately. *[Looks over I's shoulder and reads]*
40		'Hello, oh no my letter has blown away. Help catch it', 'Shall we help?'
41		Right, move you up a little bit J *[Pushes J's worksheet away from I's. J*
42		*moves to the next chair, leaving a space between herself and I]* 'cause
43		your stories are very much the same. I stood on your toe, I'm sorry.
44		*[Moves to table 1]*.

Data Extract 6.3 *UK – Kirkbright (Source: Alexander, 2000, Sequence 6.12, pp.482-3)*

```
45   K      Miss, Miss.
46   T      [Nods to K as she passes, but has noticed that F is distracted again] Right,
47          F. [F goes back to work. T sits down next to H]
48   H      I've done, 'I will too'.
49   (5) L  [Approaches from table 3] How do you spell 'can't'?
50   M      Miss Newton, Miss Newton...
51   T      Find the 'c' page in your word book. [Raises her palm in a calming
52          gesture towards M] Ssh.
53   N      [Reads to herself] 'We are working with the teacher'.
54   M      Is that how you spell 'shouted'?
55   T      [Drawing M's word book towards her] It's very much like that.
56   (6) 0  [Queuing behind L] I need 'that'
57   T      Bring me your 't' page. [O goes to fetch her wordbook. To H, in a
58          whisper] Come on, you're doing ever so well. [To M, starting to spell
59          'shouted' for him] ...
60   N      [Reads to herself] 'We are working with the teacher.'
```

Data Extract 6.3 UK – Kirkbright continued (Source: Alexander, 2000, Sequence 6.12, pp.482-3)

A, A responds and then the teacher gives feedback on this response, through 'you're doing well. Carry on'. A further example is at lines 27-30, where the teacher asks B a question, B responds and then the teacher comments 'Yes, correct'. Alexander points out that the teacher elicitations are mostly direct, that is, they involve direct questions, such as 'Why are they together?' Encouragement is provided if responses are hesitant, for example at line 10 'Well done so far, you're doing well. Carry on'.

6.7 More questions for you about the data

(vii) Now read Data Extract 6.3. What do you notice about the teacher's interventions? How would you describe them?

(viii) What do you notice about the students' interventions? How would you describe them?

(ix) Looking at all three extracts, what can you learn about whole-class teacher-student interaction in different cultural contexts?

6.8 Further discussion and conclusions

The teacher in Data Extract 6.3 has to supervise three groups and to work with two. Much of the discourse focuses on the mechanics of the learning activity rather than on the substance of the learning task. For example, at lines 5-7 the teacher explains who she will be working with. In this way, the focus is significantly different from that in Data Extracts 6.1 and 6.2, where the emphasis is on teaching specific content knowledge, sounds, and names for sounds.

In margin	
T	Teacher
A, B, C	Pupils, named and identifiable
(P)	Pupil, not identifiable (e.g. off camera)
PP	Several pupils simultaneously
PPP	Whole class simultaneously
	Omitted section of discourse
In text	
(...)	Indecipherable
/	Pause of less than 2 seconds
//	Pause of more than 2 seconds
bold	Word(s) given particular emphasis
<u>underlining</u>	Overlapping turns/simultaneous utterances
...	Interrupted or unfinished utterance, or explicit cueing for next turn
A, B, Ю, YO	Letter *names* as spoken
a', 'b', 'yo'	Letter *sounds* as spoken
C-A-T	Spelling, spoken letter by letter
'c'-'a'-'t'	Spelling, spoken sound by sound
[*italics within square brackets*]	Explanation, translation, or contextual information

Figure 2 *Transcription conventions (Source: Alexander, 2000, Figure 16.1, p.440)*

Alexander identifies several significant features of the teacher's discourse in Data Extract 6.3. First, he points to the oblique way in which the teacher controls the class, as exemplified at lines 3-5, where the teacher talks of the curtain she is drawing rather than saying, for example, 'Be silent!' or 'Can you be quiet now?' Second, he signals the inclusive use of 'we', rather than a direct signalling of their distinct positions in the discourse through I/you. This is exemplified at lines 12, 26, 33. Third, he notes the indirect 'management of turns', exemplified, for example, at line 26 with 'Shall we see if it's in here?' And, finally, he argues that the teacher seems consciously to avoid specialist terminology, as illustrated by her 'w' and 'w'-'h' page (lines 33-4). Compare this with the Russian teacher's and children's use of the terms 'consonant', 'vowel', 'voiced', 'unvoiced' in Data Extract 6.2.

Rather than viewing these features of talk as specific to the individual teacher or one specific classroom, Alexander seeks to locate them within the teacher's personal-cultural history. Alexander uses the term 'psychobiography' to emphasise that a teacher's behaviour and talk in classrooms are part of their larger life histories.

> The notion of 'psychobiography' reminds us that in classrooms, as in every walk of life, language and the meanings it expresses are embedded in individual experience. (p.485)

The teacher has come to use language in particular ways according to her values and beliefs about teaching and learning. But these apparently individual practices are embedded within broader historical trends in different cultural contexts. Thus Alexander locates the interaction in Data Extract 6.3 in a specifically UK context, emphasising two key factors. The first is the recent UK governments' Literacy Hour initiative. The Literacy Hour is a recently introduced national educational initiative that lays down prescriptions about the content and the classroom organisation relating to the teaching of reading and writing. Data Extract 6.3 illustrates one of the prescribed elements of the Literacy Hour, which is

> independent reading, writing or word work, while the teacher works with at least two ability groups each day on guided text work. (p.483)

While the recently prescribed Literacy Hour requires teachers to explicitly introduce linguistic-specific terminology, this does not easily happen because of a second key factor influencing the teacher's behaviour. This is the

> deeply-seated collective professional beliefs about the nature of childhood which go back via the English progressive movement and Piaget to the Froebelian garden and Rousseau. (p.485)

(Froebel uses the metaphor of teacher as gardener who nurtures the children as one would plants.) Alexander explains the decision not to use subject-specific terminology in the interaction in Data Extract 6.3 as reflecting this nurturing, child-centred approach to teaching and learning prevalent in UK classrooms, which in practice often leads to the following: (a) the teacher allowing the child to use familiar notions and wordings to engage in learning; (b) the teacher aiming to get as close as possible to the child's understanding and to begin her teaching from that point.

The UK approach, according to Alexander, stands in contrast to the cultural practice exemplified in the Russian data extract, in which the teacher's professional beliefs involve a particular perspective on 'dialogue'. Dialogue in Russian classrooms, Alexander notes, can be understood as sustained and focused questioning which leads students to use, for example, subject-specific terminology as in Data Extract 6.2. Also, Alexander states that Data Extract 6.2, where the teacher directed questions at specific students, illustrates a style in Russian classrooms where teacher-pupil discourse is of a more public and formal nature. He contrasts this public discourse, where individual students respond in front of all students, with the more private discourse between individual student and teacher that occurs in many UK and US classrooms.

6.9 Your view

(x) How useful do you think the I-R-F framework is for analysing classroom discourse?

(xi) To what extent do you agree with Alexander's analysis of Data Extracts 6.1 and 6.2?

(xii) To what extent do you agree with the differences Alexander notes between all three extracts?

(xiii) Do you agree with Alexander's explanation of the differences between the Russian and UK discourse practices?

(xiv) Can you see any similarities or differences between the three extracts that haven't been mentioned?

(xv) How might you use this approach to carry out research in your own context?

6.10 Examples of studies using a similar approach

All three examples appear in the companion volume to this Workbook:

S. GOODMAN, T. LILLIS, J. MAYBIN and N. MERCER (eds) *Language, Literacy and Education: A Reader*, Stoke-on-Trent, Trentham.

Two further studies that draw on a neo-Vygotskian framework to explore specific cultural contexts are:

ROJAS-DRUMMOND, S. (2002) 'Guided participation, discourse and the construction of knowledge in Mexican classrooms', (Chapter 3)

MACHADO DE ALMEIDA MATTOS, A. (2000) 'A Vygotskian approach to evaluation in foreign language learning contexts', (Chapter 4) reprinted from *ELT Journal*, vol.54, no.4, p.335-45.

A paper that draws on a slightly different framing from sociocultural theory is:

GUTIÉRREZ, K., BAQUEDANO-LÓPEZ, P. and TEJADA, C. (2000) 'Rethinking diversity: hybridity and hybrid language practices in the Third Space', (Chapter 12) reprinted from *Mind, Culture and Activity*, vol.6, no.4, p.286-303.

PART 2
APPROACHES TO WRITTEN TEXTS

Introduction

Any kind of written text can become the object of analysis and there are a number of distinct analytic approaches that can be used. In this part of the workbook, we outline the key features of the following distinct approaches: corpus linguistics, systemic functional linguistics, contrastive rhetoric and discourse analysis. While focusing centrally on written texts, all the examples discussed seek to connect analysis of specific written texts to the social and cultural contexts in which such texts are written and/or read. They do this in different ways. Examples 7, 8, 12 and 13 illustrate the tradition of analysing publicly available written texts to identify the particular world view, or ideology, that is being constructed in the text. In these analyses the emphasis is on the relationship between the linguistic features of the written texts and the society in which they are produced. Thus, in Example 7 Stubbs uses corpus linguistics to analyse two official letters of an international youth movement and to explore how a particular ideology about men's and women's roles in society is represented and constructed through the language of the texts. In Example 8 we take you through Purser's analysis of informational texts in an Australian museum. Purser uses 'systemic functional grammar' (Halliday, 1994) to highlight how particular socio-historical groups are differentially represented in the texts. Example 12 illustrates how particular concepts from Bernstein (1996) can help to make visible the thinking underpinning educational policy on English as an additional language in the UK. In Example 13 we take you through Chouliaraki and Fairclough's use of 'critical discourse analysis' (see Fairclough, 1992, 2001) to analyse a magazine advertisement which, they argue, illustrates the changing nature of language practices at the beginning of the twenty-first century.

Examples 9, 10 and 11 all focus on texts written by students in formal educational contexts. Examples 9 and 11 explore adult students' writing. In Example 9, Scollon *et al.* draw on key concepts from Bakhtin (1981, 1986), such as 'voices' and 'intertextuality', to explore how the written texts of a group of Hong Kong students echo wordings and ideas from the specific cultural context that they inhabit. Example 11 illustrates the tradition of contrastive rhetoric, whereby written texts and practices are examined cross-culturally (see Connor, 1996). Connor *et al.* compare job applications written by students in the USA with those written by Flemish students in Belgium. Example 10 focuses on a key concern in the teaching of writing to younger children: punctuation. Hall combines text analysis with talk around the texts – that is, interviews with children, to explore why they punctuate as they do.

7: Corpus linguistics: official letters

7.1 Key features of the approach

'Corpus' means 'a body' and 'corpus analysis' thus refers to the analysis of a body of language data. A corpus can be small (for example one speech or article) or large (several million words of naturally occurring spoken or written language). Currently, corpus analysis usually makes use of computer tools in the analytic process. The computer tools designed for this kind of analysis include concordances programmes that can, for example, pick out particular words selected by the researcher and show how frequently these words are used. Analyses of large corpora of spoken and written English have shown the frequency and co-occurrence of many different lexical (vocabulary) and grammatical items. These analyses have been able to tell us a lot about language that we could not know intuitively (for a brief overview of corpora databases and computer tools for carrying out analyses, see Hockey, 1998).

Corpus analysis research often involves analysing how certain words occur in a particular text, and then comparing these patterns of occurrences with patterns that have been identified in existing large corpora of spoken and written language.

7.2 Example

STUBBS, M. (1996) *Texts and Corpus Analysis*, Oxford, Basil Blackwell [Chapter 4 'Baden-Powell: a comparative analysis of two short texts'].

Stubbs uses corpus analysis in a critical way, that is, in order to show how the lexis (vocabulary) and grammar of a text contribute to the representation of a particular ideology. Stubbs believes that texts need to be studied within the institutional contexts of their production. In other words, we need to consider who produced the text, who reads the text (for example, the age of the readers and size of readership) and how it is distributed. In this example, he focuses on two official letters from an international youth organisation. He begins with a general analysis of the content of the texts under study. He then moves on to examine in detail the occurrence and use of particular lexical items, that is, different word forms that are clearly related in meaning (for example, walk, walked, walks). Stubbs is particularly interested in using the tools of corpus analysis to explore the ideological uses and connotations of words which, at first sight, do not seem to be obviously 'ideologically loaded'. For example, the meaning of the word 'work' varies in its social significance: housework, for example, is often construed as 'women's work' and is not viewed as 'proper – that is, paid – work'. In this sense, the word 'work' can be viewed as ideologically loaded.

7.3 The aims of the researcher

Stubbs aims to:

- show how *patterns* of vocabulary and grammar, not just individual words, convey ideological positions

- demonstrate that 'sexist imbalances' (Stubbs, 1996, p.82) are constructed by the way language is used in the texts, rather than just through the use of obviously sexist words.

7.4 Data extracts *(see data extracts 7.1-7.4)*

My Dear Guides, This is just a farewell note to you, the last that you will have from me. It is just to remind you when I have passed on that your business in life is to be happy and to make others happy. That sounds comfortable and easy, doesn't it? You begin making other people happy by doing good turns to them. You need not worry about making yourselves happy, as you will very soon find that that comes by itself; when you make other people happy, it makes you happy too. Later on, when you have a home of your own, by making it a bright and cheery one you will make your husband a happy man. If all homes were bright and cheery, there would be fewer public houses and the men would not want to go out to them but would stay at home. It may mean hard work for you, but it will bring its own reward then, if you keep your children healthy and clean and busy they will be happy. Happy children love their parents. There is nothing can give you greater joy than a loving child. I am sure God means us to be happy in this life. He has given us a world to live in that is full of beauties and wonders and He has given us not only eyes to see them but minds to understand them if only we have the sense to look at them in the light. We can enjoy bright sunshine and glorious views. We can see beauty in the flowers. We can watch with wonder how the seed produces the young plant which grows to a flower which in its turn will replace other flowers as they die off. For, though plants, like people, die their race does not die away but new ones are born and grow up to carry on The Creator's plan. So, do you see, you women are the chosen servants of God in two ways: first to carry on the race, to bring children into the world to replace the men and women who pass away; secondly, to bring happiness into the world by making happy homes and by being yourselves good, cheery comrades for your husbands and children. That is where you as Guides especially come in. By being a 'comrade', that is, by taking an interest in your husband's work and aspirations, you can help him with your sympathy and suggestions and so be a guide to him. Also, in bringing up your children, by strengthening and training their minds and characters as well as their bodies and health, you will be giving them to the better use and enjoyment of life. By giving out love and happiness in this way, you will gain for yourselves the return love of husband and children, and there is nothing better in this world. You will find that Heaven is not the kind of happiness somewhere up there in the skies after you are dead but right here now in this world in your own home. So guide others to happiness and you will bring happiness to yourselves and by doing this you will be doing what God wants of you. God be with you. Baden-Powell.

Data Extract 7.1 Baden-Powell's last message to the Girl Guides (Source: Stubbs, 1996, Text G, pp.98-9)

Dear Scouts, If you have ever seen the play 'Peter Pan' you will remember how the pirate chief was always making his dying speech because he was afraid that possibly when the time came for him to die he might not have time to get it off his chest. It is much the same with me, and so, although I am not at this moment dying, I shall be doing so one of these days and I want to send you a parting word of goodbye. Remember, it is the last you will ever hear from me, so think it over. I have had a most happy life and I want each one of you to have as happy a life too. I believe that God put us in this jolly world to be happy and enjoy life. Happiness doesn't come from being rich, nor merely from being successful in your career, nor by self-indulgence. One step towards happiness is to make yourself healthy and strong while you are a boy, so that you can be useful and so can enjoy life when you are a man. Nature study will show you how full of beautiful and wonderful things God has made the world for you to enjoy. Be contented with what you have got and make the best of it. Look on the bright side of things instead of the gloomy one. But the real way to get happiness is by giving out happiness to other people. Try and leave this world a little better than you found it and when your turn comes to die, you can die happy in feeling that at any rate you have not wasted your time but have done your best. 'Be prepared' in this way, to live happy and to die happy – stick to your Scout Promise always – even after you have ceased to be a boy – and God help you do it. Your friend, Robert Baden-Powell.

Data Extract 7.2 *Baden-Powell's last message to the Boy Scouts (Source: Stubbs, 1996, Text S, pp.99-100)*

hat your business in life is to be happy and to make others happy. That soun
is to be happy and to make others happy. That sounds comfortable and easy,
it? You begin making other people happy by doing good turns to them. You ne
not worry about making yourselves happy, as you will very soon find that th
itself; when you make other people happy, it makes you happy too. Later on,
e other people happy, it makes you happy too. Later on, when you have a home
y one you will make your husband a happy man. If all homes were bright and c
hy and clean and busy they will be happy. Happy children love their parents.
clean and busy they will be happy. Happy children love their parents. There
hild. I am sure God means us to be happy in this life. He has given us a wor
happiness into the world by making happy homes and by being yourselves good,

who pass away; secondly, to bring happiness into the world by making happy
nt of life. By giving out love and happiness in this way, you will gain for
ind that Heaven is not the kind of happiness somewhere up there in the skies
your own home. So guide others to happiness and you will bring happiness to
rs to happiness and you will bring happiness to yourselves and by doing this

Data Extract 7.3 *Concordance, Happy and happiness in Girl Guides text (Source: Stubbs, 1996, Text S, p.86)*

o think it over. I have had a most happy life and I want each of you to have
and I want each of you to have as happy a life too. I believe that God put
d put us in this jolly world to be happy and enjoy life. Happiness doesn't c
our turn comes to die, you can die happy in feeling that at any rate you hav
'Be prepared' in this way, to live happy and to die happy – stick to your Sc
this way, to live happy and to die happy – stick to your Scout Promise alway

world to be happy and enjoy life. Happiness doesn't come from being rich, n
self-indulgence. One step towards happiness is to make yourself healthy and
loomy one. But the real way to get happiness is by giving out happiness to o
to get happiness is by giving out happiness to other people. Try and leave

Data Extract 7.4 *Concordance, Happy and happiness in Boy Scouts text (Source: Stubbs, 1996, Text S, p.88)*

7.5 Questions for you about the data

(i)   Read Data Extracts 7.1 and 7.2. What kind of texts do you think these are?

(ii) What does each text say about the role of women and men in society?

(iii) Do you think the two texts are written for different readers?

(iv) What kind of reader do you think each text is written for?

7.6 Some points from the researcher's analysis

The two texts are Baden-Powell's last messages to the Girl Guides (Data Extract 7.1) and Boy Scouts (Data Extract 7.2). Baden-Powell (1857-1941) was a British general who founded a youth movement known as the Boy Scouts Association:

> This was a movement which he set up in 1908, to develop boys' character and practical outdoor skills such as camping and hiking. Baden-Powell's principles of self-reliance and healthy living, based on love of God and country, and also on his military experience in southern Africa, are set in his *Scouting for Boys*. (Stubbs, 1996, p.82)

Shortly after the successful start of the Boy Scouts movement, he founded the Girl Guides in 1910 (Stubbs, 1996, p.82). The texts in Data Extracts 7.1 and 7.2 have been widely circulated and read by hundreds of thousands of children and adults. The last message to Girl Guides was published in 1941 and only reprinted once, but the last message to Boy Scouts has been reprinted several times since it was published in 1942, and is still available on a postcard in Scout Association shops.

Stubbs begins his content analysis of the texts with the assumption that the sexism of the texts is obvious when reading the texts today (over 50 years after they were written); they may seem offensive or just ridiculous, even humorous. Stubbs thus identifies sexism as the ideological position to be analysed. He shows that the texts reveal different assumptions about their readerships: Data Extract 7.1 is longer and more complex both in the words used (lexically) and in its sentence structure (syntactically), when compared with Data Extract 7.2. Stubbs suggests that perhaps Scouts are assumed to have shorter attention spans!

Stubbs shows that the message to Guides is full of references to men, either as 'men' or 'husbands', and contains many words showing relations between people, or people and God: husband, parents, comrade, servant. He contrasts this with the message to Scouts, in which there are no references to women and almost none to outside relations (the references to 'other people' and the fictional 'pirate chief' are the only ones). In Data Extract 7.1, Guides are defined in relation to home, husband and children, while the Scouts are not defined in relation to any particular thing, except perhaps to their careers (one reference). Both texts support the preservation of the *status quo*: in Data Extract 7.2, Scouts are encouraged 'to be contented with what you have got', and in Data Extract 7.1, Guides are referred to 'God's plan' and what God wants. Stubbs points out that the fact that these texts seem so dated now highlights that the concepts of women, men and children are historically variable, and are historically constructed and naturalised – rather than being natural – through repetition in texts such as these.

7.7 More questions for you about the data

(v)   Circle any words in Data Extracts 7.1 and 7.2 that you think are ideologically loaded (for an example of an ideologically loaded word, see Section 7.2 above).

(vi) What are the two most frequent lexical words (that is, content words, rather than grammatical words such as 'and' or 'of') used in each text?

(vii) Look at the two concordance sheets (Data Extracts 7.3 and 7.4). Consider the uses of 'happy' and 'happiness' in the concordances of each text.

(viii)How are these words being used? Can you find any differences between uses of these words in Data Extracts 7.1 and 7.2?

7.8 Further discussion and conclusions

Stubbs identifies 'happy' as the most common lexical item in both texts and goes on to analyse the use of 'happy', even though it is not an obviously ideologically loaded'word. Stubbs points out that in Data Extract 7.1, 'happy' is used as an adjective ten times in the first third of the text; it is not used at all in the middle third of the text and in the last third it is used in the form of the noun 'happiness' – that is, it is 'nominalised'. Stubbs describes the changing use of the word form from 'happy' to 'happiness' in the text as the 'micro-history' of the words in this text. The concordance lines of the use of happy (see Data Extract 7.3) show the syntactic context – that is, its position in the sentence – of the word more easily. It occurs in the following constructions and phrases (number of occurrences given in parentheses): MAKE happy [Noun Phrase] (6); MAKE happy [Noun] (1); BE happy (4); BRING happiness (2); GIVE OUT happiness (1); GUIDE to happiness (1). Stubbs points out that in most cases in the text addressed to guides, happiness involves other people.

> The grammar of *happy* in this text implies that it is something one can be, or be made by others, and that *happiness* is an object which one can give to someone, or a place to which one can guide someone. (p.87)

In contrast Stubbs shows that in Data Extract 7.2 there is no such shift from the use of happy as an adjective to nominal happiness, as the words are mixed throughout the text. He shows further that unlike Data Extract 7.1, only one of the uses of happy/happiness, 'giving out happiness', implies the involvement of other people. In the concordance for the Scout's message (Data Extract 7.4), every use of 'happy' is collocated with 'life', 'live' or 'die' within three words to the left or right. Happy is thus used as a feature of life and death while happiness is an object or a place.

Stubbs compares Baden-Powell's use of happy and happiness with a larger English corpus of 1.5 million words. Stubbs uses both the London-Lund corpus of 35,000 words of spoken British English and the Lancaster-Oslo-Bergewn (LOB) corpus of 1 million words of spoken British English. He finds that while Baden-Powell's use of the words is not strange or unusual, he does make selections from a range of potential uses that reinforce the different patterns in Data Extracts 7.1 and 7.2. In relation to the corpus, Baden-Powell uses nominals more ('happiness' rather than 'happy') and the collocations 'make' and 'life' more than in the general corpus. For example, 'make happy' accounts for 44% of collocations in Data Extract 7.1 compared with 4% in the corpus, and 'happy' and 'life' collocate 50% of the time in Data Extract 7.2 but only 5% of the time in the corpus.

Stubbs thus argues that

> from the potential available in the language, these texts use particular actual selections, which attach particular connotations to the lemma [happy]. (p.89)

Meanings are conveyed not only by individual words and grammatical forms, but also by the frequency of collocations and by the distribution of forms across texts. Word meanings are thus created in texts, each instance has a history in text, and ultimately word meanings change because the way they are used in texts changes. One of the implications arising from this is, Stubbs points out, that we can't completely remove sexism from language by removing sexist language forms, such as false generic 'he'. The way any word is used can be sexist, even when the words do not seem to be sexist. In this case, although there is nothing inherently sexist about the word 'happy', it can be used in sexist ways, as Stubbs's analysis of the difference between Data Extracts 7.1 and 7.2 indicates.

7.9 Your view

(ix) How useful do you find this type of analysis?

(x) Do you think there are advantages of combining content analysis with corpus analysis?

(xi) Do you agree with Stubbs that the corpus approach helps to identify the ideological function of words that are not ideologically loaded?

(xii) For what other kinds of research do you think this sort of analysis would be useful?

7.10 Examples of studies using a similar approach

Another example of a critical approach to written data, using corpus analysis, is:

KRISHNAMURTHY, R. (1996) 'Ethnic, racial and tribal: the language of racism?', in C.R. Caldas-Coulthard and M. Coulthard (eds) *Texts and Practices: Readings in Critical Discourse Analysis*, London, Routledge.

Examples of corpus approaches to spoken data are:

CARTER, R. (1998) 'Common language: corpus, creativity and cognition', *Language and Literature,* vol.8, no.3, pp.195-216.

LINDEMANN, S. and MAURANEN, A. (2001) "It's just real messy: the occurrence and function of just in a corpus of academic speech', *English for Specific Purposes,* vol.20, no.S1 (Supplement no.1), pp.459-75.

8: Systemic functional linguistics: information texts in a museum

8.1 Key features of this approach

Systemic functional linguistics is a particular approach to the analysis of 'texts'- spoken and written language – which is most notably associated with the work of M.A.K. Halliday (1978, 1989). Systemic functional linguistics is a theory of language, that is, a way of thinking about why language is as it is. A basic premise of this particular theory is that language is *functional*; that is, it is a resource for meaning-making that has evolved, and continues to evolve, to meet human needs.

Systemic functional linguistics provides a complex set of tools, linguistic terminology, categories and frameworks, for analysing texts. It is important to note that these are not simply alternative labels for traditional grammatical terms. While traditional grammars tend to focus on language forms (for example, noun, verb, parts of speech), the aim of Hallidayan systemic functional grammar is to develop an analytical and labelling system that treats form as always bound up with function and meaning-making. Grammatical choices are therefore understood as choices not simply about form but also about meaning and, indeed, about the representation of particular world views.

8.2 Example

PURSER, E. (2000) 'Telling stories: text analysis in a museum', in E. Ventola (ed.) *Discourse and Community. Doing Functional Linguistics*, Tubingen, Gunter Narr Verlag, pp. 169-98.

In this example, Purser focuses on one key system within the systemic functional approach to language to explore how particular meanings are constructed in written information texts in a museum. This is the 'system of transitivity', which means, briefly, the representation of 'who is doing what to whom'. At clause level, therefore, transitivity involves meanings that are organised in terms of 'actors' (who), 'processes' (is doing), and 'goal' (what). This roughly corresponds in traditional grammar to the subject, verb and object of a sentence. Thus, in the clause *I kicked the ball* – 'I' is the actor, 'kick' is the process, and 'ball' is the goal.

The original texts were in German and Purser analysed the transitivity in the clauses of both the German texts and the English translations. Here we focus only on the English version of the texts.

8.3 The aims of the researcher

Purser aims to:

- explore the ways in which the written texts of a museum exhibition reinforce the messages of the visual displays
- analyse the texts from a systemic functional perspective
- explore how the textual organisation of the museum information is connected with a particular perspective on the world, or ideology

8.4 Data extract *(see data extract 8.1)*

THE SOUTH SEAS EXHIBITION

[...]

(4) This exhibition aims to give an overview of the individual cultures of these peoples, (5) as they were developed (6) when Whites discovered the country (7) and began with the transformation of the former way of life[1].

[...]

(15) The cultures of the South Seas had already experienced several changes over the millennia as a result of mutual contact, sometimes over very great distances. (16) Hence the 'Europeanisation' of Oceania was no fundamentally new type of development. (17) However it did surpass all previous inter-cultural movements in its geographical expanse, and most particularly in its manner, intensity and speed. (18) It began in the 16th century with the discovery of the Pacific by the Spanish and with the first circumnavigations of the globe. (19) The European ships (20) which headed for the South Pacific in the 16th, 17th, and 18th centuries left behind many tools and implements, items of clothing and things[6] in exchange. (21) Islanders in many regions learned of iron, (22) so that, for example, on Tahiti the technique of making basalt axe heads had already been abandoned between the years 1769 and 1777. (23) Whites had also, for philanthropic reasons, been bringing domesticated plants and animals to many islands since the second half of the 18th century, especially to Polynesia.

(24) The Christian mission in the Pacific began in the 17th century (on the Marianas). (25) In accordance with their beliefs, missionaries of various confessions had been attempting, especially since the end of the 18th century, to radically change the traditional way of life (26) wherever they were able to settle, (27) and on many islands they came into considerable power. (28) Since the early 19th century, deserted sailors and escaped convicts had also been living on several islands, (29) and soon traders settled on very many of the islands of Oceania.: (30) By the end of the 19th century 'South Pacific trade' was in full bloom (with coconut oil, copra, pearls, trepang, sandalwood etc.), (31) whalers were bartering supplies in many places, (32) and the ships of brutal labour recruitment ("slave catchers") had already visited upon a number of islands.

[...]

(36) The thesis that Oceania is no zoological garden and that one cannot, in our times of globalising technology, preserve the old world is undoubtedly correct. (37) Missionaries themselves certainly thought that this old world, measured by its own standards, had a

---

right to exist: 'superseded laws, cults, social groupings and moral expectations which the group put upon its members sufficed to meet and satisfy the demands of life' (H. Strauss on the Mbowamb in New Guinea). (38) Yet in every community there has been, since the first contact with Europeans, a lively interest in the goods of the Whites, (39) and the islanders thus themselves encouraged the transformation of their own culture. (40) The natives were also initially friendly towards the invaders in many places, (41) or even regarded them as gods. (42) Whites are still greatly overvalued even today on the remote islands. (43) These islanders know hardly anything about the extensive degree of specialisation in Europe and North America. (44) They can all plant, (45) fish, (46) build houses and boats, (47) and so they believe that every single European and American can themselves make ships, aeroplanes, radios, bicycles and torches.

[...]

(62) Everyday life increasingly changed: (63) metal tools came into use everywhere, (64) the calico clothing 'prescribed' by the missionaries was willingly adopted, (65) imported foods (rice, sugar, preserves) were much sought after, (66) tin cans replaced wooden vessels and ceramic, (67) imported wood, corrugated iron and cement were used for house building whenever possible, (68) churches were erected everywhere, (69) schools built, (70) and health care was also improved, (71) once innumerable infectious diseases had been introduced (72) and entire island populations decimated. (73) Independent nations have now emerged in Oceania (e.g. Tonga, West Samoa, Fiji, Nauru), (74) and development in that direction, from colonial, protectorate and trustee government, is the general trend.

Data Extract 8.1 *The South Seas Exhibition (Source: Purser, 2000, pp. 194-6)*
(The numbering corresponds to the clauses anaylsed)

8.5 Questions for you about the data

Data Extract 8.1 is from an information sheet accompanying a number of artefacts (tools, weapons, jewellery) in an exhibition about peoples of the Pacific in a major European museum. Purser states that the overall function of the written texts is not to describe the objects but rather to provide 'general background reading' (p.176).

As stated above, Purser focuses on transitivity in the texts – who (actor) is doing (processes) what (goal). Let's consider an example of representations of actors in a text. In the clause *I kicked the ball*, 'I' is clearly the actor with agency (causing the kicking). In an alternative wording, *the ball was kicked by me*, the 'actor' is put in the background and the agency thus less emphasised. In a third possible representation, the actor can be made completely invisible; in the passive construction, *the ball was kicked*, there is no mention of an actor and, therefore, agency (who the ball was kicked by) is obscured.

(i)   Look at Data Extract 8.1. Underline the 'actors' in the clauses.

(ii) What kinds of 'actors' do you notice? Are they visible or invisible? Is agency (who is doing what) explicit or obscured?

(iii) How do the choices made about representing actors and agency contribute to the perspective being offered in the exhibition?

8.6 Some points from the researcher's analysis

Purser makes several points about actors and agency in the texts being analysed. First, the participants whose actions affect other participants are almost exclusively European (examples: whites discover the islands, bring plants and aim to get power; European ships leave tools; missionaries change traditional life). Second, the islanders' agency is obscured. Thus while presumably the islanders were involved in adapting to new ideas, materials or practices (islanders are involved in abandoning their own technology, adopting European clothes, using traditional objects), this is not made explicit in the text.

8.7 More questions for you about the data

Now consider the kinds of processes that are in the text. Many different types of processes have been identified and categorised within systemic functional linguistics, but we will focus on two here: *material processes*, which are action verbs like 'kick' and involve an actor with agency; and *relational processes*, which are verbs like 'is', 'seems' (she *is* angry), which attribute a quality to somebody or something or identify the participant with a role.

(iv) Look at the data extract again. Underline three material processes.

(v) Underline three relational processes.

(vi) What do you notice about the kinds of processes that different actors are engaged in?

8.8 Further discussion and conclusions

Purser makes the following points on the use of material processes:

- the Europeans are shown doing very specific activities – their ships head for the Pacific, missionaries settle, sailors live and trade

- islanders do less clear-cut activities – although they do some specific activities, such as fishing, building, irrigating, the activities they are mostly involved in are more often represented as abstractions, such as cults, nations, cultural elements, traditional life.

On the use of relational processes, Purser states that:

- relational processes are used throughout 'to classify, locate, define and evaluate the Pacific cultures being described' (p.181). This emphasis on classification involves a high level of grammatical metaphor, that is, activities are represented metaphorically. For example, of the clause 'Metal tools *came into use*', Purser states '[this] gives an image of indigenous people not explicitly participating in the use of new materials'.(p.181).

The general point that Purser makes on the basis of her analysis of the extract (and other extracts) is that however 'well meaning' or 'objectively' one aims to write about the cultural practices of other people

> Representing and making sense of another culture is never neutral – there is unavoidable bias and inequality of position. (p.185)

However, as she argues, readers are not forced to comply with particular representations of events, people and cultures, and can come to look critically at texts. One way in which we can develop as critical readers is to identify the grammatical strategies used in constructing texts, one of which is transitivity, the focus of her analysis here.

8.9 Your view

Having read Purser's analysis of the different kinds of participants and processes:

(vii) How useful do you find the categories of the system of transitivity (as illustrated briefly here) – actor and process – for looking in detail at the written text?

(viii) To what extent, in your view, do the grammatical choices reflect a particular ideology on the Pacific, its history and its peoples?

(ix) To what extent do you agree with Purser's general position that there is no such thing as neutral description?

(x) Can you think of an analysis you might carry out in your own context, using the categories of 'actor' and 'process'?

8.10 Examples of studies using a similar approach

Systemic functional linguistics has been used to analyse a wide range of written texts in many contexts. For useful edited collections of studies, see:

MARTIN, J.R. and VEEL, R. (eds) (1998) *Reading Science: Critical and Functional Perspectives on Discourses of Science*, London, Routledge.

VENTOLA, E. (2000)(ed.) *Discourse and Community. Doing Functional Linguistics*, Tubingen, Gunter Narr Verlag.

For an introduction to systemic functional grammar, see:

BLOOR, T. and BLOOR, M. (1995) *The Functional Analysis of English*. A Hallidayan Approach, London, Edward Arnold.

9: Bakhtinian discourse analysis: students' written texts

9.1 Key features of this approach

'Discourse analysis', as stated in the main introduction, is used to refer to three broadly distinguishable approaches to language analysis: the analysis of stretches of language longer than a single utterance or sentence; the analysis of specific ways of using language in particular contexts; and the analysis of different ways of representing social reality through language. A combination of the first two of these approaches to discourse involves analysis of language – texts – in context. The third approach involves drawing on social theory and philosophy in order to theorise about the social and cultural meanings that are being constructed in a text. In this way, key concepts of a particular social theory or philosophy are used as a lens through which to analyse specific texts.

Key concepts from the work of the literacy theorist and philosopher of language Mikhail Bakhtin (1895-1975) are increasingly being used in studies of language, including analyses of written texts. A central notion in Bakhtin's work is that language is 'dialogic'. Briefly this means that all specific uses of language or 'utterances', to use Bakhtin's preferred term, embedded as they are in sociocultural and historical contexts, are dynamic in their contribution to meaning-making. Bakhtin says:

> The living utterance, having taken meaning and shape at a particular historical moment in a socially specific environment, cannot fail to brush up against thousands of living dialogic threads, woven by socio-ideological consciousness around the given object of an utterance; it cannot fail to become an active participant in social dialogue. (Bakhtin, 1981, p.276)

9.2 Example

SCOLLON, R., TSANG, W.K., LI, D., YUNG, V. and JONES, R. (1998) 'Voice, appropriation and discourse representation in a student writing task', *Linguistics and Education*, vol.9, no.3, pp.227-50.

Scollon *et al.* focus on the meanings constructed in student writing. They draw on the work of several theorists, notably Bakhtin, and in particular his notion of 'voices'. They also draw on Wertsch's notion of 'communication as *mediated action*' (Scollon *et al.*, 1977, p.228) in which individuals are viewed as 'appropriating' or taking on different social voices necessary for the kind of utterance they want to produce. Scollon *et al.* are concerned to trace how an individual borrows from other voices to produce a text that performs a particular action. They thus attempt to explore the relationship between a specific utterance and its 'cultural, historical and institutional settings' (p.229). In examining this relationship, the researchers argue that people do not simply appropriate other voices, but that the act of appropriation always involves some adaptation.

The researchers apply the notions of 'voices', 'dialogism' and 'appropriation' to the production of student texts. In doing so they hope to move the focus away from the need to teach students how to 'do quotation and citation correctly' to examining the 'social practices of textual appropriation' (p.227), that is, how students engage in the use of many voices – 'polyvocality' – and other texts in their writing.

9.3 The aims of the researchers

Scollon *et al.* aim to:

- explore the extent to which Hong Kong students 'appropriate the voices of others' in their own discourse in classroom writing tasks 'relating to the transition of sovereignty from the British to the Chinese government' (p.230)

- explore the linguistic means students use to do this

- provide teachers and learners with a different way of viewing citation, 'seeing it as part of the larger, more fundamental issues of polyvocality and discourse representation' (p.229).

9.4 Data extracts *(see data extract 9.1-9.2)*

Data Extract 9.1 was one of the writing tasks given to 60 second-year university students in Hong Kong taking a course on English for Professional Communication. Data Extract 2 is one student's response to the task.

You are a Hong Kong Chinese of your parents' generation. A friend who has immigrated to Vancouver has written you a letter asking you if you plan to immigrate to Canada as well. You answer that you do not plan to do so because you believe that Hong Kong has a strong future of which you want to be part.

Write a short personal letter which gives the reasons why you feel the future of Hong Kong looks good.

Data Extract 9.1 Writing task (Source: Scollon et al., 1998, Task A, p.231)

1 Hey guy! It's nice to receive your letter as you seldom writes!

2 Ha, Ha!

3 How's your life in Vancouver? According to your letter, I guess you love it very
4 much, right? I feel so warm and appreciate much that you've concerned about my
5 future in Hong Kong, however, in my opinion, I suppose it will be a bright one.

6 Hong Kong people have been characterised as hardworking, smart and helpful group
7 and it is such properties which make Hong Kong to be such a successful city. I don't
8 think that these properties will disappear just because we have a new government/
9 ruler. Moreover I'm sure that the Chinese Government will not want to cease the
10 prosperity of Hong Kong as Hong Kong means 'a goose which lays gold eggs to her'

11 So, please don't worry about my future here as it will be great & much more brighter
12 than before.

13 Wish you a terrific life in Vancouver &...write me soon.

Data Extract 9.2 *A student's response (Source: Scollon et al., 1998, p.233)*

9.5 Questions for you about the data

(i)   Read through Data Extracts 9.1 and 9.2 – the writing task and the student's letter. How many different 'voices' can you identify in the letter?

(ii) What is the main 'voice' in this text – that is, the one that is used the most?

(iii) Underline the phrases or words in the letter where the writer seems to be directly addressing someone else.

(iv) How are the different 'voices' you identified signalled or marked in the text?

9.6 Some points from the researchers' analysis

Scollon *et al.* point out that the main 'voice' one hears in the letter is that of the fictionalised author of the letter, the pretend parent, for example in the first line of the letter and lines 3-5. They also show that the first section of the letter (lines 1-5) is dominated by dialogism where the fictionalised author is clearly addressing an imagined recipient, for example in 'Hey guy' and 'How's your life in Vancouver?' The recipient's voice also comes into the letter. For example, in lines 4-5 where the student writes 'I ... appreciate much that you've concerned about my future', the recipient's voice is implied as saying something like 'I'm concerned about your future in Hong Kong' (p.233). Scollon *et al.* thus argue that even at the most basic level, the student letters are polyvocal, containing 'a fictionalized writer responding to a fictionalized reader' (p.233).

Within these two main voices, the researchers identify further evidence of different 'voices'. Line 6, Scollon *et al.* argue, is not in the author's voice but is rather an example of 'a more general, anonymous, public voice' (p.234). In the phrase 'and it is such properties' (line 7) Scollon *et al.* reason that the voice is ambiguous; it could be the author's voice ('I think it is such properties ...') or it could be a continuation of the public discourse ('Hong Kong people are also characterised as ...'). They thus describe this utterance as polyvocal, both the voice of an anonymous public discourse on Hong Kong people and the voice of the fictionalised author.

Scollon *et al.* also characterise the utterance 'Hong Kong means 'a goose which lays gold eggs to her' (lines 9-10) as polyvocal: the 'voice of tradition' is marked off by scare quotes around the saying, but the awkward phrasing of the expression 'a goose which lays the gold eggs to her' also shows the author's voice as an ESL writer coming through (p.234)

9.7 More questions for you about the data

Scollon *et al.* draw on Fairclough's notion of 'discourses of representation', and in particular on the distinction that Fairclough makes between 'manifest intertextuality' and 'interdiscursivity' (Fairclough, 1992). 'Manifest intertextuality' involves the use in one text of actual words from another: an obvious example is when the words of a politician used in a speech are quoted in a newspaper article. 'Interdiscursivity', in contrast, is a more abstract kind of echoing in a text that involves the use of styles, genres and ideological positions: for example, a specific text may echo or represent the ideology of racism.

(v) Read through the letter quickly again and look at where the different voices come in. Can you identify the different ways in which other voices are introduced into the text?

(vi) What different 'discursive frames' (that is, styles, genres, general ideological positions) can you identify in the letter?

(vii) The letter was written in English despite the fact that no directive was given as to the language it should be written in. Why do you think English was chosen by the student?

9.8 Further discussion and conclusions

Scollon *et al.* identify a number of ways in which manifest intertextuality is evident in the total set of 60 letters in their analysis. We will only look at the examples that come up in the one letter above – that is, an extract from the data. One example is the use of scare quotes around the phrase 'a goose which lays gold eggs to her' in lines 11-12. Scollon *et al.* argue that the use of scare quotes is a subtle form of discourse representation that allows the author to distance him/herself from the voice that has been appropriated, either to emphasise it as authoritative, as in this example, or as euphemistic. Another example is the use of the passive, as in 'Hong Kong people have been characterised ... group'. Here an anonymous voice is cited but the passive voice gives the statement an authoritative air (see Example 8 for another example of the passive). The researchers argue that analysing how intertextuality works in this way helps to show up how different voices are embedded within texts.

Scollon *et al.* point out that it is more difficult to trace interdiscursivity than manifest intertextuality, and especially to trace its sources. However, they identify four different kinds of interdiscursivity in the student letters: the use of English; the form of a university assignment; the style of a personal letter; and a public discourse register. Scollon *et al.* argue that the discourse on English as the preferred medium is present in all 60 of the students' use of English to write the letters, despite the fact that a letter written by their parents to a Chinese friend would probably never be written in English. Not surprisingly, they explain this as arising from the fact that the task was given by an English lecturer during the English curriculum time – this is 'the situational frame' (p.242). The frame of the university assignment was also very strong; despite the fact that students knew the task was to be unassessed, they completed it according to the instructions given and none changed the task at all. Because the task was understood as a classroom assignment, Scollon *et al.* argue that the perceived demands of such an assignment overrode the 'demands of the fictionalized situation in the task itself' (p.243) – that is, writing as a parent to a friend. Another indicator of this influence was found in the use of wordings from the task in the actual letters written by the students. The letters also clearly draw on the typical style and form of a personal letter with opening and closing greetings. A final marker of interdiscursivity which the researchers identify is that of a public discourse register – 'the public discourse of Hong Kong's transition to Chinese Sovereignty' (p.244). References to Hong Kong's prosperity (see lines 11-12) are apparently typical of the discourse used in public debates, political speeches and media reports, and such phrases are most likely to be originally in Chinese.

Scollon *et al.* presented their analysis to the students whose texts they had examined, along with Fairclough's categories and a sample of letters for them to analyse. The students' analysis not only confirmed the researchers' but the students also identified further voices that the researchers had not identified. Not only was the writing confirmed as even more polyvocal than the researchers thought, but the students also displayed a strong awareness of the different use of voices, showing this to be often deliberate and conscious. Scollon *et al.* thus conclude that their students' writing, even on artificial tasks such as the one discussed here, are highly intertextual and interdiscursive. They argue that 'the rather commonly stated concern that our students do not know how to do quotation and citation is somewhat misplaced' (p.248).

9.9 Your view

(viii) How useful do you find the notion of 'voices' to look at what is going on in student writing?

(ix) To what extent do you agree with Scollon *et al.*'s identification of manifest intertextuality in the students' texts?

(x) To what extent do you agree with Scollon *et al.*'s identification of interdiscursivity in the students' texts?

(xi) Scollon *et al.* give the students (their research subjects) an opportunity to analyse the data they produced using the same categories as the researchers did. They also present their own analyses to the students. What do you think the advantages and disadvantages of such a process might be?

(xii) Can you think of any way in which you might apply this approach to your own context?

9.10 Examples of studies using a similar approach

For a further example of the use of Bakhtin's work to explore student writing, see:

LILLIS, T.M. (2001) *Student Writing. Access, Regulation, Desire*, London, Routledge.

For examples of studies using Bakhtin's work to explore spoken language, see:

HAWORTH, A. (1999) 'Bakhtin in the classroom: what constitutes a dialogic text – some lessons from small group interaction, *Language and Education*, vol.13, no.2, pp.99-117.

MAYBIN, J. (2002) 'Voices, intertextuality and induction into schooling', in S. Goodman, T. Lillis, N. Mercer and J. Maybin (eds) *Language, Literacy and Education: A Reader*, Stoke-on-Trent, Trentham.

10: Talk around texts: punctuation in young children's writing

10.1 Key features of this approach

'Talk around texts' involves researchers encouraging the producers of texts to comment explicitly, in a variety of ways, on their texts. As a method, it has been used for different purposes with different underlying theoretical positions: as a way of gaining access to the tacit knowledge that people bring to their writing (see Odell, Goswami and Herrington, 1983); as a way of emphasising the perspectives of literacy users (see Hamilton, 1994); as an acknowledgement that people are active meaning-makers who are constantly attempting to impose an order on their activities and understanding (for children, see Wells, 1986; for adults, see Ivanič, 1998; Lillis, 2001).

10.2 Example

HALL, N. (1999) 'Young children's use of graphic punctuation', *Language and Education*, vol.13, no.3, pp.178-93.

Hall sets out to explore why young children in UK primary schools use what he refers to as 'unconventional punctuation' in their writing, for example the use of full stops or commas in places where experienced users of punctuation might least expect them. His interest is in both describing how children between the ages of 5 and 7 years use unconventional punctuation and exploring why. Rather than treating unusual or unconventional punctuation as arbitrary or meaningless, Hall looks for reasons for such punctuation, citing Ferreiro and Teberosky, who state 'what appears as confusion is actually the child's systematisation, operating from bases very different from the adults' (Ferreiro and Teberosky, 1984, cited in Hall, 1999, p.180). Starting from the premise that learning does not take place in a vacuum but always within a specific and influential context, Hall aims to identify how the learning environment may be contributing to the particular punctuation patterns that the children are adopting.

To study this context, what Hall refers to as 'the ecology of learning to punctuate' (p.180), he and his co-researchers spent a good deal of time – two and a half days a week over a period of two years – observing and making field notes of activities in the classroom. In addition, a large amount of children's writing was collected and interviews with children and teachers were carried out. Interviewing pupils about their writing was an important way of exploring the reasons underlying their use of punctuation.

10.3 The aims of the researcher

The general aims of Hall's research are to:

- describe the range of unconventional punctuation that occurs in young children's writing

- understand the principles underlying such punctuation

- consider the influence of teaching on children's punctuation practices.

In the data examples we consider here, the main focus of Hall's interest is on the way in which children use the full stop.

10.4 Data extracts *(see data extract 10.1-10.4)*

Data Extract 10.1 *Punctuation in writing (Source: Hall, 1999, Figure 1, p.182)*

Data Extract 10.2 *Punctuation in writing (Source: Hall, 1999, Figure 2, p.183)*

I like you you have niys. **(1)**	(I like you you have nice)
sewiws I reley like Gen mack. **(2)**	(shoes I really like Ginn maths)
I wesh I can do sum avrey**(3)**	(I wish I could do some every)
day Becauc. **(3)** it is guder it is	(day because it is good it is)
may frayvret I like paying I **(4)**	(my favourite I like playing I)
payti girl I feck I am gud at them	(??? girl I think I am good at them)
Do you I like. **(5)** the tyrep the basd	(do you I like the trip the best)
it was the basd I capt on gowng, (6) on the slid	(it was the best I kept ongoing on the slide)
and I naver got of it bcaus	(and I never got off it because)
it gud I cul it a twece tweley. **(7)** bcause it	(it good I call it a twirly whirly because it)
Looks like a twele Dos it to you it das to me. **(8)**	(looks like a twirly does it to you it does to me)
you have niys clws	(you have nice clothes)
I like. **(9)** the treps wot you tac us on	(I like the trips what you took us on)
I like the Naym. (10) wot you have got	(I like the name what you have got)
by L. **(11)**	

Data Extract 10.3 *Punctuation in writing (Source: Hall, 1999, pp.184-5)*

Res:	Why did you put one there? It's such a tiny one isn't it, I can hardly see that. Do you want make it a bit bigger? Why did you put one there? **(2)**
L:	Because it's a bit long.
Res:	Because it's a bit long. OK then. (*Long pause as she reads and then she puts in another one.*) OK, why did you put that one there, after 'because' **(3)**?
L:	'Cos I didn't put one in that line, (*she refers to the line above*) so I did it there.
Res:	OK so you didn't put it at the end of that line, after 'every', you put it in the middle of the next line after 'because'. Is that right? OK. (*Long pause while she reads silently.*)
L:	I've forgotten what it says.
Res:	I think it says 'it is good' but you wrote 'gooder'. (*reads*) 'It is good'. (*pause*) OK, so you are putting one after 'I'. **(4)** What mark is it that you're putting there, do you remember?
L:	A full stop.
Res:	A full stop. That's right. (*Long pause while she rereads silently*) OK, you've put one after 'I like' **(5)** there. Why have you put that one there?
L:	'Cos it's a bit long. From there, there a lot of words, to there.
and a little later:	
Res:	And why that one there? **(8)**
L:	I didn't put one into that line, so I've put one there.

Data Extract 10.4 *Talk around writing (Source: Hall, 1999, p.185)*
(The numbers refer to the line numbers of the written text in Data Extract 10.3)

10.5 Questions for you about the data

(i) Look at Data Extracts 10.1 and 10.2. What do you notice about the punctuation?

(ii) Look at Data Extract 10.3. What do you notice about the punctuation here? In what ways is it similar to or different from the patterns in Data Extracts 10.1 and 10.2?

(iii) Read the discussion in Data Extract 10.4. What do the child's comments tell you about her reasons for punctuating as she has done?

10.6 Some points from the researcher's analysis

Hall states that Data Extracts 10.1 and 10.2 exemplify the practice of 'end-line punctuation', whereby the child puts some form of punctuation, usually a full stop, at the end of each line of writing. The fact that children are using an end-line punctuation rule is also highlighted when some children talk to the researcher about where full stops should go. As can be seen in Data Extract 10.2, some children don't restrict their end-line punctuation to the full stop.

In Hall's study, at least, end-line punctuation occurred when children were writing only two or three lines of text. What was more common in the children's writing was for no punctuation to be included initially and for them to add a full stop at the end of a piece or at the end of a page. This seems to reflect the children's concern to meet the demand to get a full stop in somewhere: one child even put a full stop halfway down a blank page before writing anything and remarked 'I've done my full stop' (p.183).

Data Extract 10.3 is an example of a less-common practice of punctuating, punctuating according to what Hall refers to as 'length of unit'. In Data Extract 10.3, when the child was asked if there was anything she wanted to change or add to her writing, she added the full stops as indicated. These are not added according to an end-line rule, but rather seem to reflect a concern to break the text up into appropriate chunks. As Hall points out, the explanations that the child gives in her talk about the punctuation in Data Extract 10.4 focus on length and space: 'long', 'from there to there', 'not putting one in the line above' (p.185).

All these approaches to punctuation: end of line, end of piece, and according to length, reflect what Hall refers to as 'graphic punctuation' or 'punctuation according to graphic principles', which seems to govern much punctuation in young children's writing.

> I define graphic punctuation as the use of, or belief about the use of, punctuation which is dominated by the positioning of the marks on the page according to space rather than any underlying linguistic principle. (p.181)

10.7 More questions for you about the data

(iv) Look again at the data extracts. Why do you think children seem to punctuate according to graphic principles – that is, they use punctuation to mark space –

rather than according to any linguistic principles, such as the use of a full stop to mark a clause boundary?

10.8 Further discussion and conclusions

Hall argues that children learn to treat punctuation as a graphic phenomenon from their teachers. From his observations he points to the ways in which punctuation as a graphic phenomenon is emphasised in teaching. First, teachers stress 'endedness' in their talk; consider, for example, the teacher comment 'What comes at the end of a sentence then?' Second, there was little emphasis on exploring why punctuation occurs at particular points. Third, great importance was attached to noticing and naming; consider, for example, the teacher comments 'What's that one there?' and 'What did we call that?'

Hall also points to the way in which many of the books in the classrooms reinforce the notion of punctuation as a graphic phenomenon. For example, he states that many of the books used with the children tend to present the sentence as a visually discrete unit. This is exemplified in the following extract:

> Once there was a young prince who lived in a castle.
>
> He had a very special pet. (p.189)

The problem Hall sees with this kind of emphasis is that

> it actually draws children's attention away from the demarcatory function of sentence punctuation. The principal function of punctuation is not to mark endings, but to demarcate elements of text which have particular kinds of relationship with each other. Thus a full stop between two pieces of text denotes a different kind of relationship between them than would a comma ... (p.189)

Hall argues that while the principle of graphic punctuation is a temporary phenomenon for many children, it can persist for an unnecessarily long and unhelpful period of time. He therefore questions whether teachers' emphasis should be on the graphic aspect of punctuation and suggests that there should be shift towards an emphasis on the linguistic function of punctuation in writing.

10.9 Your view

(v) How useful do you think 'talk around texts' is in exploring children's perspectives on punctuation? What are its limitations?

(vi) What does the analysis of written texts enable the researcher to discover?

(vii) To what extent do you agree with Hall's argument that children are punctuating on the basis of graphic rather than linguistic principles?

(viii) To what extent do you agree with Hall's explanation for children's emphasis on graphic punctuation?

(ix) Can you think of ways in which this approach might be useful in your own context?

10.10 Examples of studies using a similar approach

For another study using talk around text in relation to punctuation, see:

IVANIČ, R. (1996) 'The logic of non-standard punctuation', in N. Hall and A. Robinson (eds) *Learning about Punctuation*, Clevedon, Multilingual Matters.

For an influential article on the value of researching talk around texts, see:

ODELL, L., GOSWAMI, D., and HERRINGTON, A. (1983) 'The discourse-based interview: a procedure for exploring the tacit knowledge of writers in non-academic settings', in P. Mosenthal, L. Tamor and S.A. Walmsley (eds) *Research on Writing. Principles and Methods*, New York, Longman.

See also Example 21 in this workbook:

LILLIS, T. (2001) *Student Writing: Access, Regulation and Desire*, London, Routledge.

11: Contrastive rhetoric: job applications

11.1 Key features of the approach

Contrastive rhetoric involves studies of 'rhetoric', or what might be broadly referred to as the representation of meaning in writing, in different languages. It also includes research in second-language (L2) writing acquisition. In contrastive rhetoric, language and writing are considered to be cultural phenomena. Written texts are seen as following different rhetorical conventions – that is, specific ways of making meaning that are related to the culture in which they are produced.

Contrastive rhetoric as an approach to analysis is interdisciplinary, drawing on and combining insights from a number of different kinds of research. The insights drawn on – along with the research disciplines in parentheses – include the following:

- language and writing patterns are specific to the culture they are produced in (theory of linguistic relativity)

- writing is communication, and often persuasion, which is affected by its audience (rhetoric)

- writing as a text varies systematically and this variation can be analysed (text/applied linguistics)

- writing reproduces as well as creates different genres and discourses (theory of discourse types and genres)

- writing as an activity is 'embedded in culture' (theory of literacy)

- texts can be translated across cultures, even though these translations may be somewhat different from the original (theory of translation) (Based on Connor, 1996, 9)

11.2 Example

CONNOR, U., DAVIS, K.W. and DE RYCKER, T. (1995) 'Correctness and clarity in applying for overseas jobs: a cross-cultural analysis of US and Flemish applications', *Text*, vol.15, no.4, pp.457-75.

Researchers within contrastive rhetoric typically focus on written texts produced in a range of contexts for a number of purposes, and they draw on tools from the disciplinary contexts described above in analysing texts. In this specific example, Connor *et al.* develop a multi-levelled framework for analysing differences and similarities between US and Flemish job applications written in English.

Note: The two letters discussed here were randomly selected by the researchers from the 74 letters that were analysed as part of their study. Since the analysis is based on the total collection of letters, you will not see evidence of all the features mentioned.

11.3 The aims of the researchers

The aims of Connor *et al.* are to:

- analyse similarities and differences between US and Flemish job application letters written in English, in order to determine whether there are any significant, culturally specific differences between the two groups

- compare the letters according to the categories of 'correctness' – that is, the number and type of errors present, for example punctuation and spelling, words, sentence structure and paragraph structure – and 'clarity' – content, organisation and length – to see whether there are any general differences between the texts produced by US students and those produced by Flemish students.

11.4 Data extracts *(see data extracts 11.1-11.2)*
Note The roman numerals given in square brackets at the end of each paragraph refer to the coding scheme and analytical framework in Figure 3.

1	Dear Dr. Davis
2	In reply to your advertisement in wich [sic] you offer a business education
3	Internship at your Indiana University, I would like to apply for the
4	job. [I/II]
5	I am doing my second year at the Antwerp University of Economics and
6	you will find a full account of my qualifications on the attached personal
7	record sheet. [III]
8	If you feel that my qualifications meet with your requirements, I shall be
9	pleased to be called for an interview. [IV]
10	Sincerely yours

Data Extract 11.1 Flemish applicant (Source Connor et al., 1995, p.467)

1	Dear Sirs:
2	Dr. Ken Davis, Professor of English W-331 at Indiana Unversity-Purdue
3	University at Indianapolis, has provided me with your job description
4	for the position of Assistant to the Tourist Information Manager for the
5	City of Antwerp, Belgium. This position greatly interests me because in
6	[sic] encompasses both my work experience and my interest in interna-
7	tional culture, as indicated on the attached resume. [I/II]
8	I have had over twelve years of experience in the public relations/market-

9	ing field. During that time, I have served as the Marketing Director for
10	a major Indianapolis chiropractic clinic with responsibilities for develop-
11	ing marketing plans and public relations venues for four clinics. I also
12	assisted with, produced and directed a local radio talk show for the clinics.
13	My employment duties have included a variety of coordination duties
14	for clients and dignitaries, including travel and hotel accommodations.
15	As an assistant to the Practice Development Director at a major
16	Indianapolis law firm, my duties included organization of client recep-
17	tions, travel arrangements for attorneys and clients, and intercommunica-
18	tion with attorneys and clients, some of whom have been in foreign
19	countries. [III]
20	I have a special personal interest in European culture, based upon my
21	experience as a host parent for the Youth for Understanding international
22	youth exchange program. During my involvement with this group, I have
23	hosted children from Denmark, Finland and Germany, as well as Chile
24	and Japan. [III]
25	I will be available for interview at any time, I may be reached at my
26	place of business at (XXX) XXX-XXXX from 8.00 a.m. (USA time)
27	until 5:30 p.m., Monday through Friday, or at home at (XXX) XXX-
28	XXXX at any time. [IV/V]
29	Thank you for your review of this application. [VI]
30	Sincerely

Data Extract 11.2 *US applicant (Source Connor et al., 1995, pp.467-8)*

I	Identify the source of information. (Explain how and where you learned of the position.)
II.	Apply for the position. (State desire for consideration.) a. direct stategy: 'I apply for this position ...' b. indirect strategy: 'I would be a good candidate ...'
III.	Provide supporting arguments for the job application. (Describe your qualifications, personal and professional. Describe reasons for application. Describe benefits to you and/or prospective employer.)
IV:	Indicate desire for interview.
V.	Specify means of further communication. (Indicate how you can be contacted or when you will contact the prospective employer.)
VI.	Express politeness (pleasantries) or appreciation.

Figure 3 *Meaning components of a letter of application: a coding scheme (Source: Connor et al., 1995, Table 1, p.464)*

11.5 Questions for you about the data

(i) Both of the letters in Data Extracts 11.1 and 11.2 are job application letters. The first is written by a Flemish business student writing in English. He has had at least six years formal instruction of English. The second was written by a US business student whose first language (L1) is English. Write down any differences and similarities between the two letters that immediately stand out.

(ii) Compare the letters using the category of 'correctness': identify any errors in spelling, punctuation, word choice, sentence structure and paragraph structure. Do these differ between the two letters or not?

(iii) Compare the letters using the category of 'clarity'. You will notice that the sections in the letters are numbered from I to VI. These numbers show the different steps of the letter as outlined in Figure 3. Go through each section and identify the different steps. (Count the number of words in each section and write down the total figures.)

(iv) Now compare the letters section by section; can you find any similarities and differences for each section in the length of the sections; the kind of information given; and the way the information is organised?

11.6 Some points from the researcher's analysis

The most obvious difference between the Flemish and US letters was in their overall length: the average Flemish letter was much shorter (104.9 words) than the average US letter (196.6 words). This difference is illustrated in the two letters here, where the Flemish letter is 78 words and the US letter is 253 words.

As far as 'correctness' is concerned, the most common errors for both US and Flemish letters were mechanical: punctuation, spelling and 'typos' – typing errors. This is illustrated in the letters here, where both the Flemish (line 2 'wich' instead of 'which') and the US (line 5 'in' instead of 'it') letters contain typos. However, the Flemish letters in the total data set showed many more errors than those written by the US students, especially at the word and sentence level. Connor *et al.* found that the Flemish applicants made on average 7.1 errors for every 100 words written, while the US sample made only 1.9.

Under 'clarity', Connor *et al.* found that apart from steps I and IV, the steps in the US letters were longer than in the Flemish. The biggest difference was found in category III, where writers give supporting arguments for their application. In III, the US writers gave lengthy discussions of their personal and professional qualifications for the job as well as the benefits to themselves and the employer, while the Flemish letters tended to give only a general statement of qualifications. This contrast can be seen in the letters here. The US applicants were also more likely to express appreciation to the reader than Flemish applicants. This is illustrated in the examples where step VI is absent in the Flemish letter but present in the US letter: 'Thank you for your review of this application.' Connor *et al.* thus conclude that the US candidates are better at writing the kind of self-promotion required and in 'using the letter as a sales instrument' (1995, 473).

11.7 More questions for you about the data

(v)　Look specifically at step IV in Figure 3. 'Indicate desire for interview'. Which of the letters is more direct and which more indirect in this step?

(vi)　Do you think that the differences between the two letters stem from cultural differences between the US and Flemish applicants, or do you think they are merely a result of L1 versus L2 differences – that is, Flemish speakers writing in their second language?

11.8 Further discussion and conclusions

A further contrast that Connor *et al.* identify between the Flemish and US letters under the category of 'clarity' is the 'degree of directness of expression' in asking for an interview. The Flemish letters were generally more direct in asking for an interview than the US letters, and several of the US letters avoided the word 'interview' altogether. The US letters tended to give information about how and when to make contact, rather than to request an interview directly. In the examples here, the US letter does use the word interview, but it is still more indirect in approaching this topic ('I will be available for interview') than is the Flemish letter ('I shall be pleased to be called for an interview').

A summary of the differences Connor *et al.* found between the US and the Flemish letters shows that, on average, the US applicants write more, and make fewer mistakes, than their Flemish counterparts. Specifically, US applicants are more informative about their qualifications and suitability for the position and are less direct in requesting an interview.

The question that Connor *et al.*'s findings raise is whether the differences identified are evidence of cultural differences, which contrastive rhetoric aims to explore, or whether they are simply a result of L1/L2 speaker contrast. Connor *et al.* argue that the differences in error and general length point to L1/L2 differences rather than cultural differences. However, specific differences under clarity – that is, content and amount of information given in specific steps – are similar to findings from other cross-cultural research on business letters. An example of such research is Jenkins and Hinds's (1987) study of US and French business letters, where the US letters were longer, more specifically directed at the reader and more individual in content, whereas the French letters were briefer and less personalised. Connor *et al.* also explain the differences in step III as evidence of cultural differences; the US letters engage more in self-promotion, whereas the Belgians generally do not provide supporting arguments and refer readers to their resumé. They discuss research which shows that Belgians (including Flemings) are not generally boastful about their own achievements and are more likely to rely on others to read between the lines of a job application to find out about them. They thus see the features of the Flemish letters as fitting in with this cultural style:

Belgians' typical reliance on others also entails a heavier reliance on past achievements (including university degrees, qualifications, and the like) rather than on current accomplishments. This preference may also explain why our Antwerp students put more emphasis on the resumé ... than on the letter. (p.473)

11.9 Your view

(vii) How useful do you find the key analytic categories that Connor *et al*. used, such as 'correctness', 'clarity' and 'degree of directness of expression'?

(viii) To what extent do you agree with Connor *et al*.'s comparative analysis of the Flemish and US texts?

(ix) Some of the earlier works in contrastive rhetoric have been criticised for treating 'culture' too simplistically. For example, the classic article by Kaplan (1966), in which he characterised different thought patterns for 'English', 'Semitic', 'Oriental', 'Romance' and 'Russian' students based on their writing in English, was criticised for two main reasons: first for privileging the writing of English native speakers in his article and, second, for overgeneralising about groups (for example, 'Orientals' included writing from a number of cultural and linguistic contexts, such as Chinese, Thai and Korean writers, which have their own differences). Do you think the analysis described here avoids the problems criticised in Kaplan's early work?

(x) How convincing do you find the claim that the differences between the letters are cultural, and not just L1/L2 differences?

(xi) What other kind of analyses could this approach be used for?

(xii) How useful might this approach be in your own context?

11.10 Examples of studies using a similar approach

For a further study in letter writing, see:

OKAMURA, A. and SHAW, P. (2000) 'Lexical phrases, culture and subculture in transactional letter writing', *English for Specific Purposes*, vol.19, no.1, pp.1-15.

For another study looking at student writing, see:

CRISMORE, A., MARKKANEN, R. and STEFFENSEN, M.S. (1993) 'Metadiscourse in persuasive writing: a study of texts written by American and Finnish university students', *Written Communication*, vol.10, no.1, pp.39-71.

For an example of a study of children's writing, see:

REPPEN, R. and GRABE, W. (1993) 'Spanish transfer effects in the English writing of elementary school children', *Lenguas Modernas*, vol.20, pp.113-28.

12: Bernsteinian discourse analysis: educational policy

12.1 Key features of this approach

Analysis of educational policy discourse is an important aspect of educational research. By 'educational policy discourse', we mean any text that states a position or a set of goals relating to an aspect of education, for example, prescriptions about the curriculum, staffing or pedagogy. Such texts can be either written or spoken, but, probably because of ease of access, researchers often focus on written texts. Through such analysis researchers aim to make visible fundamental ideas that are influencing educational policy and practice in a particular context. Analysis of policy documents typically involves content analysis – a focus on what is being said – and textual/linguistic analysis – a focus on how things are being said.

In approaches to discourse that seek to combine text analysis with social theory or philosophy, key concepts from a particular social theory are often used as a lens through which to analyse specific texts. This was exemplified in Example 9, in which concepts from the work of Bakhtin were used. Another writer whose theories have been influential for some time in education is the sociologist Basil Bernstein. His work has made a significant impact on debates about the relationship between language and education, and his more recent work is increasingly being drawn on to theorise both educational practice and policy (Bernstein, 1996).

12.2 Example

LEUNG, C. (2001) 'English as an additional language: distinct language focus or diffused curriculum concerns?', *Language and Education*, vol.15, no.1, pp.33-55.

Leung focuses on policy and research documents from the UK, Australia and the USA to compare policies on English as an additional language (EAL) in state education. In particular, Leung draws on Bernstein's concepts of 'competence' and 'performance' to explore and theorise educational policy on EAL in the UK.

12.3 The aim of the researcher

Leung aims to:

- 'offer an analytical account of the current conceptualisation of EAL as a curriculum policy and provision' (p.34).

12.4 Data extracts *(see data extracts 12.1-12.6)*

Learning is best achieved through enquiry-based activities involving discussion...

To learn a language it is necessary to participate in its meaningful use ... The curriculum itself is therefore a useful vehicle for language learning ... A main strategy ... for both curriuclum learning and language learning is the flexible use of small group work ... (Bourne, 1989: 63)

Data Extract 12.1 *Research-based principles (Source: Leung, 2001, p.35)*

Like all pupils, bilingual pupils should have access to a stimulating curriculum which, at the same time, helps their language development...

- Oral and written responses at different attainment levels can be encouraged by the use of a balance of open-ended and structural tasks.

- Matrices, true/false exercises ... can help to ensure that achievement is not entirely dependent on proficiency in English.

- Exercises with some repetitive element, such as science experiments ... provide a pattern which supports language development. (NCC, 1991: 1-2)

Data Extract 12.2 *Policy document (Source: Leung, 2001, p.35)*

Effective planning ... makes use of variation in teaching styles, including direct instruction and one-to-one tuition, which offer pupils learning EAL opportunities for concentrated listening as well as participation in group talk requiring interaction. (SCAA, 1996: 13)

Data Extract 12.3 *Policy document (Source: Leung, 2001, p.36)*

... a student will be able to

Use and respond to the linguistic structures and features of some social and school-based texts and extend their application to some unfamiliar texts.

---

this will be evident when, for example, the student:
In a controlled context
... uses and responds to compound or complex utterances ....
uses some cohesive devices to link ideas in utterances, e.g. personal pronouns (it, she, they), demonstrative pronouns (this, these, those) ... (Board of Studies, 1996: 95)

Data Extract 12.4 *Policy document (Source: Leung, 2001, p.36)*

The ESL Development Project's brief was to work towards:

- an increased capacity to measure proficiency development ...

- a better understanding of the interrelationship between mother tongue/English as a Second Language/English Language development issues ...

- assistance to teachers in maximising effectiveness of instruction for students of non-English speaking background ... (McKay, 1992, 1:1)

Data Extract 12.5 Policy document *(Source: Leung, 2001, p.37)*

Descriptors	Sample Progress Indicators
→ following oral and written directions, implicit and explicit → requesting and providing clarification ...	→ asks a teacher to restate or simplify directions → join in a group at the appropriate time ... (TESOL, 1997:45)

Data Extract 12.6 Policy document *(Source: Leung, 2001, p. 38)*

12.5   Questions for you about the data

(i)   Look at Data Extracts 12.1-12.3. What do the extracts say about learning? About language?

(ii)   In Data Extracts 12.1-12.3, what do you notice about the perspective on the teaching and assessment of English as an additional language?

(iii)   Now look at Data Extracts 12.4-12.6. What do the extracts say about learning? About language?

(iv)   In Data Extracts 12.4-12.6, what do you notice about the perspective on the teaching and assessment of English as an additional language?

12.6 Some points from the researcher's analysis

Data Extracts 12.1-12.3 are from research and policy documents on the teaching of EAL in UK schools. Data Extract 12.4 is from an Australian document outlining the learning outcomes expected for EAL students at particular stages. Data Extracts 12.5 and 12.6 are from North American ESL (English as a second language) policy documents stating what EAL students are expected to achieve and how they will be assessed. Leung contrasts the extracts from policy and research documents in the UK context with those from the Australian and North American contexts and argues that they reflect very different perspectives on how best to approach the teaching of EAL students in schools. The first perspective, evident in Data Extracts 12.1-12.3, is that successful EAL learning will take place in learning environments where students are encouraged to participate in meaningful and motivating activities. Students who are using English as an additional language are not treated differently from their peers and no specific language-focused tuition is presumed to be needed. In contrast, policy statements in Data Extracts 12.4-12.6 exemplify the view that there needs to be a focus on the specific language needs of EAL speakers. Leung identifies two distinct discourses on EAL provision in the policy and research documents: what he refers to as 'EAL as a diffused curriculum' in the UK documents and what he refers to as EAL as explicit language teaching in the US and Australian documents.

Leung points out that these differences clearly demonstrate the culturally specific nature of EAL provision. For example, there are specific cultural and historical reasons for the perspective evident in the UK research and policy documents: progressive pedagogy that emphasises student learning as a process of individual discovery; a theory of language learning that emphasises language acquisition as part of other activities, rather than explicit teaching; reaction against the marginalised educational provision in the 1960s and 1970s for immigrant students, which led to campaigns to provide mainstream rather than separate provision, so that the students learned alongside their English peers.

12.7 More questions for you about the data

(v) Look again at Data Extracts 12.1-12.3. What kinds of assumptions do you think are implicit in the statements about learners, learning contexts, access and opportunity?

(vi) Look again at Data Extracts 12.4-12.6. What kinds of assumptions do you think are implicit in the statements about learners, learning contexts, access and opportunity?

12.8 Further discussion and conclusions

Having made the contrast between two discourses on EAL – EAL as a 'diffused curriculum' and EAL as explicit language teaching – Leung focuses on two key concepts from Bernstein, which he uses to explore the educational assumptions underpinning the perspectives evident in the policy and research documents. The two concepts he uses are 'competence' and 'performance', which Bernstein sees as fundamental in Western European and North American educational thinking. Competence, explains Leung, is an abstract notion referring to practices, including learning, that are 'tacitly acquired'. 'Performance', in contrast, emphasises the output or outcomes, and the skills necessary to achieve these. From this perspective, the UK discourse on EAL can be said to be competence-oriented whereas the Australian and North American discourse on EAL emphasises performance. But what does the application of the notions of competence and performance add to our understanding about educational policy on EAL?

Leung draws on Bernstein's notion of 'social logic' to explore the implicit assumptions underlying competence and performance oriented models of EAL. By 'social logic' Bernstein is 'referring to a set of founding assumptions which shape and form the concept' (Leung, 2001, p.42). Briefly, key assumptions of the social logic underlying the competence model are as follows:

- all students can achieve competence in EAL

- students acquire language tacitly

- acquisition is not influenced by differential power relations, diversity, ethnicity or social class

In contrast, key assumptions of the social logic underpinning the performance model, argues Leung, are as follows:

- outcomes depend on a range of factors, including starting points, age, contexts, focus of teaching and previous educational experience

- the specific focus of instruction influences outcome

- distinctions between individuals and groups, such as educational experience, differential power relations, affect outcomes

Leung states that Bernstein's focus on the 'social logic' of competence and performance helps to 'make explicit the underlying assumptions of different conceptualisations' (p.44), thus making visible the assumptions underlying policies and practices of EAL teaching. Leung accepts that the discourse of EAL as a 'diffused' curriculum in the UK has enabled students to gain immediate access to mainstream classrooms, and acknowledges that this policy of open access has led to significant educational achievements for some minority ethnic students in the UK. But he also raises questions about this policy. A key concern is that the needs of EAL learners become almost invisible in the curriculum: just as there is no EAL curriculum, there are no specialist EAL teaching courses (and non-specialist teachers may mistakenly attribute language development issues to learning difficulties); given the lack of nationally agreed EAL assessment targets, EAL students are assessed following a curriculum aimed at first-language speakers of English and may be judged unfairly. Leung concludes that the competence/performance concepts help to raise questions about the effectiveness and desirability of current policy and practice.

12.9 Your view

(vii) To what extent do you agree with the differences Leung identifies between the discourses on EAL in the UK, Australia and the USA?

(viii) What, if any, do you consider to be limitations in his analysis?

(ix) How useful do you consider the application of Bernstein's notions of 'competence' and 'performance' to EAL policy discourse?

(x) How might you use this approach in your context?

12.10 Examples of studies using a similar approach

For further studies of language policy on English and bilingualism, see:

GRANVILLE, S., JANKS, H. and MPHAHLELE, M. *et al.* (1998) 'English with or without g(u)ilt: a position paper on language in education policy for South Africa', *Language and Education*, vol.12, no.4, pp.254-72.

NWENMELY, H. (1999)'Language policy planning in St Lucia: stagnation or change?', *Language and Education,* vol.13, no.4, pp.269-79.

STROUD, C. (2001) 'African mother-tongue programmes and the politics of language: linguistic citizenship versus linguistic human rights', *Journal of Multilingual and Multicultural Development,* vol.22, no.4, pp.339-55.

13: Critical discourse analysis: a magazine text

13.1 Key features of this approach

Researchers working within critical discourse analysis (CDA) are particularly interested in the ways in which discourse practices reproduce and/or transform power relations within society. To explore the relationship between the micro study of texts, focusing on the details of how texts work, and the macro politics of society, analytic frameworks developed by the linguist Norman Fairclough have been particularly influential. The three-dimensional approach to language taken by critical discourse analysts is outlined by Fairclough as follows:

> Any discursive 'event' (that is, any instance of discourse) is seen as being simultaneously a piece of text, an instance of discursive practice, and an instance of social practice. The 'text' dimension attends to language analysis of texts. The 'discursive practice' dimension [...] specifies the nature of the processes of text production and interpretation, for example which types of discourse [...] are drawn upon and how they are combined. The 'social practice' dimension attends to issues of concern in social analysis such as the institutional and organisational circumstances of the discursive event and how that shapes the nature of the discursive practice. (Fairclough, 1992, p.4)

A critical discourse approach therefore involves explicit attention to the linguistic analysis of specific texts as well as the theorisation of the social and cultural contexts in which texts are produced and interpreted. Key foundational social theorists within critical discourse analysis are Marx, Gramsci and, particularly in the case of Fairclough, Foucault. Key notions from the work of such social theorists are drawn on in order to explore the relationship between language and power relations within society (see Fairclough, 1992).

13.2 Example

CHOULIARAKI, L. and FAIRCLOUGH, N. (1999) *Discourse in Late Modernity. Rethinking Critical Discourse Analysis*, Edinburgh, Edinburgh University Press [Chapter 1 'Discourse in late modernity'].

Chouliaraki and Fairclough focus on one particular text from a weekly UK magazine. They draw on key existing ideas from work in critical discourse analysis as well as offering new analytic frames.

13.3 The aim of the researchers

One of Chouliaraki and Fairclough's stated aims in examining and discussing this text is to:

- use one text to illustrate the nature of discourse practices at the beginning of the twenty-first century.

13.4 Data extract *(see data extract 13.1)*

13.5 Questions for you about the data

(i)   Look at Data Extract 13.1. How would you label/describe this text?

(ii) What is the purpose of the text? (Advertising, information, pleasure?)

(iii) What kind of publication do you think this text is from?

(iv) What are the most salient features of the text?

(v)   What makes them salient?

(vi) How would you describe the language used in the text?

13.6 Some points from the researchers' analysis

The text is an advertisement from *The Big Issue in the North*. This is a weekly magazine sold in the streets by homeless people in the UK. The aim of the magazine is to 'enable homeless people to earn an income through self-help' (http://www.bigissue.co.uk/bigissue.html). Similar magazines are sold on the streets in many parts of the world and in many languages. Chouliaraki and Fairclough use this text to illustrate what they consider to be some significant characteristics of discourse practices at the beginning of the twenty-first century.

A key characteristic they emphasise is the mixture of discourses in the text.

Charity discourse

One discourse they identify is a 'charity discourse': an obvious feature of this discourse practice is the cut-off slip at the bottom of the text where the reader is asked to make a financial donation. Chouliaraki and Fairclough also point to the following explicit appeal as indicative of charity discourse: 'Please support our Christmas Appeal and help us help vendors leave the streets for good'. They identify several other discourses in the text – these are 'advertising discourse', 'academic social science discourse', 'everyday discourse' and 'political or socially engaged discourse'.

Advertising discourse

Advertising discourse is identified by Chouliaraki and Fairclough in the heading, which consists of two parallel phrases, designed to attract the reader's attention; the use of first- and second-person pronouns where the reader is addressed directly – 'we could try to guilt trip you'; the image of the young man, whose gaze is directed at the reader, thus contributing to the effect of the reader being addressed.

Data Extract 13.1 The Big Issue *Christmas appeal (Source: Chouliaraki and Fairclough, 1999, Figure 1.1, p.11)*

Academic social science discourse

The following wordings are identified by Chouliaraki and Fairclough as features of academic social science discourse: 'challenge stereotypes', 'sense of self-worth', 'culture of long-term homelessness'. They point to the use of nominalisations, which are common in academic discourse, such as 'homelessness' and 'self-worth'. 'Nominalisation', broadly defined, refers to the turning of processes into abstract nouns: so for example, 'homelessness' is a nominalisation of a clause such as 'I don't have a home', where both the agent (I) and the process (don't have) is present.

Everyday discourse

They point to the following as examples of everyday discourse: 'earning a living', 'find homes', 'jobs'.

Political discourse

By political discourse, they mean language that challenges a notion of individual blame and advocates change. Examples they give are as follows:

> 'The Big Issue exists to challenge stereotypes and to help homeless people reclaim their sense of self-worth and dignity by earning a living – all year round.'

> 'But we are committed to providing homeless people with the resources they need to break out from the damaging culture of long-term homelessness and find homes, jobs and better futures.'

13.7 More questions for you about the data

(vii) How useful do you find Chouliaraki and Fairclough's descriptive analysis – that is, the identification of different discourses in the text?

(viii) Are you surprised to find so many discourses in one text?

(ix) On the basis of this text, what conclusions do you think it is possible to reach about discourse practices at the turn of the twenty-first century?

13.8 Further discussion and conclusions

In identifying a number of discourses within this one text, Chouliaraki and Fairclough are interested not only in description but also in explanation, that is, they are interested in explaining why such mixing of discourses occurs and in exploring the social significance of this mixing. They use their analysis of this particular text to make several general points about discourse practices in 'late modern' society. First, they argue that the mixing of discourses in one text – 'hybridity' – is a dominant feature of current 'late modern' society. Such hybridity means that it is difficult to fix meanings in texts in any straightforward way or to argue that one particular meaning is being advanced in a text. So, in this example, it is not easy to argue that the text is doing one particular thing – making a charitable appeal – because it is also making a political statement. The hybridity exemplified in this text signals, Chouliaraki and Fairclough argue, significant tensions at the heart of society, not least tensions between consumerism and political action. Second, they point to what they refer to as 'the commodification' of language. By this they mean the ways in which language has itself become a commodity that is used to sell products. The aesthetic design of the text is all-important. This is the case, they argue, as much in politically engaged texts as in texts aimed at selling goods. Language is consciously chosen to maximise the aesthetic appeal. They give as an example in this text the heading 'Homeless this Christmas. But not for life'. This juxtaposition of short positive and negative statements serves as a way of attracting attention. Third, Chouliaraki and Fairclough point to what they refer to as the 'reflexivity' in discourse practices. This refers to explicit commentary on the use of language and the production of texts. An example they give from this text is the statement 'we could try to guilt trip you', which is an explicit reference to the production of the text itself. It is also an implicit reference to what other charity texts aim to do (and hence an intertextual reference), that is, to secure donations by making readers feel guilty about either their own material circumstances in relation to other social groups, or their daily lack of action in relation to individuals who are worse off than themselves (see Example 9 for intertextuality). Chouliaraki and Fairclough argue that such 'heightened reflexivity' (explicit attention to discourse practices) is a feature of commodification – useful for selling goods – as well as providing an opportunity for greater individual control over discourse practices.

13.9   Your view on this approach

(x)   How justified do you think Chouliaraki and Fairclough are in claiming that this text illustrates the discourse practices of 'late modern' society?

(xi)   How convincing do you find their arguments about the social significance of 'hybridity', 'commodification' and 'reflexivity'?

(xii)   What kinds of texts do you think you could use this approach for?

(xiii) What are the limitations of and/or tensions in this approach?

(xiv) How might you draw on this approach to research an aspect of your own context?

13.10   Examples of studies using this approach.

For examples of other CDA approaches to media analysis, see:

FAIRCLOUGH, N. (1995) *Media Discourse,* London, Edward Arnold.

FOWLER, R. (1991) *Language in the News,* London, Routledge.

For examples of uses of CDA more generally, see:

CALDAS-COULTHARD, C. and COULTHARD, M. (eds) (1996) *Texts and Practices. Readings in Critical Discourse Analysis,* London, Routledge.

For an example of some of the debates surrounding critical discourse analysis, see:

BILLIG, M. and SCHEGLOFF, E.A. (1999) 'Critical discourse analysis and conversation analysis: an exchange between Michael Billig and E.A. Schegloff', *Discourse and Society,* vol.10, no.4, pp.543-82.

PART 3
MULTIMODAL APPROACHES

Introduction

The term 'multimodal' may be unfamiliar to some readers. In this workbook we are using it to mean approaches that involve the analysis of more than one mode of communication, or a number of 'semiotic modes'. Thus, while the emphasis in Parts 1 and 2 has been on the verbal mode (spoken and written language), the examples in this part of the workbook focus on analysing verbal language alongside other semiotic modes, such as visual, material, movement and sound. Kress and van Leeuwen, two influential researchers in this area, emphasise the importance of adopting a multimodal approach to the analysis of communication:

> Language, whether in speech or writing, has always existed as just one mode in the totality of modes involved in the production of any text, spoken or written. A spoken text is not just verbal but also visual, combining with 'non-verbal' modes of communication such as facial expression, gesture, posture and other forms of self-presentation. A written text similarly involves more than language: it is written *on* something, on some *material* ... and it is written *with* something; with letters formed in systems influenced by aesthetic, psychological, pragmatic and other considerations; and with a layout imposed on the material substance, whether on the page, the computer screen or a polished brass plaque. (Kress and van Leeuwen, 1996, p.39).

Kress and van Leeuwen argue that the multimodality of texts has largely been ignored by those working within the different fields of language study (i.e. applied linguistics, sociolinguistics), but that, because of developments in information technology, multimodality is increasingly visible and hence subject to analysis (see Kress and van Leeuwen, 1996, 2001).

In this part of the workbook we focus on examples that are explicitly referred to by researchers as 'multimodal'. This is the case in Example 15, in which Kress *et al.* compare the visual and verbal elements of science textbooks from the 1930s and the 1990s, and in Example 16, in which Ormerod and Ivanič examine the material aspects of topic-based projects of primary school children. Other examples in this part have not been explicitly labelled as multimodal by the original researchers but are included here because their analyses focus on more than one semiotic mode. Thus in Example 14 we discuss Swann's analysis of the function of the teacher's gaze alongside verbal language in her research on gender in classroom talk. In Example 17 we outline Iedema's analysis of an Australian documentary film, which involves an analysis of the relationship between different semiotic modes used in film: words, image, sound and movement. In Example 18 we illustrate the emerging trend in research of exploration of computer-mediated communication (CMC) by taking you through Sugimoto and Levin's cross-cultural analysis of the use of symbolic images ('emoticons') in email.

Unsurprisingly, there are a number of difficulties associated with presenting multimodal analyses in the form of a written text, whether in books and journal articles written by the original researchers or in this workbook. At a theoretical level it is important to recognise that multimodal analysis is still in its infancy. At a practical level there are several significant constraints. Most obviously there is the difficulty of discussing multimodal research when we have only one mode (the written) in which to present the data. This is particularly difficult when we wish to represent non-verbal aspects of spoken interaction, such as gesture and facial expression, or moving visual images. Apart from these practical constraints, you will often find that published analyses of multimodal texts, such as webpages and films, do not include examples of data because of copyright laws. In the examples in this section we show how researchers have their own different ways of dealing with these problems.

14: Non-verbal behaviour and interaction: teacher gaze and student participation

14.1 Key features of this approach

The study of patterns of participation in classrooms has been the focus of much educational research. Of particular interest has been the differential participation of boys and girls in classroom discussion. Two main approaches have been used to investigate this. First, there has been a feminist educational research approach, which has involved quantifying patterns of participation, exploring questions such as: Who gets to speak? When? Who does the teacher address? How often? (see, for example, Clarricoates, 1983; Spender, 1982). Second, significant contributions have been made from an interactional sociolinguistic approach, which, as discussed in Example 2 in Part 1, involves a focus on how participants negotiate spoken interaction. Studies focusing on gender and interaction have consistently pointed to differences between males' and females' interaction, yet at the same time have shown that any differences are not absolute in nature but vary according to context (see, for example, Cameron, 1992; Coates and Cameron, 1988; Johnson and Meinhof, 1997). Identifying differential patterns of participation between girls and boys in classrooms, and analysing exactly how these are brought about, is considered to be particularly important in educational contexts because of the different opportunities for learning that such patterns may afford.

14.2 Example

SWANN, J. (1998) 'Talk control: an illustration from the classroom of problems in analysing male dominance of conversation', in J. Coates and D. Cameron (eds) *Women in Their Speech Communities. New Perspectives on Language and Sex*, London, Longman, pp.122-40.

In this example, Swann draws on the analytical tradition of interactional sociolinguistics (IS – see Example 2) to analyse the participation of boys and girls in classrooms. In IS, careful attention is paid to the specific ways in which interaction is negotiated between participants. Swann's approach differs, however, from traditional IS studies on gender (which frequently make use of audio recording of data) in that she emphasises the role that non-verbal features and contextual factors play in enabling boys to dominate classroom conversation. Such features include: participants' gaze during the conversation (who is looking at whom); the hand-raising behaviour of pupils; seating arrangements; and other forms of body language. In this example, Swann focuses particularly on the teacher's gaze. Quantitative analysis (for example, counting the number of conversational turns of different speakers and the number of words in each turn) is combined with qualitative analysis (for example, analysing how and why a particular speaking turn may occur) in this approach.

14.3 The aims of the researcher

Swann aims to analyse:

- 'the mechanisms [including non-verbal] of turn allocation and turn exchange that support male dominance of classroom talk'

- 'the roles played by ... girls, boys and the class teacher in the achievement of such interactional dominance' (Swann, 1998, p.130).

14.4 Data extracts *(see data extracts 14.1-14.2)*

In Data Extract 14.1, Swann has quantified two videoed sequences of classroom talk after transcribing the talk.

Contribution to classroom talk from girl and boy pupils in 'pendulum' and 'mining' sequences			
Pupils		Amount spoken	
	Total words spoken	Total spoken turns	Average words per turn
'Pendulum' sequence			
Sarah	79	17	4.6
Laura	20	5	4.0
Donna	37	5	7.4
Unidentified girls	18	9	2.0
Total girls	**154**	**36**	**4.3**
Matthew	133	23	5.8
Trevor	83	20	4.1
Peter	55	10	5.5
Unidentified boys	48	20	2.5
Total boys	**319**	**73**	**4.4**
'Mining' sequence			
Kate	127	9	14.1
Lorraine	13	7	1.8
Anne	23	8	2.9
Emma	8	4	2.0
Unidentified girls	–	–	–
Total girls	**171**	**28**	**6.1**
Mark	47	9	5.2
Ian	80	23	3.5
John	35	5	7.0
Darren	101	15	6.7
Unidentified boys	3	2	1.5
Total boys	**266**	**54**	**4.9**

Data Extract 14.1 Contribution to classroom talk from girl and boy pupils in 'pendulum' and 'mining' sequences (Source: Swann, 1998, Table 9.1, p.132)

14.5 Questions for you about the data

Read through Data Extract 14.1 and compare the contributions to classroom talk made by the different pupils in the 'Pendulum' and 'Mining' sequences.

(i) Who contributes the higher number of speaking turns in each sequence, girls or boys?

(ii) Who contributes the higher number of words uttered in each speaking turn and overall, boys or girls?

(iii) Look for intragroup differences (that is, among the girls and among the boys). Number the three most talkative pupils for each sequence.

14.6 Some points from the researcher's analysis

Swann points out that, at the most general level, the table in Data Extract 14.1 shows that, on average, boys contributed more in the two talk sequences, in terms of both the number of turns taken and the number of words uttered. This finding was in line with other research on classroom talk carried out with larger samples of pupils. The quantitative analysis also highlights important intergroup differences: there were girls who were more talkative (for example, Sarah in the 'Pendulum' sequence and especially Kate in the 'Mining' sequence) as well as quieter boys (for example, John and Mark in the 'Mining' sequence).

14.7 More questions for you about the data

Read through Data Extract 14.2 of classroom talk from the 'Pendulum' sequence where Swann also coded the teacher's gaze, that is, when the teacher is looking at the boys and when she is looking at the girls. Swann notes that the seating arrangements made it easier for the teacher to face the boys than the girls. As you read the extract, look at the transcription key in Figure 4 (p.105).

(iv) Who does the teacher direct her gaze at more overall, the boys or the girls?

(v) Identify all the teacher's questions in the extract (they are marked from 1-12). Identify where the teacher's gaze is directed for each question. At whom is her gaze more often directed when asking questions?

(vi) How often do the boys chip in? And the girls?

14.8 Further discussion and conclusions

Swann points out that the transcript shows the teacher's gaze is directed far more often towards the boys and that the teacher is also most frequently looking at the boys 'at critical points', in this case when she is asking questions (p.136). Eight questions are directed to the boys and four to the girls. Swann explains that two of the questions directed at the girls (4 and 6) took place after a last-minute switch of gaze from the boys and one (8) functioned more as an aside. From the spoken interaction it seems that the boys are contributing more by simply chipping in but Swann's analysis of the teacher's gaze shows she is directing more of her attention (and her questions) to the boys. Their

Questions are numbered in sequence.
.... = teacher's gaze towards the girls
----------- = teacher's gaze towards the boys
(Where gaze is not marked this is because the teacher is looking elsewhere – for instance, at the overhead projector.)

Teacher: If you have a pendulum (.) which we established last

week was a weight a mass (.) suspended from a string

or whatever (.) and watch I'm holding it with my hand

so it's at rest at the moment (.) what is it that makes

the pendulum swing in a downward direction for

instance till it gets to there? [1][(.) just watch it

Matthew: [gravity

Teacher: What is it Matthew? [2]

Matthew: Gravity

Teacher: [Yes (.)]now we mentioned gravity when we were
Boy: [((xxx))]

Teacher: actually doing the experiments but we didn't discuss it

too much (.) OK so it's gravity then that pulls it

down (.) what causes it to go up again at the other

side? [3]

Data Extract 14.2 *Teacher-pupil talk (Source: Swann, 1998, pp.133-5, 140)*

Boy: ⌈Force   the force⌉

Boy: ⌊The string   Miss⌋it gets up speed going down.

Teacher: It gets up speed going⌈down (.) does⌉anyone know the

Boy: ⌊(force)(xxx)⌋

Teacher: word for it when you get up speed? [4] (.) as in a car

when you press the pedal? [5]

Boy: ⌈accelerate⌉

Boy: ⌊momentum⌋

Teacher: You get momentum (.)⌈Matthew (.)⌉it accelerates

Matthew: ⌊(xxx)⌋

Teacher: going down doesn't it and it's the (.) energy the force

that it builds up that takes it up the other side (.)

watch (.) and see if it's the same (.) right (.) OK (.)

em (.) anything else you notice about that? [6] (.) so

it's gravity what about the moon? [7] (.) that's a bit

tricky isn't it? [8] (.) is ⌈there grav⌉ity on the

Boys: ⌊(xxx)⌋

Teacher: moon? = [9]

Boys: = No no it would float

Data Extract 14.2 *Teacher-pupil talk continued (Source: Swann, 1998, pp. 133-5, 140)*

Teacher: There isn't gravity on the moon? [10] (.)

Several: No

Matthew: There is a certain amount

Teacher: A certain amount Matthew? = [11]

Matthew: = ⌈ (xxx) ⌉

Boy: ⌊ Seven ⌋ times less

Teacher: You reckon it's seven?[12]

Boy: Times less than on earth

-----------------------···························· --------------------

Teacher: Yes (.) well it's a it's a difficult figure to arrive at but

----

it is between six and seven

Data Extract 14.2 *Teacher-pupil talk continued (Source: Swann, 1998, pp.133-5, 140)*

verbal behaviour can be seen as responding to her direct questions. Swann points out that there is also more general muttering from the boys than from the girls, which suggests that they may be attracting more of the teacher's attention through this. Swann thus argues that the interaction of the boys' behaviour and the teacher's behaviour guaranteed the boys more speaking turns.

While acknowledging the boys' overall dominance, Swann shows that there are significant intragroup differences in the data (with more-talkative girls and quieter boys): 'differences between boys and girls are not categorical' (p.138). Different mechanisms also contribute to the boys chipping in more (for example, the teacher's gaze and the informal atmosphere of the conversation, which encouraged chipping in). Swann thus concludes that

> There is an interaction between the behaviour of all participants: for instance, the greater attention paid by teachers towards boys may encourage boys' fuller participation, which in turn encourages greater attention from the teacher, and so on. (p.139)

Extended square brackets mark overlap between utterances e.g.:

A: he's going to the   funeral
B: oh my god

An equals sign at the end of one speaker's utterance and at the start of the next utterance indicates the absence of a discernible gap, e.g.:

A: after all she's dead   =

B: = mm

Pauses are indicated by (.) (short) or (–) (longer).

Double round parentheses indicate that there is doubt about the accuracy of the transcription:

A: she lived in Brisbane, ((they were at Brisbane))

Where material is inaudible or impossible to make out, it is represented as follows:

A: but sorry ((xxx))

Single round parentheses give clarificatory information, e.g.:

A: he's dead, isn't he (laughs).

Material in square brackets is phonetic, e.g.:

A: the [θɪ] the theory goes

Underlining indicates that words are uttered with added emphasis, e.g.:

A: then they'd <u>know</u> that you hadn't come.

A small cross indicates the end of a tone-group, e.g.:

A: I'll never get out +

The symbol (pp) precedes words where the speaker speaks very quietly, e.g.:

A: (pp) I don't know

.... = teacher's gaze towards the girls

------- = teacher's gaze towards the boys

        (Where gaze is not marked this is because the teacher is looking elsewhere – for instance, at the overhead projector.)

Figure 4: *Transcription notation (Source: Swann, 1998, pp.175-6)*

Swann does raise the question, though, that if inequalities between girls' and boys' talk are seen as natural by those involved, a change in behaviour by girls 'to adopt conversational tactics more commonly associated with boys' (p.140) may not be well tolerated.

14.9 Your view

(vii) What methodological problems can you foresee in attempting to analyse all forms of non-verbal behaviour in classroom talk?

(viii) What are the strengths of this approach? And its weaknesses?

(ix) What do you think of Swann's argument that, rather than the boys 'dominating' classroom talk, the behaviour of all participants interacting together (including the teacher and the girls) ensures that boys talk more?

(x) Can you think of an example of research that could be carried out using this approach in your own context?

14.10 Examples of studies using a similar approach

For examples of studies focusing on gender differences in conversation, see:

TANNEN, D. (1998) 'The relativity of linguistic strategies: rethinking power and solidarity in gender and dominance', in D. Cameron (ed.) *The Feminist Critique of Language: A Reader* (2nd edn), London, Routledge.

WOODS, N. (1988) 'Talking shop: sex and status as determinants of floor apportionment in a work setting', in J. Coates and D. Cameron (eds) *Women in Their Speech Communities*, London, Longman.

For further study of the importance of physical movement in classrooms, see:

KRESS, G., JEWITT, C., OGBORN, J. and TSATSARELIS, C. (2000) *Multimodal Teaching and Learning: Rhetorics of the Science Classroom*, Continuum, London.

15: Verbal and visual analysis: textbooks in the science classroom

15.1 Key features of this approach

A key claim made by Kress and others is that there has been a change over time in the way communication functions, notably, that verbal language is no longer the central mode of communication, the visual mode having become equally important. They argue that many texts, such as newspapers, magazines and websites, as well as educational texts, for example, science and geography textbooks, have changed to reflect the deep shifts in the social world and the world of communication. The dominance of mono-modality in Western culture, they argue, is in decline:

> Not only the mass media, the pages of magazines and comic strips for example, but also the documents produced by corporations, universities, government departments etc., have acquired colour illustrations and sophisticated layout and typography. And not only the cinema and the semiotically exuberant performances and videos of popular music, but also the avant-gardes of 'high culture' arts have begun to use an increasing variety of materials to cross the boundaries between the various art, design and performance disciplines ... (Kress and van Leeuwen, 2001, p.1)

Kress and van Leeuwen state that language is always 'only one of a number of semiotic (communication/representational) modes in use in any act of communication'. Other modes include gesture, use of objects and images, and tone and pitch of voice. They point out that not only are these other, often more visual, modes important in their own right but they also have an effect on the meanings made available through language.

15.2 Example

KRESS, G., OGBORN, J and MARTINS, I (1998) 'A satellite view of language: some lessons from science classrooms', *Language Awareness*, vol.7, no.2/3, pp.69-89.

In this specific example, Kress *et al.* are particularly interested in the semiotic modes of educational texts. They attempt to counter the assertion, which seems implicit in much educational research, that all the important things that go on in the classroom are expressed through verbal language. The focus of analysis in the example discussed here is on the visual and verbal features of science textbooks.

15.3 The aim of the researchers

Kress *et al.* aim to:

- explore the shifts in verbal – i.e. written – and visual modes in textbooks over time. They are particularly interested in analysing evidence for the shift from the dominance of the verbal mode to an increasing specialisation of visual and verbal modes, and in examining the different functions that these modes are performing.

15.4 Data extracts *(see data extracts 15.1-15.2)*

The focus of analysis here is on extracts from two science textbooks aimed at 14-year-olds. Data Extract 15.1 is old (published in 1938) and Data Extract 15.2 is newer (published in 1988).

15.5 Questions for you about the data

(i) Read through both texts: what similarities and differences can you note?

(ii) How is the visual image used in Data Extract 15.1? What is the relationship between the visual image and the written language in the text?

(iii) How are visual images used in Data Extract 15.2? What is the relationship between the images and the written language in the text?

(iv) Can you see any differences/similarities in the relationship between written text and image in Data Extracts 15.1 and 15.2?

15.6 Some points from the researchers' analysis

Kress *et al.* point out that in Data Extract 15.1, the image illustrates the text and partially repeats information provided by the written text. In contrast to this, in Data Extract 15.2, the images are not repeating aspects of the written text but are, in fact, conveying new information which is the core of the curriculum content. For example, the explanation of the circuit is not in the written text at all but is represented by the image. The visual mode has thus developed a more specialised function, representing meanings that are not available in the written text.

Kress *et al.* argue that the different communicative function of the visual images in Data Extracts 15.1 and 15.2 illustrates significant changes in school textbooks over time. They argue, furthermore, that the changes evident in the specific context of these school science textbooks indicate historical changes in the social and communicational world more generally.

15.7 More questions for you about the data

(v) Look at the language used in Data Extracts 15.1 and 15.2; how do you think the language use differs?

(vi) Specifically, compare the first paragraph at the top of Data Extract 15.2 ('In your first ... diodes') with the sentence in the last paragraph of Data Extract 15.1 beginning 'When a current is passed ...' What do you notice?

MAGNETISM AND ELECTRICITY

the magnetic poles. Fig. 62(c) shows the combined field of (a) and (b) when the wire is placed between the poles.

Note that, in Fig. 62(a) and (b), the lines of force on the left of the wire are in the same direction as those of the external field, while those on the right of the wire are in the opposite direction. Consequently in the combined field of Fig. 62(c) the field to the left of the wire is strong—there are a large number of lines, while the field to the right is weak.

If we assume, with Faraday, that the lines of force are in tension and trying to shorten (see p. 18), we should expect the wire to be urged to the right. This is precisely what we find by experiment.

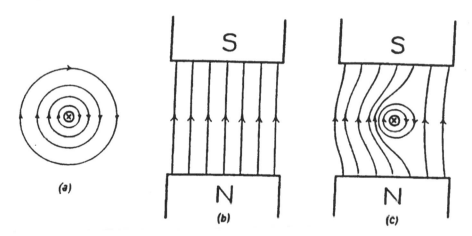

Fig. 62. (a) Magnetic field due to current in straight wire. (b) Field due to magnetic poles. (c) Combined field of (a) and (b).

The principle of the electric motor.

The simple electric motor consists of a coil pivoted between the poles of a permanent magnet (see Fig. 63). When a current is passed through the coil in the direction indicated in the figure we can show, by applying Fleming's left-hand rule, that the left-hand side of the coil will tend to move down and the right-hand side to move up. (Remember that the direction of the field due to the permanent magnet is from the N. to the S. pole.) Thus the coil will rotate in a counter-clockwise direction to a vertical position.

Data Extract 15.1 *Example from a science textbook of the 1930s (Source Kress et al., Figure 1, 1998, p.75)*

12·9 *Electronics*

Circuits

In your first circuits you used torch bulbs joined with wires. Modern electrical equipment uses the same basic ideas. But if you look inside a computer there are not many wires or torch bulbs. The wires and bulbs have been replaced by electronic devices like transistors, chips and light-emitting diodes.

Transistors and chips are examples of *semi-conductors*. They are made from special crystals like silicon. Transistors work because they only conduct electricity in the right conditions. They are useful because they can turn on and off very fast, and they need very little electricity.

An electronic light

● You can make electronic circuits with wires like the circuits you made before. The difficulty is that the contacts are poor, and sometimes things do not work. It is far better to *solder* the components.

Here is a simple circuit to operate a light-emitting diode (LED).

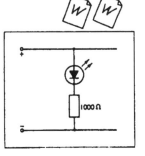

This design shows the same circuit soldered on matrix board. The board is cheap and can be re-used.

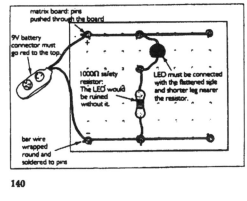

140

Transistors

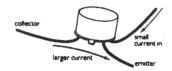

A transistor is a special semi-conductor. It has three connections: a base, a collector and an emitter. When a small current is put on the base, it lets a much larger current flow between the collector and the emitter. So a tiny current can control a much larger one.

● Try this water-detector circuit.

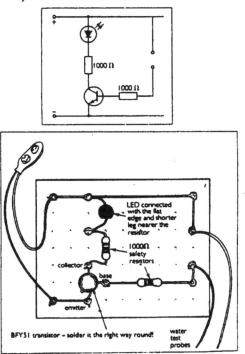

When the probes touch something wet, a very small current goes from the battery through the water to the base of the transistor. This current is big enough to make the transistor work, so the LED lights up.

Data Extract 15.2 Example from a science textbook of the 1980s (Source Kress et al., 1998, Figure 2, p.76)

15.8 Further discussion and conclusions

Kress *et al.* point out that in the extract from the science textbook of 1938, the sentences used contain a higher number of clauses. They argue that the syntax in this text (the sentence structure) is complex, conveying a complex conceptual structure. In Data Extract 15.1, language is used to convey both actions in the world as well as the structure of objects. The language is generally formal, which, as they point out, is typical of scientific writing.

Kress *et al.* contrast this with the language of the newer textbook, Data Extract 15.2. Here the sentence structure is much simpler, with many sentences containing just one or two clauses. This, they argue, is related to the fact that the conceptual information conveyed is simpler. They explain that this is mainly because, in the second extract, language is used to convey processes, events and actions (for example, 'You did this ... now do that ... if you do that'), and the information about the structure of objects is now provided in the visual image. They note that, in general, the language used is less formal and more speech-like in Data Extract 15.2 than in Data Extract 15.1.

Kress *et al.* argue that this analysis provides evidence of the increasing specialisation of visual and verbal modes in textbooks over time, and that this specialisation is a response to changes in the larger social world. Their argument implies that changes in the social world result in changes in the representational world. One relevant example of such change they give is that the audience of science textbooks in the 1990s has changed dramatically from that of the 1960s: science is now taught to the general population in Britain, not just to a small elite.

15.9 Your view

(vii) To what extent are you convinced by Kress *et al.*'s analysis of the different functions of the images and written texts in the two textbook examples?

(viii) Are you convinced by Kress *et al.*'s argument that the changes identified in the 1980s science textbook are typical of science textbooks in general? And of other textbooks?

(ix) What do you think is the relevance of this approach, if any, to education?

(x) Does a multimodal approach to textbook analysis invalidate analyses based on verbal language only?

(xi) Have you noticed a shift in communication to more visual modes of communication?

(xii) How might you explore the nature and extent of these changes in your own context?

15.10 Further studies

For further examples of studies focusing on the science curriculum and classrooms, see:

KRESS, G., JEWITT, C., OGBORN, J. and TSATSARELIS, C. (2000) *Multimodal Teaching and Learning: Rhetorics of the Science Classroom*, Continuum, London.

LEMKE, J. (2000) 'Multimedia demands of the scientific curriculum', *Linguistics and Education*, vol.10, no.3, pp.247-71.

For an example of a multimodal analysis in a TESOL (teaching of English to speakers of other languages) classroom, see:

ROYCE, T. (2002) 'Multimodality in the TESOL classroom: exploring visual-verbal synergy', *TESOL Quarterly*, vol.36, no.2, pp.191-205.

16: Texts as material objects: children's project writing

16.1 Key features of this approach

A key focus within multimodal research is the analysis of verbal and visual features of texts and the relationship between such features. All kinds of texts have been analysed, including school textbooks, magazines, storybooks, posters and computer websites. Many such analyses focus on texts as one-dimensional objects. That is, whether the focus is on verbal or visual representations, and even where dimensionality is analysed as a feature of the text, the texts themselves are overwhelmingly viewed as being one-dimensional. More recently, an interest has developed in texts as three-dimensional objects and in developing ways of analysing texts from this more concrete and material perspective. The 'materiality' of texts refers to the materials used in text construction. In written texts, for example, it could refer to the kind of paper, pens and pencils, as well as colour and shape. In spoken language it could include the sound of the voice. A basic premise of this approach is that the materiality of texts carries meaning in itself and contributes, along with other semiotic resources – words, visuals – to the meanings of the texts as a whole (see Kress and van Leeuwen, 2001). Key frameworks from Hallidayan linguistics that have traditionally been used to explore verbal texts are increasingly being used to explore visual and also material aspects of texts. In particular, Halliday's notions of the three 'metafunctions' of language are being used, that is, the three organising functional principles behind all language use. These are the 'ideational' – the expression of what is happening – the 'interpersonal' – how interpersonal relationships are expressed – and the 'textual' – how texts are constructed to form coherent meaning (see Halliday 1994).

16.2 Example

ORMEROD, F. and IVANIČ, R. (2002) 'Materiality in children's meaning-making practices', *Visual Communication*, vol.1, no.1, pp.65-91.

The specific focus of this research is the project work of children aged between 8 and 11. 'Project work' is a term used to refer to an activity that is common in UK primary schools. Briefly, children are told to choose a particular topic they would like to know more about, to study this topic and then to produce a written project as an outcome. Apart from the children's writing, this written report will usually also include visuals, such as drawings, pasted-in pictures from magazines, and so on.

In their research, Ormerod and Ivanič, set out to explore the materiality of 37 children's projects. In this paper they focus in particular on the projects as 'textual objects'. By this they mean that their aim is to explore how a text

> through its linguistic, visual and physical characteristics, carries meaning about a topic and reflects the author's meaning-making processes (Ormerod and Ivanič, 2002, p.69)

The data consists of the children's actual projects as well as interviews with the children about their projects. In this way, the researchers aim to get close to the authors' intended meanings in the texts and the reasons for using particular semiotic resources.

Note: A substantial database from this project is available on the following website: http://www.ling.lancs.ac.uk/lever/projects/53

16.3 The aims of the researchers
The aims of Ormerod and Ivanič are to:

- explore what it means to conceptualise and study a text as a textual object – that is, to focus on the material nature of the text rather than on particular semiotic modes of a text, such as the writing or the visuals

- gain an insight into the kinds of choices that children feel are open to them for making meaning in texts, rather than the kind of choices that teachers consider acceptable

- build a corpus of data that enables researchers to study literacy practices over a long period of time and to explore the kinds of changes that occur

16.4 Data extracts *(see data extracts 16.1-16.5)*
Because we can only represent the texts in a one-dimensional way, we have included some of Ormerod and Ivanič's descriptions of the three-dimensional features in the captions to the data extracts.

16.5 Questions for you about the data
(i) Look at Data Extract 16.1. What do you think the topic of Robbie's project is? How can you tell? Why do you think he includes actual wax in his project?

(ii) Look at the details of Data Extract 16.2. What do you think Denise's project topic is? How can you tell? Why do you think she attaches egg shells and feathers to pages of her project?

(iii) Look at the details of Data Extracts 16.3 and 16.4. What do you think Ray's project is about? How can you tell? How do the physical characteristics of the visual – the black bats against the yellow moon – contribute to what Ray is saying in his project?

Data Extract 16.1 Robbie's wax (Source: Ormerod and Ivanič, 2002, Figure 1, p.70) ('on one of the pages ... Robbie carefully smeared some of the blackcurrant-scented rollerblade wax which he uses to lubricate the edge of the pavement, so as to facilitate particular movements when out rollerblading with his friends', p.69)

Data Extract 16.2 Denise's feathers (Source: Ormerod and Ivanič, 2002, http://www.ling.lancs.ac.uk/lever/projects/53) ('Denise attached feathers and broken eggshells to pages', p.69)

Data Extract 16.3 *Ray's front cover of 'Bats' (Source: Ormerod and Ivanič, 2002, Figure 2, p.72) ('[Ray used] black felt-tip pen and pencil to create a glossy surface that shimmers against the image of the yellow moon in the starry night sky', p.73)*

Data Extract 16.4 *Ray's echolocation chart (Source: Ormerod and Ivanič, 2002, Figure 3, p.73)*

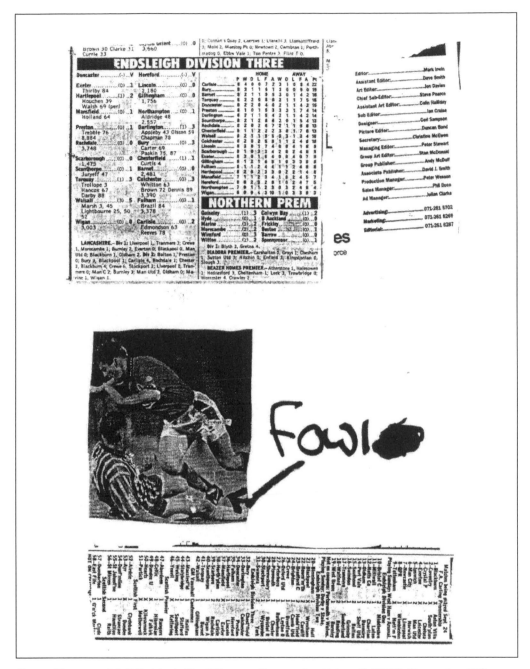

Data Extract 16.5 *Robbie's 'fowl' (Source: Ormerod and Ivanič, 2002, Figure 6, p.77)*

1.	CARRYING MEANING ABOUT THE TOPIC
1.1	Representation through 'real-life' examples
1.2	Representation through three-dimensional construction
1.3	Representation through two-dimensional construction
2	CARRYING MEANING ABOUT ATTITUDE TOWARDS THE TOPIC
2.1	Expression of attitude through the physical construction of pictures
2.2	Expression of attitude through the physical construction of words
3	CARRYING MEANING ABOUT THE TEXT
3.1	Physical distinction between verbal and other elements
3.2	Physical distinction between types of visual image
3.3	Physical distinction between areas: space and framing
3.4	Physical indications of emphasis
4	PROVIDING TRACES OF DESCISION-MAKING PROCESSES IN THE CONSTRUCTION OF A MEANINGFUL MESSAGE
4.1	Physical evidence of changes to wording
4.2	Physical evidence of changes to spelling
4.3	Physical evidence of changes to visual images
4.4	Physical evidence of changes to layout
5	POINTING TO CONNECTIONS BETWEEN THIS MESSAGE AND OTHERS IN THE WIDER SEMIOTIC ENVIRONMENT
5.1	Physical features of imported textual artefacts
5.2	Physical evidence of importation
5.3	Physical indications of new 'ownership'

Figure 5: *Types of meaning carried by physical characteristics of text (Source: Ormerod and Ivanič, 2002, Table 1, p.68)*

16.6   Some points from the researchers' analysis

One of Ormerod and Ivanič's reasons for focusing specifically on the project work of primary-school age children is that project work spans the divide between home and school, because children are allowed to focus on their own interests and develop their project both at home and at school. Choices that children make about the texts they produce are therefore shaped both by home and school practices.

In choosing particular semiotic resources, Ormerod and Ivanič argue that

> the children are choosing to share with the reader some aspect of the subject matter which may not easily lend itself to representation in visual or verbal form ... (p.70)

For example, through the smooth greasiness and sickly smell of the rollerblade wax, Robbie wants to share with the reader not only a verbal description of rollerblading in his project on 'aggressive blading' but also something of the physical experience of rollerblading. Denise, in her project on birds, wants to convey something of the material nature of birds rather than just giving verbal descriptions. Ormerod and Ivanič state that the essential meaning they want to convey lies in the object's material entirety; its whole physical 'reality'. (p.69)

The materiality of the text thus contributes to the ideational meanings of the text – that is, what the children are saying about a particular topic.

A significant finding from the project is that younger children use a greater range of material objects than older children do in constructing texts. There is a notable shift from meaning-making in three dimensions to two dimensions by the age of 10. Ray's drawing of bats for his project on bats in Data Extract 16.3 exemplifies a two-dimensional representation. It also seems to be an example of a case where a child has successfully exploited material resources in order to create a three-dimensional perspective: Ray uses thick and thin felt-tip pens, black for the bats and yellow for the moon 'to create a glossy surface that shimmers against the image of the yellow moon in the starry night sky' (p.73). Ray thus successfully uses the technological resources available to him, a range of pens and colours, to represent something of the materiality of bats in the sky.

16.7 More questions for you about the data

Look at Ormerod and Ivanič's framework for studying how physical characteristics of texts contribute to meaning-making, *Types of meaning carried by physical characteristics of text*, Figure 5. As well as contributing to what the children are saying about a topic, the physical characteristics contribute to the children's feelings about or attitudes to their topic and how they are conceptualising the purpose and nature of their texts. The first three categories in the table correspond broadly to Halliday's three main categories for conceptualising meaning-making – meaning about the topic (ideational), meaning about attitude towards the topic (interpersonal) and meaning about the text (textual) (see Halliday, 1994).

(iv) Look at Data Extracts 16.3 and 16.4. What does the physical construction of the texts tell you about Ray's attitude towards his topic? What do the choices he makes about the particular pens, pencils and colours he uses tell you about his understanding of how texts work?

(v) Look at Data Extract 16.5. What does the caption 'Fowl' tell you about Robbie's attitude towards his topic of football? What do the choices he makes about the juxtaposition of a visual against a heavy caption tell you about his understanding about how texts work?

(vi) Look at Data Extracts 16.1-16.5 again. What, if anything, can you learn about the processes of the texts' production by looking at the texts?

16.8 Further discussion and conclusions

Ormerod and Ivanič argue that the physical characteristics of texts tell us about the attitude of the children towards their topics. Thus in Ray's careful drawing of a bat with outstretched wings in Data Extract 16.3, the broken, hesitantly controlled lines seem to express his fascination with the intricate construction of the bats' wings, and the mechanics of their action (p.76)

In contrast, they suggest, the heavy black fibre-tipped caption 'Fowl' that Robbie sets against the photograph communicates both his confidence about the rules of the game and disapproval of the action. Ormerod and Ivanič state

> It is as if the child is saying, 'This is the worst thing that a footballer can do; it is a really serious offence.' (p.77)

Just as the physical characteristics communicate attitudes towards a topic, they also show children's understandings about how texts work. Compare, for example, Ray's thick use of felt-tip pen for the cover page of his project with the precise use of pencil for his detailed drawings. He knows that different kinds of resources can communicate different things about a topic. The different material resources used help to demand a different response from the reader towards the text. Thus, Ormerod and Ivanič state

> The detailed delicate little drawings quietly encourage us to look closely and care-fully at each one in turn, whereas the dramatic, shadow-like images of bats on the front cover create a strong and immediate impact without requiring or rewarding further effort. (p.79)

Ormerod and Ivanič argue that the texts also tell us something about the processes surrounding text production and how the texts connect with the wider 'semiotic environment'. An example of the former is Robbie's blacking out of a letter at the end of the word 'Fowl'. It is not possible to know from the text alone what Robbie was attempting to erase, but the way in which he so definitely covered it up shows some understanding of the importance of drafting and to choices in drafting. Deletions from other children's projects show the importance they attach to getting spelling and presentation right. The children's texts connect with the wider environment through, most obviously, their importation of a wide range of other texts, such as photographs, CD-ROM printouts, photocopies and postcards. How the imported materials are appropriated by children varies. Some make no comment, while others integrate them into their own text by add-ing a caption; an example is Robbie's caption set against the imported photograph of footballers.

Ormerod and Ivanič state that their analytical framework has emerged from their data analysis. On one level, the framework is therefore specific to their research project and can be treated as 'findings', that is, what they have learnt about the importance of physical characteristics of texts for meaning-making. However, it is also intended as a theoretical framework or heuristic that other researchers can use to explore the function of physical characteristics of texts in relation to meaning-making.

Ivanič and Ormerod echo Kress (1997) in viewing multimodal meaning-making as something that young children naturally engage in, in the sense that young children are naturally inclined to recognise the potential of a wide range of semiotic modes to com-municate particular aspects of a multifaceted reality. Given the changing semiotic landscape – technology is facilitating an increased use of a wider range of speech and other sounds, and still and moving visual images – the creative manipulation of resources that children engage in 'should be taken seriously, not just by academics, but by parents, teachers and educational policy makers' (p.89).

16.9 Your view on this approach

(vii) To what extent are you convinced by the importance attached by Ormerod and Ivanič to the materiality – the physical characteristics – of texts?

(viii) To what extent do you agree with their interpretation of the ways in which the texts contribute to meaning-making in relation to: (a) carrying meaning about a topic; (b) carrying meaning about attitudes towards a topic; (c) carrying meaning about how texts work?

(ix) How useful do you think the framework they have developed would be for analysing the function of physical characteristics for meaning-making in other texts?

(x) How might you draw on and/or develop Ormerod and Ivanič's approach to the study of the materiality of texts in your own context?

16.10 Examples of similar studies

For a further study focusing on materiality and education, see:

STEIN, P. (in press) 'The Olifantsvlei 'Fresh Stories' project: multimodality, creativity and fixing in the semiotic chain', in G. Kress and C. Jewitt (eds) *Learning and Multimodality: Moving Beyond Language*, New York, Peter Lang.

For multimodal analysis of a science classroom, see:

JEWITT, C. and KRESS, G. (2002) 'A multimodal approach to teaching and learning', in S. Goodman, T. Lillis, N. Mercer and J. Maybin (eds) *Language, Literacy and Education: A Reader*, Stoke-on-Trent, Trentham.

For a discussion of materiality in a prison context, see:

WILSON, A. (2000) 'There's no escape from third-space theory', in D. Barton, M. Hamilton and R. Ivanič (eds) *Situated Literacies. Reading and Writing in Context*, London, Routledge.

17: A social semiotic approach: television film

17.1 Key features of this approach

The growing interest in multimodality has led to an interest in developing ways of analysing the range of semiotic modes in communication or representation, rather than simply focusing on the analysis of verbal language. To do so, language researchers draw on work in semiotics and cultural studies (see Rose, 2001) and also on analytical frameworks from linguistics, particularly systemic functional linguistics (see, for example, Kress and van Leeuwen, 1996, 2001). A key principle underlying this latter work is that there is a need to develop an integrated approach to the analysis of the relationships between different semiotic modes – words, images, sound, movement – in order to understand how these different modes contribute to the 'stories' that are being told, whether in 'factual' accounts or fiction. A documentary film, for example, while often viewed as a factual representation, is the result of a series of choices about which semiotic resources should be used for particular purposes. As well as the more obvious choices about the words participants say, there are choices to be made about the distance between characters and camera – close-up or distance shots – the amount and speed of participants' movement on screen, the accompanying music and so on.

17.2 Example

IEDEMA, R. (2001) 'Analysing film and television: a social semiotic account of Hospital: An Unhealthy Business', in T. van Leeuwen and C. Jewitt (eds) *Handbook of Visual Analysis*, London, Sage, pp. 183-204.

Iedema sets out to explore how the different semiotic modes in a TV documentary film contribute to the construction of a particular story or perspective on medical care in hospitals. He puts forward a frame for analysing television documentary films that draws on systemic functional linguistics (see also Examples 8 and 16).

17.3 The aims of the researcher

Iedema's two key aims are to:

- develop ways of systematically describing and thus categorising the interplay between different semiotic resources in tele-film

- analyse the ways in which a range of semiotic resources – words, images, sound, movement – are used to construct meanings in documentary films.

As you will see, these aims of description and analysis seem to be closely bound together.

17.4 Data extracts *(see data extracts 17.1-17.3)*

As with all multimodal research, presenting the data is problematic in a printed text: we only have one mode available to us to discuss a range of modes. Thus, as with other examples in this multimodal section, we can access only the researcher's description and representation of the actual data. So Data Extract 17.1 consists of a description of a frame from a documentary, together with a drawing of the frame and a quoted comment from a clinician.

The data comprises an Australian documentary film called *Hospital: An Unhealthy Business*. The documentary is about 'hospital waiting lists, budget blow-outs and rising costs of health and aged care' (Iedema, 2001, p.184) and focuses on the tensions between providing adequate patient care and staying within budgetary requirements.

The following still is taken from a documentary about a Melbourne hospital. It shows a frame from a scene (about 7 munites into the documentary) in which a clinician walks through a hospital corridor while speaking over her shoulder to an interviewer who

follows her with a camera. While negotiating the maze of corridors which connect offices and wards, the clinician says:

> It's easy for some people to say, you know, this is the fine line, you don't step over it. Whereas for us, we actually see the patient, and I'd be more inclined to look for less urgent or emotive places to save money. I mean cardiology is, uh, a life threatening and an acute situation and I'd prefer not to save money there, you know, ... You don't treat public patients like second class citizens, if we can afford it. They get the best treatment in the private hospital. Why don't they get the same treatment in a public hospital? I mean, they're still somebody's mother or father, they're still deserving the respect to be treated ... [passed through door; cut]

Data Extract 17.1 *Scene from documentary (Source: Iedema, 2001, text and Figure 9.1, p.183)*

Step in the argument	Scene	Visuals	Relevant talk
A1	Introduction of the patient: Mick	Mick driving a car delivering mail; Mick entering the hospital	Voice-over: 'To balance the books the hospital must treat more patients. Those who will benefit most of this plan are people sitting on waiting lists, people like Mick, the local postman ...'
B1	Meeting where David Hillis (manager) gets Keith Stockman (clinician) to explain his budget overrun	DH at whiteboards; KS seated; DH and KS never in the same shot	DH: 'We can't afford stenting for the rest of the year'; voice-over: 'Keith Stockman is on the line'
A2	Operation: doctor speaking to Mick	Mick in bed, doctor and nurse talk to him	'We'll try and make you run on six cylinders.'
B2	KS and DH on their own; KS proposes 25% operation level	KS and DH seated in DH's office sharing desk space	DH: '20% is where I'll try and make it sit for the rest of the financial year'; 'what I'll do is just go bang and stop the lot.'
A3	Female clinician (SG) monologue	Camera follows clinician through corridor	'They're still somebody's mother or father, they're still deserving the respect to be treated.'
B3	Clinician points out cost of stents in cupboard	Clinician pointing at boxes in cupboard	'So there's an awful lot of money in this cupboard, well over a hundred thousand dollars I'd say.'
A4	Operation procedure; doctor arguing that Mick needs stent	Bloody hands manipulating tools, computer screen showing vascular details	
B4	Meeting between KS and administrator who argues that non-stenting is better for the hospital budget; the more often a patient comes back the more treatment units the hospital can mark up	Clinician on the left (Given) listening to administrator on the right (New)	
A5	The operation		'If we leave this now, this man will come back'
B5	DH tells cardiologists that he needs to put a stop on their unit's expenditure	Clinicians gathered in office; DH never in same shot as them	
A6	Operation: Mick speaks from his bed; Mick says goodbye to others in his ward		Doctor: 'You realize you're costing the hospital an arm and a leg here'; nurse says: 'It went very well' [churchy music starts again]
B6	doctors are reported to have achieved agreement on 25% operation (rather than DH's 20%)	woman walking through room full of files, picks file, then shown seated in front of computer typing in numbers	Voice-over: 'Calculate his worth': Mick filed away as $6000 cost; 'a numbers game', 'coding patients has become an obsession'

Data Extract 17.2 The section on 'stenting' (Source: Iedema, 2001, Table 9.2, pp. 196-7)

	Individual frames	Scenes and sequences	Stages and text as a whole
Representation (ideation) what is it about?	A lot of the shots that include doctors also show action or dynamic vectors (arms connecting doctor and patient, etc.); administrators -managers shots tend to lack vectors; doctors are often shown interacting with multiple others (in contrast to administrators)	Doctors enact temporally organized scenes, such as operations or patient consultations; administrators-managers are shown in less logically connected snippets of interaction (sequences)	The doctors enact curing and caring narratives centring around specific people, while the administrators enact financial management narratives centring around 'abstract ideas' and numbers
Orientation (inter-personality): how does it enact the social?	Doctors are often shown closer up, in more colourful and socially significant surroundings than the administrators -managers (who are often portrayed using a low camera angle, with relative distance, and lacking the colour and social intimacy of the doctor-centred interactions)	Doctors show their sense of social responsibility by curing patients or facilitating their death; administrators-managers enact a thematic consistency (meeting financial deadlines) but are not implicated in social relations beyond their official administrative role	The doctors are positioned as those who deal with and face what is real – life and death – and they thereby monopolize a host of inter-personalizing resources. The administrators are positioned as those who deal with what is imaginary and 'unreal' – finances, mobilizing control
Organisation (textuality): how is it put together as semiotic construct?	Initially administrators-managers are positioned as Given (left of screen) and doctors as New (right of screen); once into the documentary this pattern reverses, positioning the doctor consistently as Given	While the doctors engage in long scenes (which temporally unfold) the administrators engage in short sequences (which have no temporal but a thematic logic). Doctor scenes are constructed on the basis of less abstract ('closer-to-home') thematics (time), while administrator sequences are constructed on the basis of a conceptual thematics (finances, overruns etc.)	The doctor-centred segments punctuate the administrator-centred ones in such as way to suggest (but not state explicitly!) that, whatever cost-overruns they incur, they have 'bloody' good reasons. This implicit argument structure favours the doctors' view: 'don't bother me with your bean-counting problems'

Data Extract 17.3 *Summarising the analysis (Source: Iedema, 2001, Table 9.3, p.197)*

17.5 Questions for you about the data

Look at Data Extract 17.1 and consider the following questions:

(i)   How does the image and the accompanying description of the action help to create a particular image of the clinician?

(ii) How do the words that the clinician says help to create a particular impression of the clinician?

(iii) In what ways do you think the image and the words of the clinician relate to each other? For example, to what extent does the visual image reinforce or conflict with the words?

(iv) Now look at Data Extract 17.2. How does Iedema attempt to describe and categorise one particular section of the documentary film?

17.6 Some points from the researcher's analysis

A driving force behind this research is, Iedema argues, a need for us all to become more critically aware of the ways in which a wide range of semiotic resources contribute to the construction of meanings:

> we may be critically attuned to what is said, but less so to what is shown or 'sounded'. If we turn our attention to images or sound, we often have no other resources for dealing with them than intuition and common sense ... To mount a penetrating critique of the kind of documentary looked at here, we need ... a critical visual-audial literacy enabled by tools such as made available by social semiotics. (p.202)

Iedema uses the material in Data Extract 17.1 to make the general point that *how people are represented* is central to the construction of a particular story or point of view in tele-film. He states that this particular frame exemplifies a common pattern across the documentary as a whole: clinicians occupy a space much closer to the camera than administrators and managers; clinicians are shown in action busily doing things; clinicians are often filmed on a level with the camera (rather than from an angle). The combined effect of such visual representation is to place clinicians and their perspectives at the centre of the story being told in the documentary.

In Data Extract 17.2, Iedema provides more descriptive details about a particular section of the documentary film on stenting. Stenting is a medical procedure that involves inserting a metal tube into clogged arteries to open them up. In the table, Iedema not only provides a descriptive account of the tele-film but maps two 'voices' against the descriptions. These voices represent what Iedema identifies as a kind of 'dialogue' throughout the documentary about patient care versus costs. The voice marked 'A' by Iedema is what he calls the 'patient care' voice – its perspective centres on Mick the patient's predicament. The voice marked B is what Iedema calls the 'balancing the budget' voice, which 'centres around administrative managers telling clinicians they need to cut back the number of stents they use because of the cost' (p.195).

17.7 More questions for you about the data

Look carefully at Data Extract 17.2 to see how Iedema has described details from the tele-film and at how he has mapped the details against the two voices. Now consider the following questions:

(v) Iedema classifies the relationship between the scenes as a dialogue between the 'A' voice (patient care) and the 'B' voice (administrative manager). After reading the details about the scene, visuals and relevant talk, to what extent do you agree/disagree with his classification?

(vi) In your view, to what extent do the visuals and talk in each scene combine to offer one voice, or perspective? Can you see examples of visuals and talk in the same scene offering different voices or perspectives?

(vii) There are two scenes where there is no talk – A4 and B4. In your view, how does the visual in A4 offer a particular perspective on the patient-care versus hospital-funding debate? How does the silence of the clinician in B4 offer a particular perspective on this debate?

(viii) Do you think that Iedema provides sufficient descriptive details about the episode to inform you about what was going on and how it was being represented?

17.8 Further discussion and conclusion

As part of his developing social semiotic analysis of the documentary film, Iedema draws on Halliday's theory of meaning-making. Briefly, this is that all meaning-making (in whatever mode) involves three overarching metafunctions, as discussed in Example 16. The naming of these metafunctions varies across research. The terms Iedema, after Lemke (1989, 1992) uses are – 'representation', 'orientation' and 'organisation'.

'Representation' refers to what is being said (meant) about the world. What is the documentary about?

'Orientation' is to do with how characters are positioned – that is, made to seem to be – in relation to each other and how the audience is positioned in relation to them. For example, an administrator may be positioned as cold and distant, as compared with clinicians who may be represented as warm and caring. Such positioning is constructed not only through the words that people say but also through the ways in which they move in the environment and the settings in which they are filmed. For example, is the audience likely to be more sympathetic towards characters who are obviously very busy, rushing from place to place or towards someone sitting at a desk, rustling papers?

'Organisation' is to do with how the different elements in a film are sequenced and drawn together. The order in which something is presented affects the importance the audience attaches to it.

Iedema uses these three metafunctions – representation, orientation and organisation – to map out the viewpoint constructed in the documentary. He offers a summary of this analysis of the whole film in Data Extract 17.3.

On the basis of his analysis. Iedema argues that the viewpoint constructed through the use of the range of semiotic resources in the tele-film is that the doctors are busy, caring, concerned 'doers' and the administrators are cold, distant 'sayers'. Moreover he argues:

> What this documentary favours is the medical-clinical view on hospital organisation and health policy ... What the documentary does not show, and is structured to suppress, are issues which call clinicians' demands for clinical autonomy and unlimited expenditure seriously in question. Such issues are clinical practice variation ... wasteful practices – and the widespread occurrence of clinical practices which are not based on medical-scientific evidence but on personal or hospital-specific experiences, and which at times perpetuate questionable and sometimes even fatal treatments. (p.185)

17.9 Your view

(ix) Do you agree with Iedema's central position that we need to focus on all semiotic resources in analysing points of view represented in film?

(x) How useful do you find Iedema's descriptive analysis in Data Extract 17.2?

(xi) How convinced are you by his representation of the scenes as a kind of dialogue between two principal voices?

(xii) How useful do you find the application of Halliday's three metafunctions applied to an analysis of the film overall (see Data Extract 17.3)?

(xiii) It is difficult to represent multimodality in a predominantly monomodal text, such as journal articles or this workbook. Can you think of ways in which multimodality could be more successfully represented?

(xiv) Can you think of a similar analysis that you might carry out relating to your own interests?

17.10 Examples of similar studies

For further examples of analysing images from this perspective, see:

STENGLIN, M. and IEDEMA, R. (2001) 'How to analyse visual images: a guide for TESOL teachers', in A. Burns and C. Coffin (eds) *Analysing English in a Global Context: A Reader*, London, Routledge.

VAN LEEUWEN, T. (1996) 'Moving English: the visual language of film', in S. Goodman and D. Graddol (eds) *Redesigning English: New Texts, New Identities*, London, Routledge.

For a broader discussion of a framework for analysing images, see:

KRESS, G. and VAN LEEUWEN, T. (1996) *Reading Images: The Grammar of Visual Design*, London, Routledge.

18: New literacy practices: email communication

18.1 Key features of this approach

The emphasis in much literacy research is increasingly on the notion of 'literacies' or 'multiple literacies'. This conceptualisation of literacy as a plural phenomenon reflects the view that it is no longer meaningful to talk of literacy as if reading and writing were always one and the same thing, but rather that there are many literacies, different ways of constructing and understanding written texts, according to the sociocultural contexts in which they take place (see Barton and Hamilton, 2000; Street, 2002). 'New literacies' is a term often used to refer to literacy practices that are developing through the use of information technology, such as email, computer conferencing and text messaging. Given that much computer-mediated communication includes the use of conventional letters and characters alongside symbols, visuals and sound, it can be considered a multimodal activity requiring multimodal analysis. Frameworks for carrying out such analysis are currently being developed (see, for example, Baron, 1998; Yates, 2001).

18.2 Example

SUGIMOTO, T. and LEVIN, J.A. (2000) 'Multiple literacies and multimedia: a comparison of Japanese and American uses of the Internet', in G.E. Hawisher and C.L. Selfe (eds) *Global Literacies and the World-Wide Web*, London, Routledge, pp. 133-53.

Sugimoto and Levin focus on two particular modes evident in communication practices in email: email openings and the use of 'emoticons', as discussed below. Their approach involves identification, quantification and comparison of these particular features. The actual data the authors analyse is drawn from publicly available websites: it is a selection of pre-existing material rather than data specifically designed or collected for the research (as in Example 1). The data consist of a corpus of fifty randomly selected messages posted to eight newsgroups, four each from Japanese and American newsgroups. The four newsgroups were selected from each national context on the basis of the similarity in topics; these were books, education, humour and travel.

18.3 The aim of the researchers

Sugimoto and Levin aim to:

- examine some of the ways in which uses of the Internet are culturally grounded by comparing particular features of email communication by Japanese and American users.

18.4 Data extracts *(see data extracts 18.1-18.3)*

The actual data is not made available in the paper. Sugimoto and Levin exemplify the particular feature they are examining and then present an analysis based on their counting of the particular element across the messages of the different newsgroups. The first feature they examine is the openings of Japanese and American email messages, looking in particular at whether Japanese and American users include their names and affiliations at the beginning and/or end of an email.

X–Sender: tanaka@xx.yamada-u.ac.jp
Mime–Version: 1.0
Date: Tue, 21 Jul 1997 19:43: 16 +0900
To: taku@p.u-tokyo.ac.jp
Subject: 8/13
Status: 0

田中＠山田大学です。

8/13 の会議ですが、
何時頃までかかるんでしょうか・・・
宿泊の手配が必要かな？と思って。
- -
田中太郎 (Taro TANAKA)　　E-mail : tanaka@xx.yamada-u.ac.jp
山田大学教育学部
College of Education, Yamada Univ.
〒 321-1122　山田市弥生 3250　Tel. 0864-21-4321 (直通)
- -
Note: The meaning of the message body is:
     This is Tanaka @ Yamada University.
Regarding the meeting on 13 Aug.,
what time can I expect it to be over?
I wonder if I need to make a hotel reservation.

Data Extract 18.1 A sample email message in Japanese (Source: Sugimoto and Levin, 2000, Figure 6.2, p.141)

18.5 Questions for you about the data analysis

(i) Look at the Japanese opening exemplified in Data Extract 18.1. Are you surprised by the way in which the Japanese email user states name and affiliation? If you use emails, would you normally include your name and affiliation at the beginning of your email? Why/Why not?

(ii) Look at the analysis in Data Extract 18.2. What similarities do you notice between Japanese and American users? What differences do you notice?

	US				Japan			
	alt.books. reviews	k12.chat. teachers	rec. humor	rec.travel .usa- canada	fj. books	fj. education	fj. jokes	fj. travel
Name at beginning					13	20		1
Name + affiliation at beginning	1	2			8	6		2
Name at end	31	8	21	23	2	13	34	
Name + affiliation at end	1	21		2			1	1
Name both at beginning and end					1	3		
Name + affiliation at beginning and name at end						1		

Data Extract 18.2 *Name and affiliations in email messages (Source: Sugimoto and Levin, 2000, Table 6.1, p.142)*

18.6 Some points from the researchers' analysis

In their discussion, Sugimoto and Levin focus on the possible reasons why Japanese writers begin their emails by giving their name and affiliation, in contrast to the American writers, who do not. They point to two possibilities. First, they suggest that Japanese users may have difficulty in finding the 'From' line among the headers because Roman letters are used in email headers. Second, they suggest that Japanese users may be continuing a practice carried over from a previous virtual context. This way of opening Japanese emails was common in *'paso-kon tsushin'* (literally, personal computer communication), which was a system using commercial Japanese network-service companies, pre-dating the widespread use of the Internet. Within this network 'only nonsense strings of alphabetic characters and digits appear as the identities of the senders' (p.143), so it was customary for people to state their names at the beginning of the message.

Sugimoto and Levin argue that, contrary to the assumption that global Internet use results in one uniform practice, practices on the Internet reflect and constitute local cultural influences and interests. Thus, emerging or 'new' global literacy practices are always bound up with existing local practices.

18.7 More questions about the data

The second feature of email communication that Sugimoto and Levin seek to examine is the use of 'emoticons' by Japanese and American users. Emoticons

	USA				Japan			
	alt.books. reviews	k12.chat. teachers	rec. humor	rec.travel .usa-canada	fj. books	fj. education	fj. jokes	fj. travel
total no.	0	5	5	0	12	20	0	15
:-) "smiling"			1		1	5		1
:) "smiling"		3	1					
:-("sad face"		1						
:("sad face"		1	1					
;-) "wink"		1						1
;) "wink"		1						
?-("questioning"						1		
^^ "smile"					2	4	1	
^^; "smile with cold sweat"					6	7		4
(^.^;) "smile with cold sweat"								8
(-.-;) "silence with cold sweat"								1
^^;v "smile with cold sweat and 'v-sign'"								
m(__)m "apology or thanks"					5			
[;^J^] "a variation of the 'cold sweat' smiley"					1			
^<>^ "smile with open mouth"					1			
(^^)y" "smile with smoking"						1		
(?_?) "wondering"						1		
(;;) "crying"						1		
(_o_) "I'm sorry ..."								1

Data Extract 18.3 Use of emoticons in email messages (Source: Sugimoto and Levin, 2000, Table 6.3, p.142)

are simple character sequences that express emotions and are intended to soften the tones of written messages, thus avoiding unnecessary confrontation and arguments (p.143)

They examine the use of emoticons from across the same sample newsgroup emails.

   (iii) Look at Data Extract 18.3. Are you familiar with the range of emoticons listed in the table? Are there any that aren't familiar?

   (iv) What do you notice about the kinds of emoticons used by the Japanese and American users?

   (v) What do you notice about the number of emoticons used by Japanese and American users?

   (vi) What do you notice about the type of virtual contexts in which particular emoticons are used? And in which newsgroups?

18.8 Further points and discussion

Sugimoto and Levin make the following points based on their interpretation of the data in the table:

*   many emoticons are different in the two cultures; for example, the basic smiley in the USA is :-), whereas the basic smiley in Japan is (^-^)

*   some of the Japanese writers use 'American' emoticons such as ;-), but most Japanese use Japanese emoticons rather than American ones. No Japanese emoticons appear in the US messages.

*   although emoticons originated in the USA, particular forms and meanings have evolved in a different cultural context. The most commonly used Japanese emoticon is (^-^;) or (^^;) which, according to Sugimoto and Levin, represents a smile with 'cold sweat' on the side of its face. The most typical use of emoticon (^-^;) or (^^;) occurs when Japanese writers are afraid they are saying something too strongly and is an expression of the Japanese cultural value of modesty in communication (p.144).

18.9 Your view on this approach

   (vii) How useful do you think the focus of their analysis is – that is, email openings and emoticons?

  (viii) How plausible do you find the reasons given for the differences between Japanese and American openings in emails? How would you explain the differences?

   (ix) How would you explain the different use of emoticons in Japanese and American emails? To what extent do these differ from the email practices of other cultural groups?

   (x) How convinced are you by the reason given for the greater use of the emoticon of the 'cold sweat smile' among Japanese users?

(xi) How might you draw on this approach to explore specific aspects of email use in your own context?

18.10 Examples of similar studies

The study of communication via the World-Wide Web is a developing area of research. For examples of the range of studies, see:

HAWISHER, G.E. and SELFE, C.L. (eds) (2000) *Global Literacies and the World-Wide Web*, London, Routledge.

SNYDER, I. (ed.) (1998) *Page to Screen: Taking Literacy into the Electronic Era*, London, Routledge.

An example of work focusing on linguistic analysis is:

BARON, N. (1998) 'Letters by phone or speech by other means: the linguistics of email', *Language and Communication*, vol.18, pp.133-70.

PART 4
ETHNOGRAPHIC APPROACHES

Introduction

Ethnography is a commitment to observing real-life events as they unfold, wherein the researcher attempts to make sense of these events from the perspectives of participants. While there are debates about exactly what counts as an ethnographic method, the following features outlined by Hammersley (1994) give a strong sense of what adopting an ethnographic approach involves.

- It is concerned with analysis of empirical data that is systematically selected for the purpose.

- Those data come from 'real world' contexts, rather than being produced under experimental conditions created by the researcher.

- Data is gathered from a range of sources, but observation and/or relatively informal conversations are usually the main ones.

- The approach to data collection is unstructured, in the sense that it does not involve following through a detailed plan set up at the beginning; nor are the categories used for interpreting what people say and do pre-given or fixed.

- The focus is a single setting or group, of relatively small scale; or a small number of these. In life-history research the focus may even be a single individual.

- The analysis of the data involves interpretation of the meanings and functions of human actions and mainly takes the form of verbal descriptions and explanations, with quantification and statistical analysis playing a subordinate role at most.

Observation is central to ethnography, but there is considerable debate about what it means to 'observe'. In the past, some ethnographers claimed they were simply reporting what they had observed, 'telling it like it is'. However, most ethnographer-researchers now strongly argue that interpretation is always a part of observation and that interpretation is informed by the theoretical and ideological positions of researchers (see Clifford and Marcus, 1986). Rather than ignoring these positions, it is considered important to make explicit the basis on which interpretations are made. In this part of the workbook, you will see that different theoretical positions are illustrated.

Researchers of language and literacy are increasingly combining an ethnographic approach to the study of a particular phenomenon with a range of linguistic, or text-oriented, forms of analysis. Examples included in this part of the workbook focus on adult and community literacy practices, student writing in university and school, and informal adolescent language practices. In Example 19, we outline Zubair's analysis of the uses and perceptions of literacy in a rural Pakistani community, focusing particularly on literacy and gender. Zubair draws on work in 'New Literacy Studies' (Barton and Hamilton, 2000) to combine an ethnographic approach with an analysis of the ways in which people talk about literacy. Example 20 summarises Hamilton's exploration of the value of visual data, i.e. photographs in researching community literacy practices. Through her analysis, Hamilton problematises some core concepts used in literacy studies. Example 21 focuses on Lillis's work on student writing in higher education, and in particular on the value of 'talk around text' to explore student meaning-making. In Example 22 we take you through Haas-Dyson's analysis of primary school children's writing in the classroom. Haas-Dyson draws on Bakhtinian theory in her intricate analysis of the ways in which children draw on popular culture in their writing and in their oral responses to each other's writing. Example 23 illustrates how post-structuralist feminist theory can be combined with an ethnographic study of identity in a particular curriculum context: Lee sets out to explore the ways in which students negotiate their gendered identities in school geography lessons. And in the final example of the workbook, Example 24, we outline an approach by Rampton that integrates interactional sociolinguistics with ethnography to focus on the relationship between language, identity and ethnicity among adolescents in the UK.

19 Ethnography and new literacy studies: women's literacy practices

19.1 Key features of this approach

'New Literacy Studies' is the name often used to refer to research and writings in which literacy is viewed as a profoundly cultural and ideological phenomenon, rather than being seen simply as a technical phenomenon whereby people decode and encode symbols and letters. A key proponent of the idea that literacy is a sociocultural phenomenon is the anthropologist Brian Street, who makes a clear distinction between the two views on literacy. He refers to the view of literacy as a predominantly technical phenomenon as the 'autonomous' model of literacy, and the view of literacy as a cultural phenomenon as the 'ideological' model of literacy. He states that the ideological view of literacy

> posits that literacy is a social practice, not simply a technical and neutral skill; that it is always embedded in socially constructed epistemological principles. It is about knowledge: the ways in which people address reading and writing are themselves rooted in conceptions of knowledge, identity, being. Literacy, in this sense, is always contested, both its meanings and practices, hence particular versions of it are always 'ideological', they are always rooted in a particular world-view ... (Street, 2001, p.8)

Given the emphasis on the contexts of literacy within new literacy studies, an ethnographic approach to research is often adopted. The range of contexts studied includes home/school literacy practices (Heath, 1983), community literacies (Barton and Hamilton, 1998), academic literacies (Jones *et al.*, eds., 1999) and prison literacies (Wilson, 2000).

19.2 Example

ZUBAIR, S. (1999) 'Women's literacy in a rural Pakistani community', in T. O'Brien (ed.) *Language and Literacies: Selected Papers from the Annual Meeting of the British Association for Applied Linguistics*, University of Manchester, September 1998, BAAL and Multilingual Matters, pp.114-25.

Zubair uses an ethnographic approach to explore the uses and perceptions of literacy across genders and generations in a rural Pakistani community. She uses data derived from focus-group discussions, individual interviews, field notes and participation in literacy events to gather detailed information about the lives of participants and their community. Drawing on Street's work, Zubair explores the ways in which literacy in a particular community relates to larger sociocultural practices; she analyses the relationship between *literacy practices* and *power* in the community, family and home.

19.3 The aims of the researcher

Zubair aims to explore and to show:

* what literacy means to different users of literacy

* how gender ideologies restrict women's access to certain literacies

* 'how identity and power are negotiated through talk' (p.118).

19.4 Data extracts *(see data extracts 19.1-19.2)*

S, R and O = older woman   A = woman in her thirties
Z and N = younger women   M = moderator (Zubair)
F = male participant in early forties

038.	**R:**	[yes absolutely there was *izzat* – if someone came outside we
039.	**O:**	[very respectable people
040.	**R:**	couldn't tell whether it was a human being or an animal we
041.	**R:**	remained indoors like silent birds – <u>now</u> there's freedom children
042.	**R:**	are also being educated and we also have some awareness but
043.	**R:**	for us those times were okay=
044.	**O:**	=it was good=
045.	**R:**	=it was absolutely fine
046.	**O:**	(unclear)
047.	**R:**	those times were absolutely fine those elders did right now
048.	**R:**	there's freedom – children have an easy life now even for us it's
049.	**R:**	easier
050.	**M:**	umm would you tell me something about it? (signalling towards younger participants)
051.	**A:**	what do we know? [what shall we (unclear)
052.	**Z:**	[I think that there shouldn't be so many=
053.	**A:**	=restrictions=
054.	**Z:**	=restrictions should not be there because_(starts speaking Urdu)
055.	**Z:**	one can't sit at home (M: umm) that's our view because the new
056.	**Z:**	generation (laughs) would say that one can't sit at home there
057.	**Z:**	should be some freedom – at least to move about to meet friends
058.	**Z:**	to go out with friends to parks to see movies – there should be a
059.	**Z:**	little bit of freedom- too much of it (restrictions) is not good
060.	**Z:**	(**M**: umm) I think if there is too much pressure on a girl she
061:	**Z:**	won't be able to do what's right for her (**M**: umm) that's all
062:	**Z:**	(laughs)

Data Extract 19.1 Focus group interaction (Source: Zubair, 1999, Example 1, pp.118-19)

164.	**M:**	why didn't you?
165.	**F:**	it's okay if women are literate they become very free Islam is
166.	**F:**	about strictly observing *purdah purdah* is obligatory a woman
167.	**F:**	must cover herself if she goes out head must be covered it is
168.	**F:**	Islamic [Islam
169.	**S:**	[(laughs) see
170.	**F:**	these are the Islamic rules=
171.	**S:**	=(jokingly) he is our Islamic=
172.	**F:**	=Islam says teach up to this learn to read that you are familiar
173.	**F:**	with the religion but people forget religion and pay attention to
174.	**F:**	worldly education more they have [no respect for elders
175.	**N:**	[yeah this is also this is
176.	**N:**	written meaning that our prophet said that even if you have to
177.	**N:**	go to China to get educated you should go this means some
178.	**N:**	freedom was given=
179.	**F:**	=China that
180.	**N:**	this is all made up by them to supress to kill that 'you aren't
181.	**N:**	going out you aren't learning literacy' when Islam allows one
182.	**N:**	to go out to become literate then these these restictions are
183.	**N:**	imposed by man

Data Extract 19.2 Focus group interaction (Source: Zubair, 1999, Example 2, pp. 119-20) (In this extract, F is responding to a question about why he didn't send his daughter to school)

19.5 Questions for you about the data

(i) Read through the extracts, paying close attention to the language used by the participants.

(ii) Circle all the pronouns – *I, we, you, they, them* – in the two extracts. Look at the use of *I, we, you* and *they* in particular. In each case, who is the pronoun referring to?

(iii) What do you notice about the use of pronouns by different people and age groups in the extracts? Is there any difference between the pronoun use of F (the male participant) and the women's pronoun use?

(iv) Look for any sets of antonyms (words with opposite meanings) in the two extracts (examples of antonyms are strong/weak; good/bad; old/new). Do you think these could be evidence of conflicting ideas in the discussions?

19.6 Some points from the researcher's analysis

Zubair analyses *how* people talk about literacy/illiteracy as well as *what* they say. To do this, she combines an analysis of the language people use – word choice or lexis and use of figurative language as well as pronoun use – with a thematic content analysis of what they say. She collects a number of different kinds of data: recorded focus-group interviews and individual interviews – that is, people's talk about literacy; participant observation; literacy documents; and field notes. Because she is interested in power relations as they are played out around literacy in the community, Zubair, following Dentith (1995) adopts Bakhtin's perspective on language 'as a site of contest for power struggles between different groups in the community' (p.120).

In general, Zubair's analysis illustrates the perceptions of different members of the community regarding the acquisition and use of literacy and how this differs across generations and genders. Zubair identifies sets of antonyms (such as 'restrictions', 'pressure' and 'suppress' versus 'freedom'; 'old' versus 'new'; 'then' versus 'now') and argues that these reveal 'antithetical juxtapositions of concepts and attitudes' (p.120). She argues that the use of antonyms reflects the conflicting ideologies about the role of women in the community and the participants' preoccupations with them. For example, the young women's desire for freedom and the way this is linked to literacy conflicts with the male view expressed in the extract. The language used thus reflects the specific interests of different groups and illustrates Bakhtin's perspective on language as a site of struggle.

Looking at pronoun use, Zubair argues that the younger woman's (Z) use of *I* (Data Extract 19.1) is an indicator of her individuality and awareness of her rights, in contrast with the older generation of women who refer to themselves collectively as *we*. The middle-group woman, A (aged 30), uses *we* in the same way as the older women. Zubair points out that, in lines 54-6, the younger woman, Z, uses the plural pronoun *our* when referring to the younger generation of women and showing the separation between the age groups. Focusing on gender differences in Data Extract 19.2, Zubair shows how the pronoun *they* is used by the male, F, to refer to the women, setting up a binary 'us versus them' relationship. In F's statement 'if women are literate they become very free', F sets up educated women as threatening, a group 'struggling for power and dominance through literacy' (p.121).

19.7 More questions for you about the data

  (v)   Now read through the extracts again, paying attention to the content of the discussion rather than to language use.

  (vi) What do the extracts tell you about the participants' views on gender roles?

  (vii) How do perspectives on this differ for the groups and individuals represented: older women; younger women; the 30-year-old woman; the man?

19.8 Further discussion and conclusions

Zubair argues that the ambivalence shown by all participants, the male included, when talking about women's literacy suggests that gender roles are changing in the community. They seem to be in a process of redefinition and renegotiation, but these changes are gradual and unobtrusive. Zubair suggests that this ambivalence and uncertainty is indicative of the fact that participants are unsure of how to replace the traditional ideologies and expectations regarding gender roles that they have been socialised into. Zubair points out that in lines 52-62 and 175-183, Z and N question and challenge the dominant male values of the community, and in lines 175-183 N does this by arguing with F, who seems in this discussion to be representative of the general male view. The debate between F and N in Data Extract 19.2 indicates the way in which the acquisition of secular literacy is linked to community interpretations of sex roles in Islam and the tradition of *purdah*, or segregation of the sexes. Zubair argues that, in the participants' discourse, secular literacy is 'constructed as an empowering phenomenon' (p.123). Her analysis of these extracts thus shows that the way in which the value and promise of literacy is understood varies across age groups, gender and individuals.

19.9 Your view

(viii) How effective do you find this kind of analysis?

(ix) What are the advantages of combining different approaches – that is, a focus on how language is used and the content of what people say?

(x) Do you accept Zubair's argument that the language used in the interviews illustrates the way power is being contested in the community?

(xi) What difficulties could you envisage in conducting this kind of research?

(xii) How might you use a similar approach in your own context?

19.10 Examples of studies using a similar approach

For a further study on literacy and gender, see:

ROCKHILL, K. (1983) 'Gender, language and the politics of literacy', in. B. Street (ed.) *Cross-cultural Approaches to Literacy,* Cambridge, Cambridge University Press.

For multilingual literacies, see:

SAXENA, M. (1994) 'Literacies among Punjabis in Southall', in M. Hamilton, D. Barton and R. Ivanič (eds) *World of Literacy,* Clevedon, Multilingual Matters.

For ethnographic study of community literacies, see:

BARTON, D. and HAMILTON, M. (1998) *Local Literacies*, London, Routledge.

20: Ethnography and visual data: community literacy

20.1 Key Features of this approach

The 'new' in 'New Literacy Studies' signals an approach to literacy that differs from the conventional view of reading and writing as an individual and cognitive activity. The *new* emphasises a shift towards literacy as a fundamentally social phenomenon, with reading and writing embedded in social relationships and institutional practices, as outlined in the introduction to Part 4. Within New Literacy Studies a number of core analytic concepts have been developed that emphasise the socially embedded nature of all literacy activities. A key concept is that of the literacy event. Barton and Hamilton, who have carried out extensive research into the literacy practices of one community in the North of England, define literacy events as follows:

> Literacy events are activities where literacy has a role. Usually there is a written text, or texts, central to the activity and there may be talk around the text. Events are observable episodes. (Barton and Hamilton, 2000, p.8)

Literacy events are made up of several key elements, such as participants, settings, artefacts (or the tools of literacy) and activities (Hamilton, 2000, p.17). These elements are widely used as analytic concepts in literacy research. Another important concept is that of 'practices', which is used in two important ways. First, practices refers to an amalgam of single literacy events, such as people reading, what they read, where they read. These events are all observable, therefore literacy is observable in some way. Second, practices refers to a more abstract notion of literacy – the meanings of literacy within particular social and cultural contexts; for example, the social significance of reading in a particular way in a particular place.

20.2 Example

HAMILTON, M. (2000) 'Expanding the new literacy studies. Using photographs to explore literacy as social practice', in D. Barton, M. Hamilton and R. Ivanič (eds) *Situated Literacies. Reading and Writing in Context*, London, Routledge, pp.16-34.

Hamilton focuses on the value of visual images in research on literacy. She explains that analysing visual images is a way of learning more about people's everyday literacy practices. These include photographs from newspapers which show literacy in everyday life. She also argues that a focus on visual images can enhance key concepts developed within New Literacy Studies.

20.3 The aims of the researcher

Hamilton's overarching aim is to:

- 'trace the threads of literacy practices through contemporary social life, using visual evidence of them' (p.18).

More specifically, she sets out to:

- analyse photographs as records of literacy events and practices and to analyse photographs in order to explore ways of thinking about literacy in society

- explore the usefulness of key concepts in 'new literacy studies'.

20.4 Data Extracts *(see data extracts 20.1-20.4)*

Data Extract 20.1 *Activities in the job centre (Source: Hamilton, 2000, Figure 2.1, p.23)*

Data Extract 20.2 *Footing the bills (Source: Hamilton, 2000, Figure 2.2, p.24)*

Data Extract 20.3 *Giant cheque (Source: Hamilton, 2000, Figure 2.3, p.24)*

Data Extract 20.4 *Furness dog club (Source: Hamilton, 2000, Figure 2.1, p.25)*

20.5 Some questions for you about the data

(i)   Hamilton says that she began her photographic research with a particular idea about what constitute the key elements of a literacy event. The basic elements of a literacy event that she identified are listed in Table 20.1. Look at Data Extract 20.1 and, using Hamilton's list, make notes on the different elements in the photograph.

Table 20.1 Identifying basic elements of literacy events and practices in photographs

Elements visible within literacy events (These may be captured in photographs)	What can you see in the photograph?
1 *Participants*: the people who can be seen to be interacting with the written texts	
2 *Settings*: the immediate physical circumstances in which the interaction takes place	
3 *Artefacts*: the material tools and accessories that are involved in the interaction (including the texts)	
4 *Activities*: the actions performed by participants in the literacy event	

(Source: Hamilton, 2000, Table 2.1, p.17)

20.6 Some points from the researcher's analysis

The photograph in Data Extract 20.1 was taken in a job centre (where people seek information about possible employment) in the UK. Hamilton states that this photograph in many ways illustrates what is often thought of as a typical literacy event, with each of the four key elements listed in Table 20.1 being identifiable: the photograph shows people interacting with texts, people reading details of job vacancies and newspapers (element 1); the setting is apparent as it is possible to identify the immediate physical surroundings (element 2); the artefacts are evident, such as paper and notices (element 3); activities are evident, with people reading, writing and talking about texts (element 4).

So the photograph serves to record the specific details of elements in this particular literacy event. The four elements identified by Hamilton at the outset of her research thus seem to provide a useful framework for analysing literacy events in photographs.

20.7 More questions for you about the data

(ii)   Now look at Data Extracts 20.2, 20.3 and 20.4. Can you describe the photographs using the four elements from Table 20.1 – participants, settings, artefacts, activities?

(iii)   Do you find it difficult to identify and describe any of the elements? Which ones? Why?

20.8 Further discussion and conclusion

Hamilton argues that while the four-element framework is useful for describing and making sense of literacy events, after taking and analysing many photographs she has come to think that the elements are not as straightforward as she might have initially assumed. Here are some of the questions that emerged for her after analysing some 100 media photographs, examples of which you have seen here.

Participants – How do we decide who the participants in a literacy event are? Sometimes this can be difficult, for example, if there is a crowd in a photograph, is everyone in the crowd a 'participant'?

Settings – How do we decide on the boundaries of a setting? For example, in Data Extract 20.2 the physical setting is domestic but the document is a legal one. The domains of literacy are clearly permeable and interlinked, so it is important not to conceptualise settings as completely distinct or self-contained.

Artefacts – What do we count as artefacts in a literacy setting? For example, are shelves on which books are placed artefacts?

Activities – What do we mean by literacy activities? The literacy activities that we most obviously think of are reading and writing, but many activities involve written texts even though people are not necessarily reading or writing (as in the photograph that is Data Extract 20.3).

As well as raising questions about any presumed easy identification of the elements of a literacy event, Hamilton goes on to argue that while we most obviously think of literacy as 'interactions between people and texts', there are other important literacy practices made visible with the help of photographs. These are: *literacy in the environment* – for example, signs and labels which are in the everyday background of our lives; *literacy on the body* – writing on people's clothes, tattoos on the skin; *reproduction of documents* – images of documents reproduced in newspapers, for example a letter or a medical form.

Hamilton argues that the analysis of literacy in photographs in newspapers helps to raise important questions about core concepts used in New Literacy Studies. For example, what do we mean by 'interaction'? What do we mean by 'event'? These are questions that need further exploration and discussion. As Hamilton says:

> this study of newspaper photographs has provided visual evidence of a wide range of everyday, public literacy practices, and confronted us with the need to refine the terms we use to describe and take account of these. (p.32)

20.9 Your view

(iv) What do you think visual images – for example photographs – can tell us about literacy in people's everyday lives?

(v) How useful do you think the four elements in Table 20.1 are for analysing visual images of literacy? What are the shortcomings/problems?

(vi) To what extent do you agree with Hamilton that using photographs to explore literacy helps to problematise any straightforward view of a 'literacy event'?

(vii) How might you draw on Hamilton's approach to research an aspect of literacy in your own context?

20.10 Examples of studies using a similar approach

For overviews of research focusing on images, see:

PROSSER, J. (ed.) (1997) *Image-based Research*, London, ECL Press/Taylor and Francis.

VAN LEEUWEN, T. and JEWITT, C. (eds) (2001) *Handbook of Visual Analysis*, London, Sage.

For the use of images in the study of literacy, see:

WILSON, A. (2002) 'Researching in the third space: locating, claiming and valuing the research domain', in S. Goodman, T. Lillis, N. Mercer and J. Maybin (eds) *Language, Literacy and Education: A Reader,* Stoke-on-Trent, Trentham.

21: Ethnography and talk around texts: student academic writing

21.1 Key features of this approach

Research focusing on the reading and writing of academic texts, by students as well as by professional academics, is often referred to as 'academic literacies'. This area of literacy research draws on work in New Literacy Studies, discussed in Examples 19 and 20. In recent times, academic literacies research has been prominent in the UK (see Ivanič, 1998; Jones *et al.*, eds 1999; Lea and Stierer, eds 2000) and South Africa (Angelil-Carter, 2000; Thesen, 1997).

Talk around texts, as discussed in Example 10, has been used to explore writers' perspectives on their texts in a number of ways,. In research on academic literacies, talk around texts has been particularly important as a way of bringing to the fore writers' views on the texts they are constructing. Analysis of such talk alongside analysis of written texts enables the researcher to glimpse the reasons behind the decisions made about specific aspects of the text. When systematic talk around text is combined with an ethnographic approach through, for example, life/literacy history interviews and regular contact between researcher and participants over a sustained period of time, it is possible to explore connections between specific decisions made in writing and the individual writer's personal, social and cultural history (see Ivanič, 1998).

21.2 Example

LILLIS, T.M. (2001) *Student Writing: Access, Regulation and Desire*, London, Routledge [Chapter 4 'The regulation of authoring'].

Lillis draws on an ethnographic approach alongside a method of semi-structured talk around text to explore the experiences of non-traditional students writing in higher education. By non-traditional she means students from social groups largely historically excluded from higher education.

Her approach is ethnographic to the extent that she set out to explore participants' previous life and literacy histories and their experiences of meaning-making in writing over a period of time. Talk around text refers to the process that Lillis as researcher and participant observer engaged in with the student-writers. The talk was oriented in two different ways, depending on the purpose at the time. One kind Lillis calls 'talk as 'business as usual', where she played the role of tutor and knowledgeable insider to academic discourse helping her students to understand and meet the writing requirements of their assignments. A second kind of talk was 'talk to explore students' experiences of engaging in academic writing practices' (Lillis, 2001, p.9).

21.3 The aims of the researcher

Lillis aims to:

- explore how dominant pedagogic practices in higher education (HE) work against student-writers' learning of the literacy conventions they need to produce the expected 'essayist' literacy (Gee, 1990)

- explore how individual student meaning-making in writing is regulated

- to explore student-writers' perspectives on their meaning-making in writing

21.4 Data extracts *(see data extracts 21.1-21.4)*

Mary

Mary is a 23-year-old Black working-class student. During the first year of our talking about her writing, she was studying a Language Studies course and also working as a part-time support teacher in a primary school.

Mary was brought up in a household where predominantly Creole was spoken – by mother, grandparents, uncles and aunts. She feels very positive about this experience and continues to read and write poetry in Creole. Her mother also taught her to read in English at home. Mary remembers feeling very bored for the first two years at school:

> I think school slowed me down. Because they weren't pushing me. The level of ... look, what I knew before I went into school, it wasn't developed or advanced. It was, like, they kept me at a certain pace with some other kids who didn't know how to read or write.

Data Extract 21.1 *Extract from Mary's literacy/life history account (Source: Lillis, 2001,*

Extract from text	*Talk around*
Writing about Black children being sent to schools for the 'educationally subnormal'.	T asks M to explain how she's using Cummins' ideas.
Here the interpretation of Cummins' two concepts (CALP) and (BICS) are anticipated in the opposite direction.	M: Well Cummins' concept of surface fluency could be sort of applied to Creolised speech by West Indian children. When any person in education hears them, it gives them the impression, because of the nature of the language and its structure, it'll give the impression that this child's incapable of academic work. But sometimes people who speak Creole can read English and understand it quite well.
	T: I think you've got to say something like Cummins' concept of surface

---

Data Extract 21.2 *Talk around texts (Source: Lillis, 2001, p.94)*

Extract from text	Talk around
	fluency has got to be reinterpreted
	——
	M: I never knew that such a word existed, 'reinterpreted'.
	T: What other word would you put?
	M: I don't know. I don't think there's anything wrong with it. I think it's all right. I think it saves a lot of time. Yeah, 'cause I didn't know what word to use. I was thinking I've got this idea and I can't say it.

Data Extract 21.2 *Talk around texts (continued) (Source: Lillis, 2001, p.94)*

M: Prerequisite can be described in a lot of other ways, you see. You don't need it, it's just fancy, it's just an extra word. Reinterpreted, now, which means er being interpreted again in a different way, I can't see any other word for saying that, without having a long string of words and make it unclear.

[....]

M: A sort of stereotype I would have would be people who would use words like that are real academics and people sit down and talk about 'prerequisite' [speaking in an exaggerated RP, 'posh', accent: laughs] over coffee and tea [laughs]. And I just don't experience those kinds of things so why should I ... I could be left out from my own community, why am I talking like that for?

T: And you don't want to be part of that community?

M: No, 'cause I don't fit in 'cause I'm Black. How can I fit in there? No way, no matter how qualified, how much qualifications, they'll still see me as black and that's it. And I don't relate to those people anyway, no, no.

[....]

They'll see me differently and I don't want them to, at all. At all. [laughs] —— Oh they'll probably say something like erm, what's she using that word to me for? They probably *do* know what it means but they think there's no need for that. It's unnecessary. It's like putting on airs and graces in a way.

[....]

M: I mean, if I write like that, if I use certain words that are just unnecessary, I'm just going to feel out of it.

T: Out of what? [they laugh]

M: Sort of like I'm not me, you know? It's too much of a big stride.

Data Extract 21.3 *Talk around texts (Source: Lillis, 2001, p.95)*

Connections ...

Wordings, addressivity

Extract from an earlier draft of this chapter	*Comment by one reader on my use of the wording 'imbricated'*
This involves viewing student academic writing as a social act, imbricated in the social context in which it takes place rather than an act of autonomous and individual meaning making	*Reader:* Why are you using this word, imbricated? *Me:* I don't know. I like it ... *Reader:* Aren't you just falling into the trap of using the sort of language that your students complain about? You know, unnecessarily complex words?

I liked this word and it felt intuitively right to use in the way I was using it. But where had I actually got this word from? It clearly wasn't a word I'd normally use. And shouldn't I work out where I'd got it from in any case, in order to decide whether I wanted to consciously use it, to own it, or not?

I thumbed through numerous articles and books to see if I could find this word but couldn't. Then one day I suddenly remembered ... Berlin, it's from Berlin.

> Our consciousness is in large part a product of our material conditions. But our material conditions are also in part the products of our consciousness. Both consciousness and the material conditions influence each other, and they are both imbricated in social relations defined and worked out through language. (Berlin 1988: 489)

Data Extract 21.4 Connections (Source: Lillis, 2001, p.97)

21.5 Questions for you about the data

(i) Look at Data Extract 21.1. In what way do you think Mary is a 'non-traditional' student?

(ii) Look at Data Extract 21.2. What is the focus of the talk?

(iii) Look at Data Extract 21.3. What are Mary's criteria for taking on a new word? What reasons does Mary give for taking on the word 'reinterpret' but not 'prerequisite'?

(iv) What difficulties does Mary face in using academic discourse?

21.6 Some points from the researcher's analysis

In Data Extracts 21.2 and 21.3 Mary and Theresa (the researcher) are discussing a section from one of Mary's essays. The interaction focuses on how Mary feels about using words that are new to her. On the basis of Mary's comments, Lillis states that Mary's decisions about using new words are strongly influenced by her sense of social identity and 'how close or distant she feels particular wordings are' (p.94) to who she feels she is. Decisions about using language in particular ways, including using new words, are bound up with Mary's sense of self and of who she wants to be in HE. Thus Mary associates the word 'prerequisite' with a social group that is alien to her and she is clearly worried about what friends who have not gone on to HE will think about her if she uses words like this in conversation. ('They'll see me differently and I don't want them to' – Data Extract 21.3). She is also concerned about how she feels about herself in the academic context, and this influences her choices in writing ('I mean, if I write like that, if I use certain words that are just unnecessary, I'm just going to feel out of it' – Data Extract 21.3).

Mary seems to use the criterion of usefulness to decide whether to use a new word ('Because prerequisite can be described in a lot of other ways, you see. You don't need it, it's just fancy ... Reinterpreted, now ... I can't see any other word for saying that'). But Lillis points out that this sense of usefulness is still tied up with Mary's sense of who she is and who she wants to be in relation to HE and her community.

21.7 More questions for you about the data

(v) Read Data Extract 21.4 from the researcher's comments on her own writing. How do you think this extract relates to the data discussed above?

21.8 Further discussion and conclusions

Lillis is reflexive in her writing. Reflexivity usually refers to a critical self-awareness of your relationship to the research process – exploring how you, as researcher, have affected it and how it has affected you. Lillis uses reflexivity to let her analysis impact back on her own ways of writing, which are in turn related to how she views herself in relation to the non-traditional student-writers involved in the research as well as in relation to the academy. She is also careful to illustrate this reflexive process to the reader: in Data Extract 21.4, for example, you can see how Lillis traces her use of the word 'imbricated' back to another researcher of student writing whose work she admired, namely Berlin (1988). She follows up on further research (Elbow, 1991) which critiques Berlin's use of certain academic wordings as alienating for student readers and decides to remove the word 'imbricated' from her own text.

Lillis's concern about choice of words connects directly with the student-writers' preoccupations. After discussions with the other participants in the research as well as Mary, Lillis concludes that the student-writers tend to use previously unknown new, or academic words only as a last resort, when they cannot say what they want to say using their own repertoire of words. Lillis points out that this is connected to a wider concern of the student-writers about pretending to be someone who they are not: 'Using the minimum number of new words seems to offer the possibility of staying close to who you are, and who you want to be' (2001, p.100).

The student-writers frequently chose to disguise their own views, though, and to write what they expect the markers would value. While this use of disguise seemed to allow students to participate in higher education while still retaining their sense of self, Lillis argues that this raises two concerns. First, she questions whether it is always possible for writers to control the voices they draw on, and second, she suggests that in the students' struggle to remove their own views and selves from their writing, 'the institution loses potentially new meanings and new identities' (p.104).

Lillis finds that all the student-writers experienced problems in their meaning-making within the higher education context, not only in relation to the words they use, but also in relation to the content and nature of the task (p.105). They point to the problematic relationship between their sense of self, including their ways of writing and meaning-making, and the institutional context.

21.9 Your view

(vi) How successful do you think the talk-about-text approach as illustrated here is?

(vii) What examples of research can you think of where 'talk about text' would be a useful methodological approach?

(viii) What difficulties might you anticipate in using this approach?

(ix) What do you think of the way Lillis illustrates reflexivity in her research?

(x) How might you use such an approach in your own context?

21.10 Examples of studies using a similar approach

For studies using talk around texts or interviews to explore university-level students' writing, see:

ANGELIL-CARTER, S. (2000) *Stolen Language*, London, Longman.

IVANIČ, R. (1998) *Writing and Identity: The Discoursal Construction of Identity in Academic Writing*, Amsterdam, Benjamins.

For a study using talk around text in relation to children's writing, see Example 10 in this workbook:

HALL, N. (1999) 'Young children's use of graphic punctuation', *Language and Education*, vol.13, no.3, pp.178-93.

22: Ethnography and a Bakhtinian approach: writing in the primary classroom

22.1 Key features of this approach

An ethnographic approach to studying classroom practices has been widely used in educational research (see Hammersley, 1994, see also Introduction to Part 4). While what counts as 'ethnography' is debated, it involves a commitment to observing and making sense of real-life events, usually from the perspectives of the participants. A range of methods are used, including observation through the use of video- and audio-recording, field notes, interviews with participants and the collection of relevant documents.

When exploring and making sense of what is observed, researchers use the work of theorists from different disciplines, including sociology and philosophy. The work of Bakhtin is increasingly being used to explore language and literacy practices in a wide range of contexts. As discussed in Example 9, a fundamental Bakhtinian notion is that language is dialogic. A metaphor that Bakhtin uses to describe the dialogic nature of language is that of language as a 'chain of communication' (Bakhtin, 1981, 1986). Briefly, this means that any specific communicative act is embedded in a much broader, historical act, or chain, of communication.

> The topic of the speaker's speech, regardless of what this topic may be, does not become the object of speech for the first time in any given utterance; a given speaker is not the first to speak about it. The object, as it were, has already been articulated, disputed, elucidated, and evaluated in various ways ... The speaker is not the biblical Adam, dealing only with virgin and unnamed objects, giving them names for the first time (Bakhtin, 1986, p.93)

Researchers draw on specific areas of Bakhtin's dialogic conceptualisation of language to help them explore particular aspects of the data they collect and analyse.

22.2 Example

DYSON, A.H. (1997) 'Rewriting for, and by, the children: the social and ideological fate of a Media Miss in an urban classroom', *Written Communication*, vol. 14, no. 3, pp. 275-312.

Dyson's study takes place in one classroom of an inner-city school in a 'high poverty' area in the USA. She focuses her observation on the official 'free writing time' in the classroom, although she observed the children more generally both in the classroom and in the playground. Dyson got to know all the children in the class but found two children especially useful as 'guides' or informants who made visible for her the 'social complexities of their classroom lives'. (p.286). Dyson's data included field notes based on observation, audiotapes of the children's talk and their acting out of their stories within the classroom community, and written texts that the children composed. Dyson uses ethnography to trace the chain of communication in the rewriting of popular stories by individual children as well as the responses from other children to these.

22.3 The aims of the researcher
Dyson aims to:

- explore the ideological tensions that surfaced around the use of a particular female character – Emily, from a popular film – in the children's stories

- show 'the dialogic process through which children use known stories and story characters to mediate community conversations about ideological matters' (p.287)

- explore how children, as members of a collective group, use 'the agency of writing to question given stories and thus, their given social and political worlds' (p.284).

22.4 Data extracts *(see data extracts 22.1-22.7)*
The data discussed shows the children's use of characters and plot from a popular film at the time, *Three Ninjas*, in their free writing and in what Dyson refers to as the 'Author's Theater', where the children chose classmates to act out their stories. The data also includes discussions in which the 'audience' commented and posed questions to the author. Dyson focuses in particular on the way in which one character, Emily, enters children's writing. Dyson explains that in the film *Three Ninjas*, Emily is a 'blonde, European-American pre-adolescent' who lives next door to three brothers, Rocky, Colt and TumTum. Emily and the oldest boy, Rocky, have a crush on each other. The boys are learning the skills of the Ninja from their grandfather who was brought up in Japan. The film is about the confrontation between the grandfather and his three boys, on one side,

---

Once upon a time there was three boys. Their name was Rocky, TumTum, and Colt. And there was a girl named Emily. And Rocky was in love with her. And she was walking down the street. And then some bad guys came to get Emily. And she said, 'Help me,' she said. And then she called their names. 'Rocky, TumTum, and Colt,' she called. And they came to save [her]. And The End.

2 Chapter

And they came to get her. And she was not locked in the closet. And they said, 'Can you hear me?' Rocky said. She said, 'I can hear you,' and she got out of the closet. End. ... [spelling and punctuation corrected for ease of reading]

Data Extract 22.1 Makeda's (female) story (Source: Dyson, 1997, p.292)

> Thomas (a 'bad guy'): Why we didn't get to fight Rocky, TumTum, and Colt?
>
> Makeda: Because it [the fighting group of actors] gets too much out of hand...
>
> Thomas: All we did is pull Emily and take her.
>
> Lynn: Well, in the next chapter, chapter 3, I'd like to have a little bit of fighting because in the movie and in the video there's some fighting. A play has to have fighting.
>
> Kristin: ...Does and Author's Theater have to have fighting to make it a good Author's Theater?
>
> Many 'no's' are voiced.
>
> Sarah: I know I'm one of the people who don't like fighting.
>
> Lynn: Um, well, there might be fighting but not physical fighting, but you know, words, like I have in my story. There are not – well, there is one punch, but the rest of it is words.

Data Extract 22.2 *The children's class discussion of Makeda's 'Author's Theater' (Source: Dyson, 1997, p.293)*

> Once upon a time there were three ninjas and the bad guys. And the Grandpa taught them karate. Rocky and Colt were playing basketball to get Emily's bike back. And Rocky and Colt had won. And they gave Emily her bike back. And Emily kiss Rocky. [Emily most certainly did not kiss Rocky in the film.] [spelling and punctuation corrected for ease of reading]

Data Extract 22.3 *Sammy's (male) story (Source: Dyson, 1997, p.294)*

and a baddie (Snyder) and his group of evil Ninjas on the other. Emily has very few lines in the film and her main role is to fulfil a romantic relationship with Rocky. She is also rescued twice in the movie and has a moment of physical glory when she gives one of the baddies a kick and a punch (Dyson, 1997, p.288).

22.5 Questions for you about the data

Read through the data extracts focusing on the role that Emily is given in each.

(i) Read Data Extracts, 22.1 and 22.2: Makeda's story. How prominent is Emily's role in Makeda's story?

(ii) In what kind of role does Makeda cast Emily?

(iii) How do the children respond to Makeda's story? Do they pick up on Emily's role at all?

(iv) Read Data Extracts 22.3 and 22.4: Sammy's story. Underline the audience's responses to Sammy's story.

(v) How does Tina play the role of Emily, and why do you think she plays it this way? (Data Extract 22.4)

Sammy is presenting his 'Three Ninjas' story, which features Aloyse as Rocky, Patrick as TumTum, and Bryant as Colt. The cast is rounded out with Radha, playing Grandpa, Jonathan, playing the boys' father, and Michael playing all bad guy roles. Sammy has come to the bike scene.

Sammy (improvising but appropriating directly from the film): Rocky, Colt, TumTum, and Emily was riding their bikes, and then Emily went to school [i.e., Emily took the straight and narrow path to school, unlike Rocky and his brothers who ignored a KEEP OUT sign and took a less paved route through an abandoned lot] ....The fat boy and the skinny boy [the school bullies] had take Emily's bike.

Michael (playing both roles): Give me that bike (firmly).

Sammy: And then – and then Emily screamed and called Rocky.

Tina screams shrilly and calls out in a high-pitched, pathetic voice for Rocky. The audience laughs appreciatively.

Sammy: Rocky said, 'What's wrong, Emily?'

Aloyse: What's wrong, Emuly?

Tina (boo hoos with enthusiasm and then says in a choked-up voice): They took my bike! (More audience laughter. Tina smiles amidst her boo hoos.)

Rocky gives Emily a ride to school, where the two older brothers play a basketball game with the bullies 'to get the girl friend's bike back.' Emily is not mentioned again.

Data Extract 22.4 *Sammy's presentation of his story in the 'Author's Theater' (Source: Dyson, 1997, p.294-5)*

Once there was a girl named Emily. She was tough. Her and her boy friend was eating pizza. They love to eat pizza. So one day they were going to school. They love school. Emily's mother walks them to school. She was nice. She love little kids. Kids love her. Then they went into the room. Bad boys, they love to beat up kids .... School is over now. Rocky, Emily, TumTum and Colt. Colt was going away. Emily found him. The bad boys had him. Emily can whip some butt. So she did. So they all ran away.

Data Extract 22.5 *Tina's (female) first story (Source: Dyson, 1997, p.296)*

Batman. Once there was a man that studied bats. He loved to study bats. He was married. His wife name was Emily. She was pretty. So her husband went to the lab to study a baby bats. It was a girl. Her name was Bebe. She was very very big. She love men. She would eat the women if they would be bad to the man. Emily man came home. She was mad then happy again. The end. [spelling and punctuation corrected for ease of reading]

Data Extract 22.6 *Tina's second story (Source: Dyson, 1997, p.297)*

Tina takes her place in the front of the rug and calls her actors. Edward is to be the scientist, Makeda the wife, and Rhonda the baby bat Bebe. Tina begins to read with great expressiveness.

Tina: 'Once there was a man that studied bats. He loved to study bats. He was married ...' ['O::h,' says the audience.] 'Her name was Emily.'

Edward: Just like *Three Ninjas*! (Tina grins very widely.)

Tina: 'She was pretty. So her husband went to the lab' and was studying a bat named Bebe. (Tina stops reading and begins improvising but stays very close to her text. Her written text has confused syntax at this point and perhaps that influences her decision to abandon the text.)

Rhonda: I'm Bebe. I'm a bat. (Class laughs enthusiastically. Edward, apparently responding to the class's playful mood, gasps, runs off to the far corner of the rug, and stands shaking. Tina then responds to his actions, improvising her next line.)

Tina: He was afraid of her. She *lo::ved* him.

Peer: The bat loved him? (incredulous audience member)

Tina: Whoever messed with him she would kill them. One day the man went back home. He told his wife about the bad day he had.

Edward: I had a bad day! That bat messed up. She tried to kill me, man! (The audience laughs. Edward may have misunderstood Tina's text, since his improvisation suggests that the bat was trying to kill him, which was not the case. However, Tina once again picks up on Edward's improvisation.)

Tina: He went back to the lab. And the bat killed him. And he died. The End. (audience laughter)

Data Extract 22.7 *Tina's presentation of her story in the 'Author's Theater' (Source: Dyson, 1997, p.298)*

    (vi) How does the audience respond to her portrayal?

    (vii) Read Data Extract 22.5: Tina's story. How does Emily's role in Tina's story differ from that in Makeda's and Sammy's stories?

22.6 Some points from the researcher's analysis

Following Bakhtin, Dyson views all language as dialogic, all speaking (or writing) involves 'revoicing of others' words' (p.277) to some degree (see also Example 9). Taking control over meaning-making is not, therefore, an easy process. Dyson argues that growing up 'in an ideological sense' involves a more selective choice of the words we appropriate and pass on to others, and she is keen to explore where and how this happens in the language used by the children in her study. She also argues that the act of rewriting, whether by adults or children, reveals the ideological tensions that authors feel 'as they respond to others in their social spaces' (p.279). The ideological tension Dyson explores in this example centres on gender.

Dyson states that in Makeda's story (Data Extract 22.1) Emily features as a star but not as a superhero. As already outlined, the film places Emily in a victim role in two scenes. Makeda's story follows the film very closely by placing Emily in the victim role, but differs markedly from the film in its lack of physical fighting. Dyson reads the audience/children's response as objecting to the lack of physical fighting in Makeda's story. Dyson analyses the ideological tensions here as 'to do with the goodness of physical fighting and, also, with the unruliness of actors engaged in such fighting' (p.293). What Dyson finds interesting here is that there are no objections from the children to the role of Emily as victim.

Dyson explains that Sammy fleshed out the basketball scene and the fight scene in his Author's Theater presentation (Data Extract 22.4) both for his own pleasure and the audience's. However, Tina parodies Emily's role as pathetic for the same reasons. After the Author's Theater event she explains to Sammy that the part he cast for her was boring and that she needed to make it more interesting, even though it was only a small part. This echoed other dissent in the classroom about the fact that the Ninja's story didn't have roles for the girls.

Dyson points out that in Tina's story, (Data Extract 22.5) Emily's role is dramatically different from that of the other children's stories and of the original film. Emily is now presented as the rescuer and thus as a superhero. Dyson emphasises the way in which Tina highlights Emily's physical power in the orientation to the story (line 1), thus setting the scene for her physical confrontation with the boys. Dyson argues that Tina is using Emily 'to resist the representation of girls as 'weak'' (p.296) and thus to resist the dominant ideology of the story. It is also Emily's mother who is the major adult figure in her story (rather than the boys' grandfather). Dyson comments that in Tina's story, Emily develops some agency, as does Tina herself. [*Note*: This story was not acted for the class so there was no audience response to it.]

22.7 More questions for you about the data

(viii) Read through Data Extracts 22.6 and 22.7, which present a further story and Author's Theater by Tina, as well as some of the classroom response to this. What kind of roles do women play in Tina's story?

(ix) How does Emily feature in Tina's story?

(x) How do the roles of the characters change from the story to the Author's Theater?

(xi) How do the audience respond to the Author's Theater? (Data Extract 22.7)

22.8 Further points from the researcher's analysis

Dyson points out that during the Author's Theater performance (Data Extract 22.7)

Tina's relieved Emily, dutiful Batman, and vigilant Bebe had become caricatures (the female vampire, the nerdy scientist, the little woman at home). (p.298)

Playing to the enjoyment of the audience and the interpretations of her actors, Tina continued to reinterpret the characters during her Author's Theater. In this way, Dyson sees the children as 'capable of taking control of the stories they deem their own' (p.302).

Dyson argues that the 'appropriated heroes' (p.298) were, however, subject to some critical reflection in the classroom response. Once Tina had liberated the characters from their usual plots, a space was created to question their motivations. This was in contrast to stories that followed the original film closely, in which the characters' motivations would have been assumed. Despite her earlier complaint about the weakness of the female characters and particularly Emily in the Ninja stories, Tina was happy to sideline Emily when the actions of Batman and Bebe were generating amusement and fun. However, Lynn challenges the representation of Emily, and her silence:

> And it might've been that she [Emily] should've gotten there and saved him some way. (p.300)

Dyson's interpretation of this meant that the classroom community had changed ideologically such that it was now possible for Emily to be powerful even though she wasn't in Tina's Author's Theater. But Dyson cautions that the 'dialogic chain about Emily was not linear' (p.303). Dyson argues that the children's writing of alternative stories did not necessarily eliminate or permanently change the *status quo* in the classroom community, although alternative stories did change the community in some way in that they allowed for a questioning of taken-for-granted human relations that could no longer be taken for granted in the same way. In Dyson's view:

> this is the process through which chains of communication are established in a responsive community, including a community of children: authors' symbolic products generate ideological tensions; those tensions highlight heretofore taken-for-granted textual and social relations; others use culturally sanctioned forms of agency (in this case, writing) and garner the authority to challenge the status quo – to rewrite the story, a liberatory act. (p.303)

22.9 Your view

(xii) Based on the data given, do you think the children did engage with ideological issues through their writing, acting and talk about these activities?

(xiii) Do you think that the children exercised 'agency' in the rewriting process?

(xiv) What problems could you foresee in using such an approach?

(xv) Can you think of a research example in your own context where you might use such an approach?

22.10 Examples of studies using a similar approach

For further examples of studies of writing focusing on agency and intertextuality, see:

IVANIČ, R. (1998) *Writing and Identity: The Discoursal Construction of Identity in Academic Writing*, Amsterdam: Benjamins.

See also Example 9 in this workbook:

SCOLLON, R., TSANG, W.K., LI, D., YUNG, V. and JONES, R. (1998) 'Voice, appropriation and discourse representation in a student writing task', *Linguistics and Education*, vol.9, no.3, 227-50.

For an example of Bakhtinian analysis of spoken language, see:

MAYBIN, J. (2002) 'Voices, intertextuality and induction into schooling', in S. Goodman, T. Lillis, N. Mercer and J. Maybin (eds) *Language, Literacy and Education: A Reader*, Stoke-on-Trent, Trentham.

23: Ethnography and critical discourse analysis: gender and school geography

23.1 Key features of this approach

A key interest for language researchers in recent times has been the relationship between language and identity. Briefly, this involves a focus on the ways in which the language we use contributes to our sense of who we are and who we want to be: for example, speaking a language with a particular accent or dialect usually links an individual (by him/herself or by others) to a particular geographical region or social class, as discussed in Example 1.

For those drawing on post-structuralist writings on language, 'subjectivity' rather than 'identity' is the preferred term. There are several reasons for this. The first is that while 'identity' may suggest a sense of self that is fixed, 'subjectivity' emphasises the constant making of the self. Weedon defines subjectivity as follows:

> 'Subjectivity' is used to refer to the conscious and unconscious thoughts and emotions of the individual, her sense of herself and her ways of understanding her relation to the world. Humanist discourses presuppose an essence at the heart of the individual which is unique, fixed and coherent and which makes her what she is ... Against this irreducible humanist essence of subjectivity, poststructuralism proposes a subjectivity which is precarious, contradictory and in process, constantly being reconstituted in discourse each time we think or speak. (Weedon, 1987, pp.32-3)

A second reason why 'subjectivity' rather than 'identity' is often preferred relates to the idea that different discourses make available different kinds of 'subject positions'. For example, two obvious subject positions that the discourse of schooling makes available are those of teacher and student, which involve very specific ways of being and interacting. While discourses such as that of schooling regulate what kinds of subject positions are available to individuals, they do not completely determine what individuals can do. Fairclough refers to the 'felicitous ambiguity' of the term 'subject':

> In one sense of subject, one is referring to someone who is under the jurisdiction of a political authority, and hence passive and shaped: but the subject of a sentence, for instance, is usually the active one, the 'doer', the one causally implicated in action (Fairclough, 2001, p.32)

Individuals or subjects are thus both shaped by the discourses in which they move and shapers of those discourses.

23.2 Example

LEE, A. (1996) *Gender, Literacy, Curriculum. Re-writing School Geography,* London, Taylor and Francis [Chapter 1 'Introduction: gender, literacy, and schooling'; Chapter 3 'Reading the classroom dynamics'].

Lee adopts an ethnographic approach to the study of 15- and 16-year-old students' participation in the school subject of geography, immersing herself in a particular classroom over an extended period of time. Lee's main interest is to explore the gendered subjectivity of the students as they engage in school geography, that is, she sets out to explore how the 'doing of geography' is linked to the 'doing of gender'. Lee draws on a series of methodological and theoretical frames from interactional sociolinguistics, critical discourse analysis and feminist post-structuralist theory.

23.3 The aims of the researcher

Lee aims to:

*   explore what is differently at stake for girls and for boys as they engage in school geography

*   examine the potential of feminist and post-structuralist theory for exploring and understanding literacy and curriculum in schools

*   investigate how research into literate practices in one classroom subject, geography, can contribute to feminist work on gendered subjectivity.

23.4 Data extracts *(see data extracts 23.1-23.4)*

```
1   Katherine's work in the classroom was typical of the girls' usual approach
2   to public speech situations. Most of the time, Katherine participated in class
3   discussion only when directly called on. She regularly took steps to downplay,
4   or even refuse, possible ascriptions of authority in front of the class. This went,
5   on occasions, almost as far as a refusal of a 'knower' position. In several
6   instances in whole-class lessons, she chose to read out an answer to a question
7   from her notes when called upon for a response, even though she was in a
8   position to be able to extemporize a response more directly, as several boys had
9   already done. That is, she knew an appropriate answer as well as, if not better
10  than, they did. In addition, though a fluent reader (something I ascertained
11  during interview), she delivered the required information from her notes to the
12  class in a kind of caricature of a barely competent reader, hesitating and
13  stumbling slightly. This appeared to be a performance simultaneously of
14  compliance and refusal, where the refusal was a refusal of speech. It appeared
15  that to speak unprompted – to articulate meanings from her head – might have
16  signified one or both of two things: a public position of authority, and a position
17  of engagement with and endorsement of the dominant discursive orientation of
18  the language of classroom discussion. On occasions such as this, the subjective
19  investments in speaking and not speaking are clearly complex.
```

Data Extract 23.1 *Ethnographic description of Katherine in a geography classroom (Source: Lee, 1996, p.75)*

1	There was a powerful male physicality in the room. Boys swamped girls in
2	visible ways as well, through their numbers, the massing of their bodies in
3	clusters around the room, their occupation of most of the space. Indeed, there
4	was a strong sense of centre and periphery in the distribution of bodies in the
5	space. Girls sat together in the front left-hand corner and seldom left this space.
6	Individual boys and groups of boys, on the other hand, moved regularly around
7	the classroom space, visiting each other. Robert in particular, as the most mobile
8	student, made regular visits from his group of three boys (arguably the dominant
9	group in the class) to another group of three in the opposite corner of the
10	classroom. Robert also included Alex D in his visits and in the social talk
11	engaged in by many of the boys for much of the time. Neither Robert nor any
12	other boy approached the girls' corner in their movements around the room.

Data Extract 23.2 *Ethnographic description of boys in a geography classroom (Source: Lee, 1996, p.73)*

23.5 Questions for you about the data

(i) Read through Data Extracts 23.1 and 23.2. What do you think the aim of the researcher is in including these accounts?

(ii) Read through Data Extract 23.1. Underline where the analyst is describing Katherine's behaviour in the classroom. Underline where the researcher is interpreting Katherine's behaviour.

(iii) Read through Data Extract 23.2. Underline where Lee is describing Robert's behaviour. Underline where Lee is interpreting Robert's behaviour.

(iv) Read through Data Extract 23.3. What do you notice about Andrew's and Katherine's contributions?

(v) What do you notice about Alex D's (the teacher) participation in the talk?

(vi) What do you notice about the ways in which specialist language – the discourse of geography – is used by the three participants?

23.6 Some points from the researcher's analysis

Data Extracts 23.1 and 23.2 are from a chapter dealing with the ways in which boys and girls 'do' geography and gender in the geography classroom, that is, learn particular ways of knowing geography at the same time as learning particular ways of being a boy or a girl.

Lee includes the written accounts of the girls and boys in the classroom before the spoken interaction in Data Extract 23.3. The accounts illustrate how the ethnographer's task of 'describing' her 'observations' is not a transparent or easy one. Description is always mediated by the language that is used, the particular researcher's perspective and the theoretical (stated and unstated) approaches that the researcher is drawing on. This

Resources population and polution discussion

1	Andrew:	You have to say what a resource is. You have to say it's useful; it's a natural product.
2	Katherine:	What's natural?
3	Andrew:	That comes from the erth.
4	Katherine:	But you have to tie everything together. To see how each one relates to the other, how they affect the product and um, the uses we get from the product
5	Andrew:	'Useful commodities!'
6	Alex D:	Oh right, that's good. Useful commodities. That sounds good. Are you happy with that?
7	Katherine:	Being natural....
8	Alex D:	Yes, both natural and...
9	Andrew:	Man-made.
10	Katherine:	Artificial.
11	Alex D:	Do you mind if we say human? That means made by all people.
12	Andrew:	They might be things or, you know ... concepts.
13	Alex D:	Things or ideas. Or techniques. They might be a way of doing something.
14	Andrew:	You should put in an example there. Like, you know, ... like iron or ideas ... technology.
15	Alex D:	Right, we're getting somewhere. I think we've missed a bit of what Katherine was saying a little while ago. She said something about use. What about use?
16	Robert:	'Human consumption'. Human use.
17	Alex D:	Use for what though?
18	Andrew:	For a more technological society.
19	Alex D:	To maintain our living standard? Is that a way of putting it? What did you say Katherine? How did you put it?
20	Katherine:	To maintain a balance and ...
21	Alex D:	Yes ... I think you're a bit further down the track than we are at this point...
22	Katherine:	Like the natural things and the human things tie in together, like to benefit ... depending on how we treat them.
23	Alex D:	(writing on board): They can be combined to produce goods and services. As Andrew says, we haven't really gone into what is renewable or non-renewable, but perhaps that isn't really necessary at this point of the definition.

Data Extract 23.3 Spoken interaction in the geography classroom (Source: Lee, 1996, pp.86-7)

Broadly taking on some of the theoretical and methodological concerns of poststructuralist research traditions, the book text is subjected to a rigorous examination of its own production as a form of positioned practice as this is theorized within critical ethnography (Brodkey, 1987; Clifford and Marcus, 1986). On the one hand, in Brodkey's (1987: 71) words, the book text seeks to 'call attention to the voice in which the story is being told'. On the other, in Gebhardt's terms in the quotation at the head of this section, the data are produced 'under the hypothesis that a different reality is possible'. Within the terms of these two positions, the events that I record and report and the readings I produce take their place in the text because they exemplify ways in which individual students are positioned and take up positions within a gender/power/knowledge dynamic in and through literate practices in the classroom.

I have sought to avoid various forms of methodological reductionism currently dominant in educational research contexts. Lather (1991: 15) calls for 'a reflexive process that focuses on our too easy use of taken-for-granted forms'. Methodologically, the book seeks to work as 'rhetoric' in Cherryholmes' (1988) sense, inviting and attempting to persuade a reader to affirm or confirm the account of the necessary complexity of questions of literacy and literacy pedagogy within an acknowledgment of what Donald (1985: 242) calls 'a sense of the daily struggle and muddle of education'. In particular, the book seeks to avoid the impression of a too-neat analysis of power – to avoid the impression that 'the story is too pretty to be true' (Foucault, 1980: 209). It seeks to work with, rather than against, Schon's notion of 'zones of uncertainty' within processes of inquiry (Schon, cited in Doll, 1988:116). It acknowledges the need for, again in Lather's terms, a more hesitant and partial scholarship capable of helping us to tell a better story in a world marked by the elusiveness with which it greets our efforts to know it' (Lather, 1991: 15).

Data Extract 23.4 *Commenting on the research process (Source: Lee, 1996, pp.22-3)*

makes the task of simply recording observations impossible. However, it is possible to distinguish shifts between attempts at recording or simple description, and more obviously interpretative comments. If you look again at Data Extract 23.1, you will see that lines 2-3 provide a description of Katherine's behaviour – she only participated when asked to. Compare this with lines 3-4, where Lee offers an interpretation of Katherine's behaviour. Lee sees Katherine's behaviour as an attempt to downplay 'possible ascriptions of authority', that is, to avoid presenting herself in a public context as a knower.

Lee makes many points relating to the talk episode in Data Extract 23.3. Here are just a few. First, Katherine is 'exploratory' and Andrew is 'propositional'. Katherine's turns raise questions and signal her struggle between official discourse – what is natural – set against what is artificial. Andrew, in contrast, uses assertions and repeats technical terms (turn 5), as does Robert (turn 16), which is approved by the teacher. Second, it is Andrew's contributions that are picked up consistently by Alex D, the teacher. Third, in this talk episode (turns 5, 13, 15, 17) there is clear evidence of what Lee calls 'discursive separateness', where the participants pursue conversations as if in isolation. See, for example, Andrew's continuation at turn 3 of his own comment at turn 1, rather than responding to Katherine's question. Katherine in turn 20 produces a continuation of her strand of argument begun in turn 4.

Lee locates Andrew's and Katherine's contributions within major discursive domains of geography. Lee states that Andrew draws on a discourse that constructs a perspective on resources 'in terms of a capitalist geographical enterprise' (p.88) at turn 5 in his apparent echoing of 'useful commodities' and his responses to Alex D as resources to be used 'for a more technological society' (turn 18). Katherine, in contrast, draws on a bio-philosophical discourse that is more holistic and concerned with balance and interrelationship (turns 20, 22). They are thus both drawing on and promoting particular discourses of geography. However, Lee argues, Andrew's and Robert's discourse is that of the dominant discourse of geography in schools, and in wider society, and Katherine's is an oppositional one. Institutional support for the dominant discourse is clearly evident from Alex D's responses throughout and in the final turn, where, Lee argues, Alex D directs discussion away from concern with environmental relations towards framing definitions within capitalist industrial relations. In this way any oppositional stance is effectively marginalised and delegitimised.

23.7 More questions for you about the data

(vii) Read Data Extract 23.4. This is taken from the opening chapter of Lee's book, in which she talks about methodology and knowledge making.

(viii) What does the extract tell you about the analyst's perspective on her research, and her writing of research?

(ix) What does it tell you about her perspective on research generally?

23.8 Further discussion and conclusions

In many traditional approaches to research, a principal concern is with objectivity. Briefly stated, this concern with objectivity is part of a particular perspective on the relationship between 'researcher' and 'researched': they are conceptualised as being completely distinct and separate entities, the distance between which is necessary in order to maintain an 'objective' stance, without 'bias'. The researcher is the observer and knower and the researched is the object, what is known about.

In Lee's work, she challenges this distance between the researcher and the researched. This is perhaps not surprising, given that a key focus of her research is subjectivity – who people are, feel themselves to be and come to be – through participation in particular events within a particular context, school geography. In the process of doing this research and writing about it, she reflects on her own subjectivity, who she is and how this shapes what she is coming to see and construct. So, from her perspective, what she constructs (her written text) becomes as much an object of scrutiny as does the more obvious object (classroom geography) (see also Example 21 for a discussion of reflexivity). In this way, Lee opens up her own representation of knowledge. By referencing writers such as Brodkey, and Clifford and Marcus, she indicates that she is not alone in the academic world taking this stance. While she is talking about the way her own subjectivity shapes the construction of knowledge, a key implication is that all knowledge-making is subjective.

23.9 Your view

(x)   How useful do you consider Lee's ethnographic descriptions of boys' and girls' behaviour in the classroom?

(xi) To what extent are you convinced by her interpretation of the boys' and girls' behaviour?

(xii) To what extent do you agree with her analysis of the spoken interaction?

(xiii) What questions about research – observation, interpretation – has this example raised for you?

(xiv) How might you use such an approach in your own context?

23.10 Examples of studies using a similar approach

For examples of studies focusing on schooling, literacy and identity, see:

DAVIES, B. (1999) 'Constructing and deconstructing masculinities through critical literacy', *Gender and Education*, vol.9, no.1, pp.9-31.

See also Example 22 in this workbook:

DYSON, A.H. (1997) 'Rewriting for, and by, the children: the social and ideological fate of a Media Miss in an urban classroom', *Written Communication*, vol.14, no.3, pp.275-312.

For a discussion of post-structural research methodology, see:

BRODKEY, L. (1992) 'Articulating poststructural theory in research on literacy', in R. Beach, J. Green, M. Kamel and T. Shanahan (eds) *Multidisciplinary Perspectives in Literacy Research*, Urbana, IL, National Council of Teachers of English, pp.293-318.

24: Ethnography and interactional sociolinguistics: language and identity

24.1 Key features of this approach

Work in interactional sociolinguistics often focuses on the ways in which participants from diverse sociocultural groups negotiate communication, as discussed in Example 2. Whereas earlier studies within this tradition tended to treat aspects of social identity as given or fixed, in more recent times researchers working within interactional sociolinguistics have drawn on post-structuralist writings that point to 'identity', or 'subjectivity' (see Example 23), as something that is always developing and changing. For example, rather than exploring how men and women differentially engage in interaction, the focus has shifted to analysing how men and women 'do' gender, or social class, or ethnicity, through interaction. Such an approach is premised upon the view that by repeatedly engaging in particular kinds of talk and behaviour, individuals come to develop particular identities (and not others) (for discussion see Cameron, 1997). Much work within this field focuses mainly or solely on the oral interactions between participants and analysing how participants 'perform' aspects of their identity (see Butler, 1997; Eckert and McConnell-Ginet, 1999). Some studies, however, also use an ethnographic approach, such as interviewing and observing, to gain participants' perspectives on the relationship between specific uses of language and ways of interacting with specific aspects of identity (see Eckert, 1999).

24.2 Example

RAMPTON, B. (1995) *Crossing: Language and Ethnicity Among Adolescents*, London, Longman [Chapter 3 'Stylised Asian English (1): interactional ritual symbol and politics' and Chapter 4 'Panjabi (1): interactional and institutional participation frameworks'.]

Rampton's specific focus is on 'language crossing', that is, 'the use of language varieties associated with social or ethnic groups that the speaker does not normally belong to' (Rampton, 1995, p.14). This includes the use of Panjabi by young people of Anglo and African-Caribbean descent; the use of Creole by young people of Anglo and Panjabi descent; and the use of 'stylised Asian English' by all three. Briefly, 'stylised Asian English' includes features of English used by older members of the Asian community with limited proficiency in English, stereotypical features attributed to Asian speakers and features of a style that is overly deferential and polite in the media and in society in general. Knowledge of these different features is drawn on by the young people in their interaction. Examples of such features used are 'I no understanding English' and 'jolly, jolly good'.

The participants in Rampton's study are adolescents in an inner-city area of the UK who interact socially within the school (institutional) setting and neighbourhood, and who know each other well. Data includes: recordings of naturally occurring language use for the analysis of interaction; interviews with participants on adolescent social life, to get information on friendship networks and for reports on language use; participant observation by the researcher; local translation and commentary on the use of Panjabi in interactions.

24.3 The aims of the researcher

Rampton aims to:

- understand the use of language crossing (using Panjabi, stylised Asian English and Creole) among adolescents in a particular neighbourhood, both through interviews with young people and through the analysis of examples of such crossing in naturally occurring interaction between these adolescents in and out of school

- explore the role of crossing in inter-ethnic relationships among white Anglo, African-Caribbean, Bangladeshi, Indian and Pakistani adolescents, particularly as a tool of solidarity.

24.4 Data extracts *(see data extracts 24.1-24.3)*

Segmental phonetics

[   ] IPA phonetic transcription (revised to 1979)

The sounds of the phonetic symbols used in transcription can be roughly glossed as follows:

Vowels

[ɪ]   as in 'kit' [kɪt]
[i]   as in 'fleece' (but shorter) [fli:s]
[e]   as in 'dress' [dɹes]
[ɛ]   as in French 'père'
[æ]   as in 'trap' [tɹæp]
[a]   as in French 'patte' [pat]
[ɑ]   as in 'start' (but shorter) [stɑ:t]
[ʌ]   as in 'strut' [stɹʌt]
[ɒ]   as in 'lot' [lɒt]
[ɔ]   as in 'north' (but shorter) [nɔ:θ]
[o]   as in French 'eau'
[ʊ]   as in 'foot' [fʊt]

---

[u]   as in 'goose' (but shorter) [gu:s]
[ə]   as in 'about', 'upper' [əbaʊt]
[ɜ]   as in 'nurse' (but shorter) [nɜ:s]
[eɪ] as in 'face' [feɪs]
[aɪ] as in 'price' [pɹaɪs]
[ɔɪ] as in 'choice' [tʃɔɪs]
[ɪə] as in 'near' [nɪə]
[ɛə] as in 'square' [skwɛə]
[ʊə] as in 'cure' [kjʊə]
[əʊ] as in 'goat' [gəʊt]
[aʊ] as in 'mouth' [maʊθ]

Consonants

[p]   as in 'pea' [pi:]
[b]   as in 'bee' [bi:]
[t]   as in 'toe' [təʊ]
[ʈ]   like [t], but with the tip of the tongue curled back (retroflexed)
[ǃ]   voiceless alveolar click, the sound often made in disappointment, or, used twice, with disapproval
[d]   as in 'doe' [dəʊ]
[ɖ]   like [d], but with the tip of the tongue retroflexed
[k]   as in 'cap' [kæp]
[g]   as in 'gap' [gæp]
[x]   as in Scottish 'loch' [lɒx]
[f]   as in 'fat' [fæt]
[v]   as in 'vat' [væt]
[θ]   as in 'thing' [θɪŋ]
[ð]   as in 'this' [ðɪs]
[s]   as in 'sip' [sɪp]
[ʂ]   like [s], but with the tip of the tongue retroflexed
[z]   as in 'zip' [zɪp]
[ʃ]   as in 'ship' [ʃɪp]
[ʒ]   as in 'measure' [meʒə]
[h]   as in 'hat' [hæt]
[ʔ]   glottal stop, as in Cockney 'butter' [bʌʔə]
[m]   as in 'map' [mæp]
[n]   as in 'nap' [næp]
[ɳ]   like [n], but with the tip of the tongue retroflexed
[ŋ]   as in 'hang' [haŋ]

[ɔ] as in 'north' (but shorter) [nɔːθ]
[l] as in 'led' [led]
[ɭ] like [l], but with the tip of the tongue retroflexed
[ɫ] as in 'table' [teɪbɫ]
[ɹ] as in 'red' [ɹed]
[ɽ] like [ɹ], but with the tip of the tongue retroflexed
[ɾ] like [ɹ], but with the tongue tip tapping once against the teeth ridge (sometimes used in English 'very')
[j] as in 'yet' [jet]
[w] as in 'wet' [wet]
[tʃ] as in 'chin' [tʃɪn]
[dʒ] as in 'gin' [dʒɪn]

Conversational features

⌐ ⌐ (overlapping bracket)	overlapping turns
=	two utterances closely connected without a noticeable overlap, or different parts of a single speaker's turn
(.)	pause of less than one second
(1.5)	approximate length of pause in seconds
l.	lenis (quiet) enunciation
f.	fortis (loud) enunciation
CAPITALS	fortis (loud enunciation)
(( ))	'stage directions'
( )	speech inaudible
(text)	speech hard to discern, analyst guess
Bold	instance of crossing of central interest in discussion

Prosody

ˎ	low fall	ˈ	high stress
ˏ	low rise	ˌ	low stress
ˋ	high fall	ˮ	very high stress
ˊ	high rise	˷	very low stress
ˇ	fall rise	⌐	pitch register shift upwards
˄	rise fall	⌐	pitch register shift downwards
		↑	extra pitch height

Figure 6 Transcription key

Informant backgrounds

The ethnic background of informants is indicated as follows:

AC = African-Caribbean
An = white Anglo
Ba = Bangladeshi
In = Indian
Pa = Pakistani

(Classifying informants in terms of ethnic background raises some of the problems discussed in Chapter 1.2. The use of classifications such as these is discussed in Chapter 1, note 3.)

F = Female
M = Male

Data Extracts 24.1-24.3 constitute different types of data. The Data Extracts 24.1 and 24.2 are from an interview with the participants about their ideas on their use of stylised Asian English (SAE). Data Extract 24.3 is a transcription of actual naturally occurring conversation in the classroom where SAE (and Panjabi) are used.

Session with Ian [An M 15] and Richard [An M 15] in which findings from the 1984 research were being discussed
[simplified transcription]

Ian: if a copper comes up to you right, and you ain't done anything ((. . .)) or just say you got a supply teacher in, Ben, and she asks you a question and Asif or someone will say 'excuse me me no understanding'
Richard: yeh
Ian: and and ((laughs)) you know it w- she she knows very well that you can understand her but it get her ff- ((quietly:)) do you mind if I swear – it gets her pissed off
Richard: ((laughs))

Data Extract 24.1 *Interview data (Source: Rampton, 1995, Extract II.1, p.69)*

Rampton states that the students in this interaction generally had good, amicable relationships with the teachers involved, Ms Jameson and Mr Chambers. Asif was considered the leader of his friendship group.

This is a very small extract from the data that Rampton analyses; since his analysis is cumulative, you will only have a small glimpse of the process of analysis he uses here.

24.5   Questions for you about the data
(i)   Read through the data extracts. Look at Data Extracts 24.1 and 24.2. What reasons do the participants give for their use of SAE in these extracts?

(ii)   Now look at Data Extract 24.3. What is your general sense of what is going on in this interaction?

Interview discussion with Kuldip [In M 14] and Faizal [Pa M 14] of 1984 findings. Later on, Harbans was described as 'our clown', 'our clown of the year ((group))'. [Simplified abbreviated transcription]

Kuldip: ((smile voice)) that's what Harbans ((In M 14)) does
Faizal: yeh
Kuldip: with teachers he does that ((light laughter))
BR: he does it with the teachers?
Kuldip: ( ) he goes 'what you talking about'
               [wɒt ju tɔkɪn əbɑːt]
               ((. . .))
Faizal: Harbans, he does it all the time
BR: how do the teachers react?
Faizal: they just say 'just sit down' and he goes
        'I no understand' and they just go away then
        [aɪ no ʌnɖəstɑːɳɖ]
Kuldip: cos he does it normally with um stand-in teachers when they just,
Faizal: come in you know
Kuldip: for
Faizal: supply teachers, ( ) messes them around
Kuldip: cos he does it normally with stand-in teachers when they just
Faizal: come in
Kuldip: yeh for
Faizal: supply teachers

Data Extract 24.2 Interview data (Source: Rampton, 1995, Extract II.2, p.69)

Asif (Pa M 15, wearing radio-microphone) and his friend Alan (An M 15) are in detention for writing on desks during lessons. They are being temporarily supervised by Mr Chambers, standing in for Miss Jameson who is trying to see the Headteacher about something else. Around lines 31 or 32 their friends Salim and Kazim (both Pa M) arrive at the door at roughly the same time as Miss Jameson.

```
 1  Asif:  there's loads of writing on this table (2.0) I just wrote
 2         two words words on there and then she put me in
 3         detention [ı] (.)
 4  Alan:  ENNIT (1.0) guess what I put
 5  Mr C:  What were they (          )
 6  Alan:  I put M R
 7  Asif:  ((laughs)) I wrote mister right
 8  Mr C:  (        ) (.)
 9  Asif:  that's it (1.0)
10  Alan:  ennit that's it ('    )
11  Mr C:  what (        ) was there?
12  Asif:  what?
13  Mr C:  what (        )
14  Asif:  yeh I know Alan wrote them
15  Alan:  don't be silly
16  Asif:  ((louder)) eh don't be silly now
17         ((half laughing:)) look you're in
18         detent ⌐ ion so tell the truth
19  Alan:         ⌊you can't blame it on me now
20  Asif:  ((loud)) tell the truth Alan (2.0)
21  Asif:  she goes I don't trust you (.) she goes ⌐ well I–
22  Mr C:                                          ⌊(neither
23         do I Asif) (.)
24  Asif:  what? ⌐
25  Mr C:  I don't tr⌊ust (you    )
26  Asif:           ⌊I don't trust YOU(.)
27         ((half laughing)) I tell you straight right (7.0)
28         ((?Mr C? whistles for 4.0 secs))
29  Asif:  nobody trusts a cowboy (1.5)
30  Mr C:  (what?)
31  Asif:  ((laughing quietly)) (      ) (.)
((Kazim and Salim arrive at the door about now))
32  Mr C:  (            )
33  Alan:             ⌐(        )
34  Asif:  ((f)) Kaz ⌊ [ethe ro   ethe ro]
              ((Panj: stay here stay here))
35 Mr C:  (  see you messing   around)
36  Alan:          ⌐(      )
37  Asif:  ((chants)) ⌊ ['te'ri _____ 'a:‚di:‚di:]
```

Data Extract 24.3 *Incident report data (Source: Rampton, 1995, Extract II.3, pp.71-3)*

```
38 Ms J:    'after´you
39 Asif:    'after´you::`
            [ʌftə juʊu]
40 Salim:   ((at a higher pitch)) 'after´you::`
                                   [ʌftər juʊu]

41 Mr C:   (          ⌐        ) (1.0)
42                    ⌐((door bangs shut))
43 Ms J:    ((f)) have we got another cloth?
44 Salim:   ((f)) alright ⌐(          )
45                        ⌐((a lot of loud laughter))
46  Asif:   ((f)) Kazim you want to help us?
47Kazim:    pardon
48 Mr C:    you want another cloth do you
49  Asif:   ((f)) yeh yeh say yeh ⌐     [ɑ:  ɑ:  ɑ:  ɑ:]
                                        ((Panj: yes yes yes yes
50 Ms J:                  ⌐                (          )
51 Salim:   yeh I might ⌐(      )
52 Mr C:                ⌐(      )
53  Asif:   yeh
54Kazim:    I'll help´em
55 Salim:   yeh we'⌐ll help 'em
56 Ms J:           ⌐no you won't (.) out
57Kazim:    ((l)) come on 'en
58 Salim:   ((l)) come on
59 Ms J:    OUT (2.0)
60Kazim:    ((l)) we're not joking
61  Asif:   ((laughs))
62 Ms J:    disobedient yes
63Kazim:    I know but I (don't)
64 Mr C:    ((l)) come on Salim
65Kazim:    ((f)) so what you doing here anyway
66 Ms J:    ((f)) thank you ⌐very much
67 Salim:                   ⌐((f)) you you try to chat her up
68          ennit (        )
69 Ms J:    thank you very much
70          ((Salim and Asif (start to) leave about now))
71  Asif:   can I go now
72 Ms J:    no, and I want ⌐these desks
73  Asif:                  ⌐WHAT YOU ON ABOUT UUH
74 Alan:    ⌐Miss
75  Asif:   ⌐two words I wrote (.) You sa- is this half hour job
```

Data Extract 24.3 *Incident report data continued (Source: Rampton, 1995, Extract II.3, pp.71-3)*

(iii) In Data Extract 24.3, look at the moments in the interaction where SAE is used. How would you explain this use of SAE? What is its function?

(iv) Do you think the use of SAE fits with the interview report data on what young people say about how SAE is used?

24.6 Some points from the researcher's analysis

In the interview data, Data Extracts 24.1 and 24.2, Rampton focuses on *what* the participants have to say about their use of SAE (or, in other cases, Creole or Panjabi) rather than on *how* they say it. Thus the interview data is used as an ethnographic source for analysing the spoken interactional data. Rampton points out that Panjabi students say they often pretend to supply teachers – teachers working temporarily in a school – or new teachers that they do not know English and use SAE in these cases to support this pretence and to test the boundaries of teacher control. They also report using SAE as a form of political testing: SAE reinforces the stereotype of Asians as polite but incompetent in English. Students thus use SAE to gauge the teacher's response to this racist stereotype and detect whether they might be racist. Rampton concludes that the interview report thus supports the view that SAE is used as a form of resistance.

In Data Extract 24.3 Rampton is focusing on *how* the participants are actually using language, particularly SAE and Panjabi. Let's concentrate on SAE for the moment. SAE is used in lines 39-40 in the 'after you' episode and is mainly marked by a change from normal pitch, tone and accent in the English. Rampton points out that it occurs when Ms Jameson and Asif and Alan are entering the detention room, with the doorway clearly signifying a boundary. Rampton argues that SAE is occurring 'at a moment when boundaries were at issue' (p.73). He explains that the episode shows a stereotyped politeness that cannot be taken at face value and may be serving as an instrument of resistance in 'asymmetrical' cross-ethnic negotiation, i.e. where the adolescents have less power than the teacher.

But Rampton points out that 'resistance' doesn't seem to capture accurately what was going on at this moment, especially since the students were generally on good terms with Ms J and Mr C. He explains the switch to SAE as part of a sequence of reciprocal 'joking around', which was started by Ms J with her falsely polite use of 'after you' in line 38 – effectively she is saying 'Please do come in' and inviting the students into detention! Rampton thus characterises the use of SAE here as verbal duelling or play, rather than as political resistance, and as representing 'the kind of interactive juggling between play and seriousness' that often occurs between teachers and students. Based on this analysis, Rampton cautions against exaggerating the use of SAE as 'a language of resistance'; the context of the interaction as well as the researcher's ethnographic knowledge of the participants and the relationships between them is crucial in analysing the interaction. Thus, analysis of the interactional episode appears to support only certain aspects of the report data.

24.7 More questions for you about the data

(v) Go back to Data Extract 24.3 and look at the moments in the interaction where there is a shift to Panjabi from English (marked by translation in brackets which begins 'Panj: ...'). How would you explain the shift to the use of Panjabi?

(vi) Do you think Panjabi is used for resistance in these moments?

24.8 Further discussion and conclusion

In his analysis of the use of Panjabi in the extract, Rampton explains that Asif is playing with the boundaries of teacher control. Asif uses half-masked subversion: his repetition of 'I don't trust YOU' (line 26) could be seen as subversive, but Rampton points out that Asif could also argue, if challenged, that the comment shows he is in agreement with the teacher because he uses Mr C's words (and allegedly Miss J's words) exactly. In line 34, Asif's first use of Panjabi is addressed to the students not in detention. This follows on his subversive attempts in line 26, but could also be explained to the teacher (who doesn't understand Panjabi) as telling the others to go rather than stay. In line 49, Asif again uses Panjabi to hide his own directives and to conceal the conflict between his own authority (among his friendship group) and the authority of the teacher.

Rampton explains that line 37 constitutes a nonsensical use of Panjabi and functions differently from the other examples. This use draws on stock playground words and phrases that Alan would also have been familiar with. Thus Asif uses Panjabi here to show his own connection to 'the values and practices of peer group recreation' (p.94). The use of Panjabi here signals to Asif's friends his joke in appearing to follow the teachers in inviting them into detention (remember, only Asif and Alan are in detention). In this case, Panjabi does seem to be used as an instrument of covert opposition, although Rampton did not find that resistance to white adults was a necessary feature of cross-ethnic uses of Panjabi overall. In relation to his research question, Rampton is particularly interested in the Panjabi use in line 37 that was accessible to Alan (Anglo) and the role it plays in creating solidarity among the young people there.

24.9 Your view

(vii) What does this kind of analysis teach you about the ways in which young people are using different languages?

(viii) Are you convinced by this kind of analysis? Why or why not?

(ix) Can you think of some examples of research in your own context where this approach would be useful?

24.10 Examples of similar studies using this approach

For further work by Rampton, see:

RAMPTON, B. (1999) 'Sociolinguistics and cultural studies: new ethnicities, liminality and interaction', *Social Semiotics*, vol.9, no.3, pp.355-73.

For work on adolescent identity, see:

ECKERT, P. (1999) *Variation as Social Practice*, Oxford, Blackwell.

For an example of a study of masculinity and identity, see:

CAMERON, D. (1998) 'Performing gender identity: young men's talk and the construction of heterosexual masculinity', in S. Johnson and Y. Meinhof (eds) *Language and Masculinity,* Oxford, Blackwell, pp.47-64.

References

ALEXANDER, R. (2000) *Culture and Pedagogy. International Comparisons in Primary Education*, Oxford, Blackwell.

ANGELIL-CARTER, S. (2000) *Stolen Language*, London, Longman.

ATKINSON, J.M. (1984) *Our Masters' Voices: The Language and Body Language of Politics*, London, Methuen.

BAKHTIN, M. (1981) 'Discourse in the novel', in M. Holquist (ed.) *The Dialogic Imagination. Four Essays by M. Bakhtin* (trans. C. Emerson and M. Holquist), Austin, University of Texas Press.

BAKHTIN, M. (1986) 'The problem of speech genres' (trans. V.W. McGee), in C. Emerson and M. Holquist (eds) *Speech Genres and Other Late Essays,* Austin, University of Texas Press.

BARON, N. (1998) 'Letters by phone or speech by other means: the linguistics of email', *Language and Communication*, vol.18, pp.133-70.

BARTON, D. and HAMILTON, M. (1998) *Local Literacies*, London, Routledge.

BARTON, D. and HAMILTON, M. (2000) 'Literacy practices', in D. Barton, M. Hamilton and R. Ivanič (eds) *Situated Literacies: Reading and Writing in Context,* London, Routledge.

BERLIN, J. (1988) 'Rhetoric and ideology in the writing class', *College English*, vol.50, no.5, pp.477-96.

BERNSTEIN, B. (1996) *Pedagogy, Symbolic Control and Identity*, London, Taylor and Francis.

BILLIG, M. and SCHEGLOFF, E.A. (1999) 'Critical discourse analysis and conversation analysis: an exchange between Michael Billig and E.A. Schegloff', *Discourse and Society,* vol.10, no.4, pp.543-82.

BLOOR, T. and BLOOR, M. (1995) *The Functional Analysis of English. A Hallidayan Approach*, London, Edward Arnold.

BOARD OF STUDIES (1996) *ESL Companion to the English CSF.* Victoria: Board of Studies.

BOURNE, J. (1989) *Moving into the Mainstream: LEA Provision for Bilingual Pupils.* Windsor: NFER-Nelson.

BRODKEY, L. (1987) 'Writing Critical Ethnographic Narratives', *Anthropology and Education* 18:2, pp 67-76.

BRODKEY, L. (1992) 'Articulating poststructural theory in research on literacy', in R. Beach, J. Green, M. Kamel and T. Shanahan (eds) *Multidisciplinary Perspectives in Literacy Research*, Urbana, IL, National Council of Teachers of English, pp.293-318.

BRUNER, J.S. (1978) 'The role of dialogue in language acquisition', in A.D. Sinclair, R. Jaavelle and W. Levelt (eds) *The Child's Conception of Language*, New York, Springer-Verlag.

BRUNER, J.S. (1995) 'Vygotsky: a historical and conceptual perspective', in J.V. Wertsch (ed.) *Culture, Communication and Cognition: Vygotskian Perspectives*, Cambridge, Cambridge University Press.

BURTON, J. (1992) 'Don (Juanito) duck and the imperial-patriarchal unconscious: Disney studios, the good neighbour policy, and the packaging of Latin America', in A. Parker, M. Russo, D. Sommer *et al.* (eds) *Nationalisms and Sexualities*, New York, Routledge, pp.21-41.

BUTLER, J. (1997) *Excitable Speech. A Politics of the Performative*, London; Routledge.

CALDAS-COULTHARD, C. and COULTHARD, M. (eds) (1996) *Texts and Practices. Readings in Critical Discourse Analysis*, London, Routledge.

CAMERON, D. (1992) *Feminism and Linguistic Theory* (2nd edn), London, Macmillan.

CAMERON, D. (1997) 'Theoretical debates in feminist linguistics: questions of sex and gender', in R. Wodak (ed.) *Gender and Discourse*, London, Sage.

CAMERON, D. (1998) 'Performing gender identity: young men's talk and the construction of heterosexual masculinity', in S. Johnson and Y. Meinhof (eds) *Language and Masculinity,* Oxford, Blackwell, pp.47-64.

CAMERON, D., MCALINDEN, F. and O'LEARY, K. (1988) 'Lakoff in context: the social and linguistic functions of tag questions', in J. Coates and D. Cameron (eds) *Women in Their Speech Communities*, London, Longman.

CARTER, R. (1998) 'Common language: corpus, creativity and cognition', *Language and Literature*, vol.8, no.3, pp.195-216.

CHOULIARAKI, L. and FAIRCLOUGH, N. (1999) *Discourse in Late Modernity. Rethinking Critical Discourse Analysis*, Edinburgh, Edinburgh University Press.

CLARRICOATES, K. (1983) 'Classroom interaction', in J. Whyld (ed.) *Sexism in the Secondary Curriculum,* New York, Harper and Row.

CLIFFORD, J. and MARCUS, G. (eds) (1986) *Writing Culture: The Poetics and Politics of Ethnography,* Berkeley, CA: University of California Press.

CLIFFORD, G. and MARCUS, G. (eds) (1986) *Writing Culture: The Poetics and Politics of Ethnography*, Berkeley, University of California Press.

COATES, J. and CAMERON, D. (eds) (1988) *Women in Their Speech Communities*, London, Longman.

CONNOR, U. (1996) *Contrastive Rhetoric. Cross-cultural Aspects of Second-language Writing*, Cambridge, Cambridge University Press.

CONNOR, U., DAVIS, K. and DE RYCKER, T. (1995) 'Correctness and clarity in applying for overseas jobs: a cross-cultural analysis of US and Flemish applications', *Text*, vol.15, no.4, pp.457-75.

CRISMORE, A., MARKKANEN, R. and STEFFENSEN, M.S. (1993) 'Metadiscourse in persuasive writing: a study of texts written by American and Finnish university students', *Written Communication*, vol.10, no.1, pp.39-71.

DAVIES, B. (1999) 'Constructing and deconstructing masculinities through critical literacy', *Gender and Education*, vol.9, no.1, pp.9-31.

DENTITH, S. (1995) *Bakhtinian Thought: An Introductory Reader*, London, Routledge.

DOLL, W. E. (1988) 'Beyond Stability: Schon, Prigogine, Piaget', in W. G. PINAR (ed.) *Contemporary Curriculum Discourses*, Scottsdale, AZ: Gorsuch Scarisbrick Publishers: pp.114-33.

DONALD, J. (1985) 'Beacons of the Future: Schooling, Subjection and Subjectification', in V. Beechey and J. Donald (eds) *Subjectivity and Social Relations*, Milton Keynes: Open University Press: pp.214-49.

DYSON, A.H. (1997) 'Rewriting for, and by, the children: the social and ideological fate of a Media Miss in an urban classroom', *Written Communication*, vol.14, no.3, pp.275-312.

ECKERT, P. (1999) *Variation as Social Practice*, Oxford, Blackwell.

ECKERT, P. and MCCONNELL-GINET, S. (1999) 'New generalizations and explanations in language and gender research', *Language in Society,* vol.28, pp.185-201.

ELBOW, P. (1991) 'Reflections on academic discourse: how it relates to freshmen and colleagues', *College English,* vol.53, no.2, pp.135-55.

FAIRCLOUGH, N. (1992) *Discourse and Social Change,* Cambridge, Polity Press.

FAIRCLOUGH, N. (1995) *Media Discourse*, London, Edward Arnold.

FAIRCLOUGH, N. (2001) *Language and Power* (2nd edn), London, Longman.

FERREIRO, E. and TEBEROSKY, A. (1984) *Literacy Before Schooling,* London, Heinemann Educational.

FISHMAN, P. (1998) 'Conversational insecurity', reprinted in D. Cameron (ed.) *The Feminist Critique of Language* (2nd edn), London, Routledge, pp.253-8.

FOWLER, R. (1991) *Language in the News,* London, Routledge.

FOUCAULT, M. (1980) 'The Confession of the Flesh', in *Power/Knowledge: Selected Interviews and Other Writings by Michel Foucault*, Brighton: The Harvester Press, pp.194-228.

GEE, J.P. (1990) *Social Linguistics and Literacies: Ideologies in Discourses,* Basingstoke, Falmer Press.

GOODMAN, S., LILLIS, T., MAYBIN, J. and MERCER, N. (2002) (eds) *Language, Literacy and Education: A Reader*, Stoke-on-Trent, Trentham.

GRANVILLE, S., JANKS, H. and MPHAHLELE, M. *et al.* (1998) 'English with or without g(u)ilt: a position paper on language in education policy for South Africa', *Language and Education*, vol.12, no.4, pp.254-72.

GUTIÉRREZ, K., BAQUEDANO-LÓPEZ, P. and TEJADA, C. (2000) 'Rethinking diversity: hybridity and hybrid language practices in the Third Space', *Mind, Culture and Activity,* vol.6, no.4, pp.286-303.

HALL, N. (1999) 'Young children's use of graphic punctuation', *Language and Education*, vol.13, no.3, pp.178-93.

HALLIDAY, M.A.K. (1978) *Language as Social Semiotic*, London, Edward Arnold.

HALLIDAY, M.A.K. (1989) *Spoken and Written Language*, Oxford, Oxford University Press.

HALLIDAY, M.A.K. (1994) *An Introduction to Functional Grammar* (2nd edn), London, Edward Arnold.

HAMILTON, M. (1994) 'Introduction: signposts', in M. Hamilton, D. Barton and R. Ivanič (eds) *Worlds of Literacy,* Clevedon, Multilingual Matters.

HAMILTON, M. (2000) 'Expanding the new literacy studies. Using photographs to explore literacy as social practice', in D. Barton, M. Hamilton and R. Ivanič (eds) *Situated Literacies. Reading and Writing in Context*, London, Routledge, pp.16-34.

HAMMERSLEY, M. (1994) 'Introducing ethnography' in D. Graddol, J. Maybin and B. Stierer (eds) *Researching Language and Literacy in Social Context,* Clevedon/Milton Keynes, Multilingual Matters/Open University, pp.1-17.

HAWISHER, G.E. and SELFE, C.L. (eds) (2000) *Global Literacies and the World-Wide Web*, London, Routledge.

HAWORTH, A. (1999) 'Bakhtin in the classroom: what constitutes a dialogic text – some lessons from small group interaction, *Language and Education,* vol.13, no.2, pp.99-117.

HEATH, C. (1992) 'The delivery and reception of diagnosis in the general practice consultation', in P. Drew and J. Heritage (eds) *Talk at Work: Interaction in Institutional Settings*, Cambridge, Cambridge University Press.

HEATH, S.B. (1983) *Ways with Words: Language, Life and Work in Communities and Classrooms*, Cambridge, Cambridge University Press.

HOCKEY, S. (1998) 'Textual databases', in J. Lawler and H.A. Dray (eds) *Using Computers in Linguistics. A Practical Guide,* London, Routledge.

HOLMES, J. (2001) *An Introduction to Sociolinguistics* (2nd edn), London, Longman.

HUTCHBY, I. (1992) The pursuit of controversy: routine scepticism in talk on talk radio, *Sociology,* 26, pp 673-94.

HUTCHBY, I. and WOOFFITT, R. (1998) *Conversation Analysis. Principles, Practices and Applications,* Cambridge, Polity Press.

IEDEMA, R. (2001) 'Analysing film and television: a social semiotic account of Hospital: An Unhealthy Business', in T. van Leeuwen and C. Jewitt (eds) *Handbook of Visual Analysis*, London, Sage, pp.183-204.

IVANIČ, R. (1996) 'The logic of non-standard punctuation', in N. Hall and A. Robinson (eds) *Learning about Punctuation*, Clevedon, Multilingual Matters.

IVANIČ, R. (1998) *Writing and Identity: The Discoursal Construction of Identity in Academic Writing,* Amsterdam, Benjamins.

JENKINS, S. and HINDS, J. (1987) 'Business letter writing: English, French, and Japanese', *TESOL Quarterly*, vol.21, no.2, pp.327-50.

JEWITT, C. and KRESS, G. (2002) 'A multimodal approach to teaching and learning', in S. Goodman, T. Lillis, J. Maybin and N. Mercer (eds) *Language, Literacy and Education: A Reader,* Stoke-on-Trent, Trentham.

JOHNSON, S. and FINLAY, F. (1997) 'Do men gossip? An analysis of football talk on television', in S. Johnson and U.H. Meinhof (eds) *Language and Masculinity,* Oxford, Blackwell.

JOHNSON, S. and MEINHOF, U. (eds) (1997) *Language and Masculinity,* Oxford, Blackwell.

JONES, C., TURNER, J. and STREET, B. (eds) (1999) *Students Writing in the University: Cultural and Epistemological Issues*, Amsterdam, Benjamins.

KAMWANGAMALU, N.M. (1998) "We-codes', 'they-codes', and 'codes-in-between": identities of English and codeswitching in post-apartheid South Africa', *Multilingua*, vol.17, no.2/3, pp.277-96.

KAPLAN, R.B. (1966) 'Cultural thought patterns in intercultural education', *Language Learning,* vol.16, pp.1-20.

KRESS, G., JEWITT, C., OGBORN, J. and TSATSARELIS, C. (2000) *Multimodal Teaching and Learning: Rhetorics of the Science Classroom,* Continuum, London.

KRESS, G., OGBORN, J. and MARTINS, I. (1998) 'A satellite view of language: some lessons from science classrooms', *Language Awareness*, vol.7, no.2/3, pp.69-89.

KRESS, G. and VAN LEEUWEN, T. (1996) *Reading Images: The Grammar of Visual Design*, London, Routledge.

KRESS, G. and VAN LEEUWEN, T. (1998) 'The (critical) analysis of newspaper layout', in A. Bell and P. Garrett (eds) *Approaches to Media Discourse*, Oxford, Blackwell.

KRESS, G. and VAN LEEUWEN, T. (2001) *Multimodal Discourse. The Modes and Media of Contemporary Discourse,* London, Arnold.

KRISHNAMURTHY, R. (1996) 'Ethnic, racial and tribal: the language of racism?', in C.R. Caldas-Coulthard and M. Coulthard (eds) *Texts and Practices: Readings in Critical Discourse Analysis*, London, Routledge.

LABOV, W. (1963) 'The social motivation of a sound change', *Word*, vol.19, pp.273-309.

LABOV, W. (1972) *Language in the Inner City: Studies in the Black English Vernacular,* Philadelphia, University of Philadelphia Press.

LAKOFF, R. (1979) 'Women's language', in D.L. Butturuff and E.L. Epstein (eds) *Women's Language and Style*, Akron, OH, University of Akron.

LATHER, P. (1991) *Feminist Research in Education: Within/Against,* Geelong, Australia: Deakin University Press.

LEA, M. and STIERER, B. (2000) (eds) *Student Writing in Higher Education: New Contexts*, Buckingham, Society for Research into Higher Education/Open University Press.

LEE, A. (1996) *Gender, Literacy, Curriculum. Re-writing School Geography*, London, Taylor and Francis.

LEMKE, J. (1989) 'Semantics and social values', *Word*, vol.40, no.1/2, pp.37-50.

LEMKE, J. (1992) 'Semantics, semiotics and grammatics: an ecosocial view', paper presented at the International Congress of Systemic Functional Linguistics, Sydney, Macquarie University.

LEMKE, J. (2000) 'Multimedia demands of the scientific curriculum', *Linguistics and Education*, vol.10, no.3, pp.247-71.

LEUNG, C. (2001) 'English as an additional language: distinct language focus or diffused curriculum concerns?', *Language and Education*, vol.15, no.1, pp.33-55.

LILLIS, T. (2001) *Student Writing: Access, Regulation and Desire*, London, Routledge.

LINDEMANN, S. and MAURANEN, A. (2001) 'It's just real messy: the occurrence and function of just in a corpus of academic speech', *English for Specific Purposes*, vol.20, no.S1 (Supplement no.1), pp.459-75.

LIPPI-GREEN, R. (1996) *English with an Accent*, London, Routledge.

MACHADO DE ALMEIDA MATTOS, A. (2000) 'A Vygotskian approach to evaluation in foreign language learning contexts', *ELT Journal*, vol.54, no.4, pp.335-45.

MAKONI, S. (1999) 'Shifting discourses in language studies in South Africa', in K.K. Prah (ed.) *Knowledge in Black and White*, Cape Town, Centre for Advanced Studies of African Society.

MARTIN, J.R. and VEEL, R. (eds) (1998) *Reading Science: Critical and Functional Perspectives on Discourses of Science*, London, Routledge.

MARTIN, P.W. (1996) 'Codeswitching in the primary classroom: one response to the planned and unplanned language environment in Brunei', *Journal of Multilingual and Multicultural Development*, vol.17, pp.128-44.

MAYBIN, J. (2002) 'Voices, intertextuality and induction into schooling', in S. Goodman, T. Lillis, J. Maybin and N. Mercer (eds) *Language, Literacy and Education: A Reader*, Stoke-on-Trent, Trentham.

MCKAY, P. (1992) *ESL Development: Language and Literacy in School (vols 1 and 2)*. Melbourne: National Languages and Literacy Institute of Australia

MERCER, N. (1995) *The Guided Construction of Knowledge*, Clevedon, Multilingual Matters.

MESTHRIE, R., SWANN, J., DEUMERT, A. and LEAP W. (2000) *Introducing Sociolinguistics*, Edinburgh, Edinburgh University Press.

MYERS-SCOTTON, C. (1993) *Social Motivations for Code-switching: Evidence from Africa*, Oxford, Clarendon Press.

NATIONAL CURRICULUM COUNCIL (1991) *Circular Number 11: Linguistic Diversity and the National Curriculum*. York: NCC.

NCOKO, S.O.S., OSMAN, R. and COCKCROFT, K. (2000) 'Codeswitching among multilingual learners in primary schools in South Africa: an exploratory study', *International Journal of Bilingual Education and Bilingualism*, vol.3, no.4, pp.225-41.

NWENMELY, H. (1999)'Language policy planning in St Lucia: stagnation or change?', *Language and Education*, vol.13, no.4, pp.269-79.

ODELL, L., GOSWAMI, D. and HERRINGTON, A. (1983) 'The discourse-based interview: a procedure for exploring the tacit knowledge of writers in non-academic settings', in P. Mosenthal, L. Tamor and S.A. Walmsley (eds) *Research on Writing. Principles and Methods*, New York, Longman.

OKAMURA, A. and SHAW, P. (2000) 'Lexical phrases, culture and subculture in transactional letter writing', *English for Specific Purposes*, vol.19, no.1, pp.1-15.

ORMEROD, F. and IVANIČ, R. (2002) 'Materiality in children's meaning-making practices', *Visual Communication*, vol.1, no.1, pp.65-91.

PALINCSAR, A.S. and BROWN, A.L. (1988) 'Teaching and practising thinking skills to promote comprehension in the context of group problem solving', *Remedial and Special Education*, vol.9, no.1, pp.53-9.

POPLACK, S. (1980) 'Sometimes I'll start a sentence in Spanish y termino en Español: towards a typology of code-switching', *Linguistics*, vol.18, no.7/8, pp.581-618.

PROSSER, J. (ed.) (1997) *Image-based Research*, London, ECL Press/Taylor and Francis.

PURSER, E. (2000) 'Telling stories: text analysis in a museum', in E. Ventola (ed.) *Discourse and Community. Doing Functional Linguistics*, Tubingen, Gunter Narr Verlag, pp.169-98.

RAMPTON, B. (1995) *Crossing: Language and Ethnicity Among Adolescents*, London, Longman.

RAMPTON, B. (1999) 'Sociolinguistics and cultural studies: new ethnicities, liminality and interaction', *Social Semiotics*, vol.9, no.3, p.355-73.

REPPEN, R. and GRABE, W. (1993) 'Spanish transfer effects in the English writing of elementary school children', *Lenguas Modernas*, vol.20, pp.113-28.

ROCKHILL, K. (1993) 'Gender, language and the politics of literacy', in. B. Street (ed.) *Cross-cultural Approaches to Literacy,* Cambridge, Cambridge University Press.

ROJAS-DRUMMOND, S. (2002) 'Guided participation, discourse and the construction of knowledge in Mexican classrooms', reprinted in S. Goodman, T. Lillis, J. Maybin and N. Mercer (eds) *Language, Literacy and Education: A Reader*, Stoke-on-Trent, Trentham.

ROSE, G. (2001) *Visual Methodologies,* London, Sage.

ROYCE, T. (2002) 'Multimodality in the TESOL classroom: exploring visual-verbal synergy', *TESOL Quarterly*, vol.36, no.2, pp.191-205.

SACKS, H. (1984) 'Notes on methodology', in J.M. Atkinson, and J. Heritage (eds) *Structures of Social Action: Studies in Conversation Analysis*, Cambridge, Cambridge University Press.

SAXENA, M. (1994) 'Literacies among Punjabis in Southall', in M. Hamilton, D. Barton and R. Ivanič (eds) *World of Literacy*, Clevedon, Multilingual Matters.

SCHOOL CURRICULUM AND ASSESSMENT AUTHORITY (1996) *Teaching English as an Additional Language: A Framework for Policy.* London: SCAA.

SCOLLON, R., TSANG, W.K., LI, D., YUNG, V. and JONES, R. (1998) 'Voice, appropriation and discourse representation in a student writing task', *Linguistics and Education*, vol.9, no.3, pp.227-50.

SINCLAIR, J. and COULTHARD, M. (1975) *Towards an Analysis of Discourse*, Oxford, Oxford University Press.

SNYDER, I. (ed.) (1998) *Page to Screen: Taking Literacy into the Electronic Era,* London, Routledge.

SPENDER, D. (1982) *Invisible Women. The Schooling Scandal,* London, Writers and Readers Publishing.

STEIN, P. (in press) 'The Olifantsvlei 'Fresh Stories' project: multimodality, creativity and fixing in the semiotic chain', in G. Kress and C. Jewitt (eds) *Learning and Multimodality: Moving Beyond Language*, New York, Peter Lang.

STENGLIN, M. and IEDEMA, R. (2001) 'How to analyse visual images: a guide for TESOL teachers', in A. Burns and C. Coffin (eds) *Analysing English in a Global Context: A Reader*, London, Routledge.

STOKOE, E. (1994) 'Constructing topicality in university students' small-group discussion; a conversation analytic approach', *Language and Education,* vol.14. no.3, pp.194-203.

STREET, B. (2001) 'Introduction', in B. Street (ed.) *Literacy and Development. Ethnographic Perspectives*, London, Routledge.

STROUD, C. (2001) 'African mother-tongue programmes and the politics of language: linguistic citizenship versus linguistic human rights', *Journal of Multilingual and Multicultural Development*, vol.22, no.4, pp.339-55.

STUBBS, M. (1996) *Texts and Corpus Analysis*, Oxford, Basil Blackwell.

SUGIMOTO, T. and LEVIN, J.A. (2000) 'Multiple literacies and multimedia: a comparison of Japanese and American uses of the Internet', in G.E. Hawisher and C.L. Selfe (eds) *Global Literacies and the World-Wide Web*, London, Routledge, pp.133-53.

SWANN, J. (1998) 'Talk control: an illustration from the classroom of problems in analysing male dominance of conversation', in J. Coates and D. Cameron (eds) *Women in their Speech Communities. New perspectives on Language and Sex*, London, Longman, pp.122-40.

TANNEN, D. (1998) 'The relativity of linguistic strategies: rethinking power and solidarity in gender and dominance', in D. Cameron (ed.) *The Feminist Critique of Language: A Reader* (2nd edn), London, Routledge.

TEACHERS OF ENGLISH TO SPEAKERS OF OTHER LANGUAGES (1997) *ESL Standards for Pre-K-12 Students.* Alexandria, VA: TESOL Inc.

THESEN, L. (1997) 'Voices, discourse, and transition: in search of new categories in EAP', *TESOL Quarterly,* vol.31, no.3, pp.487-511.

THESEN, L (2001) 'Modes, literacies and power: a university case study', *Language and Education*, vol.15, no.2/3, pp.132-45.

TRUDGILL, P. (1975) *Accent, Dialect and the School,* London, Edward Arnold.

VAN LEEUWEN, T. (1996) 'Moving English: the visual language of film', in S. Goodman and D. Graddol (eds) *Redesigning English: New Texts, New Identities,* London, Routledge.

VAN LEEUWEN, T. and JEWITT, C. (eds) (2001) *Handbook of Visual Analysis,* London, Sage.

VYGOTSKY, L. (1976) *Mind in Society. The Development of Higher Psychological Processes* (ed. M. Cole, V. John-Steiner, S. Scribner and E. Souberman), Cambridge, Harvard University Press.

VYGOTSKY, L. (1986) *Thought and Language* (ed. and trans. A. Kozulin), Cambridge, MA, MIT Press.

WEEDON, C. (1987) *Feminist Practice and Poststructuralist Theory*, Oxford, Basil Blackwell.

WEGERIF, R., ROJAS-DRUMMOND, S. and MERCER, N. (1999) 'Language for the social construction of knowledge: comparing classroom talk in Mexican pre-schools', in *Language and Education*, vol.13, no.2, pp.133-150.

WELLS, G. (1986) *The Meaning Makers: Children Learning Language and Using Language to Learn*, London, Hodder and Stoughton.

WERTSCH, J.V., DEL RIO, P. and ALVAREZ, A. (eds) (1995) *Sociocultural Studies of Mind,* New York, Cambridge University Press, pp.1-34.

WILSON, A. (2000) 'There is no escape from third-space theory: borderland discourse and the 'in-between" literacies of prisons', in D. Barton, M. Hamilton and R. Ivanič (eds) *Situated Literacies. Reading and Writing in Context*, London, Routledge.

WILSON, A. (2002) 'Researching in the third space: locating, claiming and valuing the research domain', in S. Goodman, T. Lillis, J. Maybin and N. Mercer (eds) *Language, Literacy and Education: A Reader*, Stoke-on-Trent, Trentham.

WOODS, N. (1988) 'Talking shop: sex and status as determinants of floor apportionment in a work setting', in J. Coates and D. Cameron (eds) *Women in Their Speech Communities,* London, Longman.

YATES, S. (2001) 'Researching Internet interaction: sociolinguistics and corpus analysis', in M. Wetherell, S. Taylor and S.J. Yates (eds) *Discourse as Data. A Guide for Analysis*, Sage in association with The Open University, London/Milton Keynes, pp.93-147.

ZUBAIR, S. (1999) 'Women's literacy in a rural Pakistani community', in T. O'Brien, (ed.) *Language and Literacies, Selected Papers from the Annual General Meeting of the British Association for Applied Linguistics,* University of Manchester, September 1998, BAAL/Multilingual Matters, pp.114-25.

Index

academic writing 153-58
accent 3-9
advertising 92
African-American Vernacular
    English (AAVE) 9
Alexander, R. 39-49
Alvarez, A. 37
Angelil-Carter, S. 153, 158
Atkinson, J. M. 29
Australia
    and EAL 85-9
    and film 126-31

Baden-Powell, R. 54-8
Bakhtin, M., Bakhtinian 67-72, 85,
    144, 159-65
Baquedano- López, P. 50
Baron, N. 133, 138
Barton, D. 133, 141, 145, 147
Berlin, J. 157
Bernstein, B., Bernsteinian 85-9
The Big Issue in the North 92-4
Billig, M. 95
Bloor, M. 65
Bloor, T. 65
Board of Studies 86
Boy Scouts 54-7
Brodkey, L. 173
Brown, A. L. 37
Bruner, J. 31, 39
Burton, J. 10
Butler, J. 175

Caldas-Coulthard, C. 96
Cameron, D. 15, 99, 175, 185
Carter, R. 59
Chinese 68, 71, 84
Chouliaraki, L. 91-5
Clarricoates, K. 99
Clifford, J. 173
Coates, J. 99
Cockcroft, K. 17
codeswitiching 17-21
'commodofication' 95
Connor, U. 79-84
content analysis 3-4

contrastive rhetoric 79-83
conversation analysis (CA) 23-9
corpus analysis 53-9
Coulthard, M. 39, 96
Creole 175-84
Crismore, A. 84
Critical Discourse Analysis (CDA)
    91-5

Davies, B. 173
Davis, K. W. 79-84
De Rycker, T. 79-84
Del Rio, P. 37
Dentith, S. 144
dialect 3-9
discourse analysis 67-72
Disney, Walt
    films 3-9
Dyson, A. H. 159-65, 173

Eckert, P. 175, 185
Elbow, P. 157
email 133-8
emoticons 135-7
English as a Second Language
    (ESL) 87
English as an additional language
    (EAL) 85-9

Fairclough , N. 70-1, 91-5, 167
feminism 99, 168
Ferreiro, E. 73
film 3-9, 125-31, 160-1, 165
Finlay, F. 15
Finnish students 84
Fishman, P. 11-14
Flemish students 79-84
Foucault, M. 91
Fowler, R. 95
France 39-40, 83,
Froebel, 49
functional grammar 61

Gee, J. P. 154
gender 11-14, 99-106, 163-4, 167-
    73, 175, 185

and literacy in Pakistan 141-5
    see also sexism
geography 167-73
German 61
Girl Guides 54-7
Goswami, D. 73, 78
Grabe, W. 84
Gramsci, A. 91
Granville, S. 3, 90
Gumperz, J. 11, 15
Gutiérrez, K. 50

Hall, N. 73-7, 158
Halliday, M. A. K. 61, 113, 121,
    130-1
Hamilton, M. 133, 141, 145, 147-52
Hammersley, M. 159
Hawisher, G. E. 38
Haworth, A. 72
Heath, C. 29
Heath, S. B. 141
Herrington, A. 73, 78
Hinds, J 83
Hockey, S. 53
Hong Kong 68-70
Hutchby, I. 23-9
hybridity 94-5

Iedema, R. 125-31
India 39-2, 45
Initiation-Response-Follow-up (IRF)
    39, 49
interactional sociolinguistics 1-15,
    99, 175-85
interdiscursivity 70-1
internet 133-8
intertextuality 70, 165
IsiXhosa 18-21
IsiZulu 18-21
Ivanič, R. 73, 78, 113-23, 153, 158,
    165

Janks, H. 90
Japan 133-8
Jenkins, S. 83
Jewitt, C. 106, 112, 123, 152

job applications 79-84
Johnson, S. 15, 99
Jones. R. 67-72, 141, 153, 166

Kamwangamalu, N. M. 21
Kress, G. 106-13, 122-3, 125, 131
Krishnamurthy, R. 59

Labov, W. 3. 9
Lakoff, R. 14
Lea, M. 153
Lee, A. 167-73
Lemke, J. 112, 130
letters 68-71, 80-4
Leung, C. 85-9
Levin, J. A. 133-8
Li, D. 67-72, 166
Lillis, T. M. 72, 73, 78, 153-8
Lindemann, S. 69
Lippi-Green, R. 3-0
Literacy Hour 49
London-Lund corpus 58

Machado De Almedida Mattos, A.
    50
mainstream United States English
    (MUSE) 4-9
Makoni, S. 21
Marcus, G. 173
Markkanen, R. 84
Martin, J. R. 65
Martin, P. W. 21
Martins, I. 107-111
Marx, K. 91
materiality 113-23
Mauranen, A. 59
Maybin, J. 72, 166
McAlinden, F. 16
McConnell-Ginet, S. 175
McKay, P. 87
Meinof, U. 99
Mercer, N. 31-7
Mesthrie, R. 3
Mphahlele, M. 90
Myers-Scotton, C. 17

National Curriculum Council 86
National Literacy Strategy see
    Literacy Hour
Ncoko, S. O. S 17-21
New Literacy Studies (NLS) 141,
    147, 152-3
Nguni languages 21
non-verbal behaviour 99-106
Nwenmely, H. 90

O'Leary, K. 15
Odell, L. 73, 78

Ogborn, J. 106, 107-112
Okamura, A. 84
Ormerod, F. 113-23
Osman, R. 17-21

Pakistan 141-5
Palincsar, A. S. 37
Panjabi 175-84
photographs 147-52
Piaget, J. 49
'polyvocality' 68
Poplack, S. 21
project work
    in primary classrooms 113-23
Prosser, J. 152
'psychobiography' 48
punctuation 73-8
Purser, E. 61-5

racism 70
radio 23-9
Rampton, B. 175-85
reflexivity 95
Reppen, R. 84
Rockhill, K. 145
Rojas-Drummond, S. 37, 50
Rose, G. 125
Rousseau, J-J. 49
Royce, T. 112
Russia 39-40, 43-44, 48-9

Saxena, M. 145
scaffolding 32-4, 39
Schlegloff, E. A. 96
School Curriculum and Assessment
    Authority (SCAA) 86
science
    teaching 107-112
Scollon, R. 67, 166
Selfe, C. L. 138
sexism 54-8
Shaw, P. 84
Sinclair, J. 39
Snyder, I. 138
social logic 88-9
Sotho languages 21
South Africa 17-21, 153
South Seas Exhibition 62-4
Spender, D. 99
spoken language and new technology
    (SLANT) project 37
Steffensen, M. S. 84
Stein, P. 123
Stenglin, M. 131
stereotypes 4, 94
Stierer, B. 153
Stokoe, E. 29
Street, B. 133, 141

Stroud, C. 90
Stubbs, M. 53-59
stylised Asian English 175-84
Sugimoto, T. 133-8
Swann, J. 99-106
systemic functional linguistics 61-5

Tannen, D. 106
teacher's gaze 99-106
Teaching of English to speakers of
    other languages (TESOL) 112
Teberosky, A. 73
Tejada, C. 50
television 125-31
textbooks 107-111
Thesen, L. 153
Trudgill, P. 10
Tsang, W. K. 67-72, 166
Tsatsarelis, C. 106, 112, 125, 131

United States of America 39-40,
    and children's writing 159-65
    and ESL 85-9
    and the Internet 133-7
    and students' letters 79-84

Van Leeuwen, T. 107, 113, 152
Veel, R. 65
Ventola, E. 65
Vygotsky, L. S. 31, 39

Weedon, C. 167
Wegerif, R. 37
Wells, G. 73
Wertsch, J. 37, 67
Wilson, A. 123, 141, 152
Woods, N. 106
Wooffitt, R. 23-9

Yates, S. 133
Yung, V. 67-72, 166

zones of proximal development
    (ZPD) 31
Zubair, S. 141-5